BRIDGING THE GAP

Georgia Bizios & Katie Wakeford, editors

BRIDGING THE GAP

PUBLIC-INTEREST ARCHITECTURAL INTERNSHIPS

RESPONSES TO
BRIDGING THE GAP

Bridging the Gap offers tremendous value in addressing the important linkage between architectural internship and public service. As such, this discourse has the ability to positively influence the emerging generation's conception of practice and the value that design thinking has in serving society.

Clark Manus, FAIA
President, American Institute of Architects, 2011
CEO, Heller Manus

Bizios and Wakeford have assembled a timely, convincing, and highly useful collection of essays that demonstrates the power of public service to expand the education of architects through direct community engagement, greatly multiplying the dividends of internship. *Bridging the Gap* enriches the literature on public-interest practice, and establishes the relevance of social equity to our continuing discourse on professional development.

Professor Daniel S. Friedman
President, Association of Collegiate Schools of Architecture, 2010-11
Dean, College of Built Environments, University of Washington

This volume brings together a host of case studies in alternative futures for design discipline graduates. Graduates seeking meaningful, compassionate, socially relevant engagement will find this volume enlightening and a mine of trajectories. Faculty will find it a great pedagogic companion for a challenging, though opportunity-filled, future in the contemporary academy. Professionals should find it simply humbling.

Keelan P. Kaiser, AIA
President, National Architectural Accrediting Board, 2011-12
Chair, Department of Architecture, Judson University

Nineteen perspectives that will change the way you view the profession of architecture and the business behind design. Relevant to students and professionals alike, this collection highlights multiple avenues to engage in public-interest projects and careers, which are becoming ever more integral to the design of the built environment.

Danielle McDonough, Assoc. AIA, LEED AP
Vice President, American Institute of Architecture Students, 2010-11

ACKNOWLEDGMENTS

GEORGIA BIZIOS & KATIE WAKEFORD, EDITORS

We wish to offer our sincere thanks to the many individuals and institutions who contributed to this publication. We could not have done it alone!

We extend our greatest appreciation to the contributing writers for sharing not just their essays, but also their time, expertise, experience, and enthusiasm. Thank you for your dedication to the issues of architectural internship and public-interest design.

This publication grew from our work on the Home Environments Design Initiative at NC State University. We want to recognize the many students, interns, and community partners who have joined us in our explorations of public-interest architecture and informed this volume.

In preparing the manuscript for publication, several consultants provided essential assistance. To copyeditor Brent Winter, graphic designer Kelly M. Murdoch-Kitt, and proofreader Pam Morrison, we are very grateful.

This project was supported in part by an award from the National Endowment for the Arts. The NC State University College of Design's Faculty Development Program provided additional funding. The NC State University Office of Extension, Engagement, and Economic Development made it possible to develop internship opportunities that inspired this publication.

Many thanks to all.

The Editors
Raleigh, North Carolina
August 2011

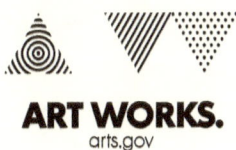

ART WORKS.
arts.gov

CONTENTS

x

FOREWORD

SERGIO PALLERONI

As an educator and practitioner of public-interest architecture, I couldn't be happier to see Georgia Bizios and Katie Wakeford's book come out. For many years now, an increasing number of us have faced the great challenge of finding ways to cultivate and nurture the lessons of public-interest design within academia and beyond. The transition to practice has been difficult for the growing number of students interested in a more publicly engaged practice, because training opportunities—true professional training, the kind you get in your first years of practice or in internships—have been scarce to nonexistent. It is in this wasteland of lack of opportunity that we lose so many of our most promising designers, despite all of our efforts as educators to instill in them the skills to make the transition.

However, as this volume makes clear, all is not lost—and far from it. The contributors to *Bridging the Gap* make convincingly clear that some of the best minds in academia and the professional world have met this challenge with great success. Within the pages of this book— which is essentially a road map to significant change—you will find a thoughtful selection of useful perspectives on the issue of public-interest internship, from the ethical reasons why we need such internships to the experiences of a star lineup of the leading figures attempting to create these opportunities. Their stories, combined with the compelling, eloquent firsthand accounts from the trenches by the interns and young practitioners engaged in these pioneering programs and practices, make this book the first one to substantively contribute to solving this difficult problem.

Given the challenges we face in our communities and in society as a whole, it is good to know that there are paths out of the woods of our current dilemma—paths that finally offer future architects the opportunity to be part of the solution.

INTRODUCTION

GEORGIA BIZIOS & KATIE WAKEFORD, EDITORS

Many in the architectural discipline see an opportunity for change in the way the profession trains our new generations and serves our communities. It is important to constantly reconsider how we educate, how we practice, and whom we serve. Internship must be included in this reassessment.[1] We believe that it is feasible and valuable for enthusiastic architecture graduates to more directly apply their energy and design skills to current social, economic, and environmental issues. We are confident that creating public-interest internship opportunities will have a powerful influence on the future of our profession and our communities.

There is a critical need for the architectural profession to contribute more effectively to the public good. Although the profession has a proud tradition of community design and many private firms are reinvesting themselves in public service, current levels of outreach and advocacy are insufficient in the face of such problems as the shortage of affordable housing, the destruction of buildings and communities by natural disasters, and the environmental toll imposed by our built environment.

There have been increased efforts at the university level to prepare future architects for public engagement. Architecture students enthusiastically participate in service-learning studios, design-build workshops, and off-campus and study-abroad experiences focused on humanitarian issues. Unfortunately, graduates discover a scarcity of similar internship opportunities. Casius Pealer has estimated that there are fewer than ten public-interest internships annually for approximately four thousand professional-degree graduates.[2] This creates a significant gap in the training of a public-interest practitioner.

The dearth of public-interest internship opportunities does a disservice to fledgling professionals, the profession, and our communities. Many civic-minded interns are left without the jobs they would most desire. The profession is denied an important opportunity to reach out to a wider audience. The shortage of public-interest internships also limits the development of public service as a legitimate architectural career track. Most importantly, our communities miss out on a rich source of creativity, design expertise, productivity, and economic development.

The essays in this collection address a broad range of considerations regarding public-interest internships. Some contributors challenge the architecture profession to embrace its ethical responsibility for contributing to the public good and train new generations to do so. Other writers present successful examples of innovative internships provided by academic institutions and nonprofits. Several authors inspire with personal accounts of the joys and satisfactions of community engagement work, even in the face of disappointments and compromises. While the collection is not intended to be exhaustive, its breadth is sufficient to fuel a vibrant conversation in the hope of inspiring the creation of new public-interest internships and informing the ongoing updates to the Intern Development Program (IDP).

The advantages to developing new public-service internships are clear. The challenges are surmountable. Let's get started.

"In light of the social, economic, and environmental issues facing us, creating new public-interest internships will not only provide opportunities for our enthusiastic architecture graduates, but it will also expand the architecture discipline's capacity to contribute to the public good and the well-being of our communities."

BEACH

FISHER

MALECHA

PYATOK

ZIMBABWE

CARUSO

PART I:
FACING
THE ISSUES

VICTORIA
BEACH

THE ETHICAL
ADVANTAGES
OF PUBLIC-
SERVICE
INTERNSHIPS

PROFESSIONAL ETHICS

From the perspective of moral philosophy, professionals have ethical obligations to serve the public, nurture their successors, care for their clients, and advance their discipline. These four core obligations are so defining that if professionals fail to fulfill even one of them, they are by definition no longer "professionals."[1] Luckily, there is an infinite number of ways to tackle each one of these four core duties separately, and many architects do just that. However, public-service internships offer a unique and underexploited opportunity to address all of the defining ethical principles in one synergistic activity.

SERVING THE PUBLIC

True professionals must provide services to those who cannot pay. For example, one would hardly argue that only rich people should have good health or be unincarcerated. That is why the medical and judicial professions provide for those with fewer resources by working *pro bono publico* (for the public good). Even if one were to argue that only some people should be healthy and free, the most effective way to ensure that "the some" do not fall victim to disease or injustice is to ensure that "the many" do not either.

Law, medicine, and all legitimate, licensed professions provide services that most cannot provide for themselves but that are absolutely vital to the survival of society. Of the four core professional duties, public service is the primary one, supported by the other three. The protection of this important service is the principal reason that the state grants professionals monopoly privilege to practice.

If a profession does not consider its services vital enough to provide them to everyone, it is in effect admitting that its importance and legitimacy are in question. It can only be a matter of time before astute legislators might also question the utility or fairness of laws protecting what would amount to a private cartel that is only out for its own interest, rather than the public's.

Some protest that pro bono work depresses the fees that professionals can charge to paying clients or that taking projects pro bono unfairly cuts into the pie of projects available for practitioners. Both scenarios would obviously jeopardize the financial viability of practicing if they ever came true, but both scenarios are fallacies. Non-paying projects do not exist without someone volunteering to do them; thus, they do not affect paying projects in any way. Pro bono work is simply not part of the pie.

Although public service is supposed to be at the very heart of a profession, it is located somewhere near the pinky toe of the Internship Development

Program (IDP) run by the National Council of Architectural Registration Boards (NCARB). Of the 5,600 hours of work required by IDP, only 80 hours, or about 1%, must be devoted to public service.[2] However, the meaningful numbers are actually 0 hours and 0% because this required service does not have to be architectural service; thus, it does not satisfy the ethical obligation to do professional pro bono work.[3]

NCARB's definition of this public-service requirement is revealing. It focuses on benefits to the interns, perhaps understandably, but it also has something of an urban safari or "ghetto tourism" flavor: "Such activities will increase your understanding of the people and forces that shape society."[4] Just as the NCARB model ethical code remains silent on the issue of pro bono work[5] and the American Institute of Architects (AIA) ethical code offers one unenforceable suggestion for its members,[6] IDP places little emphasis on the essential and defining role pro bono work plays in legitimate professions. Most counterintuitively of all, NCARB prohibits intern architects from counting any unpaid internship hours toward their public-service requirement and allows only 40 volunteer hours, or about half of one percent, to count toward overall experience in every category but community service. This rule may be intended to indirectly address firm exploitation, but it also directly thwarts pro bono professional work.[7]

Public-service internships address all these issues both directly and indirectly. Directly, they simply provide needed services to people who would otherwise not receive them, which is the very definition of *pro bono publico*. Indirectly, but just as importantly, they give participants an early foundation for a truly professional practice—the type of practice that is more likely to provide pro bono services, to work on a greater diversity of projects, and therefore to create a more significant public role for architecture in society. For these reasons, rather than effectively banning public-service internships, it would make more sense for NCARB to make them mandatory.

NURTURING SUCCESSORS

True professionals must nurture their colleagues, past, present, and future. There are pragmatic as well as ethical reasons for this. Pragmatically, nobody but the professionals themselves actually understand the field. They are the experts. Governments, therefore, must and do entrust them to self-educate and self-regulate. (Remember how ill-equipped the United States government was to deal with the clever tricks of professional accountants at Enron?)

Ethically speaking, the duty to nurture successors stems from the profession's primary duty to serve the public. A legitimate profession in service to society would be remiss in this service if its neglect of internal, organizational maintenance caused a disruption of this service. If the service itself is vital, the ongoing continuity of the service is vital.

Internship clearly represents an appropriate vehicle for professionals to provide generational continuity. IDP, the near-mandatory U.S. program, clearly states on the interns' checklist an appropriate range of skills a future architect should procure through the internship process. The efficacy of this process, however, depends on the extent to which the internship experience corresponds to its stated goals—a correspondence that, despite the best of intentions, is often far from perfect.

IDP never explains how the stating of educational goals will lead to the attaining of those goals, especially in an unregulated, unaccredited, private firm whose primary concern may be simply staying afloat. NCARB itself seems to acknowledge this inherent tension right up front. In a caveat titled "Managing Expectations," the IDP guidelines state: "You are the prime beneficiary of the IDP. To gain the greatest benefit from participation, you should pursue it as a cooperative arrangement with your employer. Recognize that your employer cannot charge clients for IDP training costs."[8] This premise depicts the training period as a somewhat selfish endeavor, guided by the trainees and financially burdening to the trainers. This might be true if architecture were purely a profit-making business, but it is completely false if architecture is a true profession that sees training its members as an act of public service that is ethically required—even at a cost.

Despite this pivotal caveat, in the adjacent paragraph NCARB claims that the intern's supervisor is "required" to help administer IDP and is "responsible" for "providing reasonable opportunities...meeting regularly with you...encouraging you," and so on.[9] But who actually "requires" the supervisor to administer IDP? And to whom is the supervisor "responsible"? Neither state licensing boards, nor the AIA,[10] nor NCARB[11] itself has the authority to hold internship supervisors fully accountable. As there is no other relevant authority, it falls to the interns in a "cooperative arrangement" to, in effect, supervise their supervisors.

Such reversal of hierarchy may not be completely ill-advised; some interns undoubtedly have the personality for it. But as a general rule, it is an inappropriate foundation for a mandatory program. The interns most in need of a program's assistance would be precisely those least likely to be comfortable overturning corporate hierarchies armed only with a checklist.

"Public-service internships offer a unique and underexploited opportunity to address all of the [professional] ethical principles in one synergistic activity."

An unfortunate effect of IDP's flawed approach is the establishment of a required three-year limbo in which many interns become vulnerable to labor and wage exploitation. Perhaps it is only natural that, given the national shortage of drafters and other support personnel for architects, firms need recent architecture graduates to fill these roles. But even when these interns receive a license to practice in a timely fashion, underpaid years focusing on bathrooms in the bowels of a corporate hierarchy—the paradigmatic "bathroom stall detail"— may preclude independence, much to the contrary of IDP's laudable purpose: "The IDP is designed to make your internship a meaningful experience by exposing you to many aspects of the profession so that you are prepared to practice architecture independently."[12]

IDP might have a greater chance of success if the realities of architectural practice were more like those of other professions. In his article "Professions and Their Discontents: The Psychodymanics of Architectural Practice,"[13] Robert Gutman described architectural practice as strikingly different from legal and medical practice in its high degree of professional hierarchy. Law firms and hospitals are hierarchical, but they are not professional hierarchies; instead, they are differentiated hierarchies, where professionals do the work they were trained to do and other experts (lab technicians, nurses, paralegals) do the differentiated, supporting work that they were trained to do. For architects, this means that the nefarious bathroom stall detail would be performed by a draftsperson—or, in the future, perhaps a computer.

In the differentiated scenario, there is less hierarchy and more collegiality among the professionals, and the roles played by the junior professionals closely mimic the roles of the senior professionals. For example, medical interns in hospitals are addressed as "Doctor," and they independently perform full patient rounds that are evaluated afterward, not directed in advance. In the absence of full collegial status for junior architects and the nonhierarchical collegiality that characterizes professions, architecture must provide major reforms of or alternatives to IDP.

For those aspiring to the status of full professional rather than support staff, public-service internship programs can provide an alternative or supplement to IDP. These programs can provide meaningful exposure to and integration of all project phases, and they can offer training in independent leadership. Perhaps most consequentially, they bring dignity to the emerging architect and to architecture as a whole by showing future practitioners the true impact and worth of their design work.

Public-service internship programs can select or design projects on the basis of different criteria from those used by commercial firms. Presumably, such programs would generally operate as nonprofit organizations, with their pro bono work receiving support from charitable resources; this would uncouple profit and project, allowing organizations to focus on projects that benefit both the public and the interns. Only projects that provide an appropriate client, scale, content, and team structure for educational purposes need be considered.

With a feasible project selected, public-service internship programs can give intern architects lead roles in executing the work. Involvement can begin as early as site selection and programming, and it can end with occupancy, much like design-build practices. When clients have been carefully selected and are aware that they may receive "unseasoned" services, gratitude for the help tends to far outweigh any concerns about the quality of the intern's work. Most concerns about interns tend to come not from clients but from practicing architects called upon to supervise them. Skepticism about the value or efficacy of internship can deepen into legal fears about liability. Good legal advice and the proper structuring of the administering organization can allay these worries.

Pennsylvania has a comprehensive "Good Samaritan" law that protects volunteers from nonprofit organizations who are rendering public services.[14] Many other states have similar laws, though they may be restricted to emergency situations. In 1997, the U.S. Congress passed the Volunteer Protection Act, giving all states a consistent, and often higher, standard of liability protection for nonprofit and government volunteers.[15]

In principle, U.S. residents clearly have legal support for their efforts to help one another. Wherever such support does not exist, it still falls to the profession to reform any law that impedes its ethical obligations to society.

With logistical hurdles aside, a public-service internship program offers an ideal model for independent practice. Right from the outset of a project, interns are given a broad range of responsibilities without having to beg for them. Interns then lead while experts assist, not the other way around. They learn by doing rather than by watching, as in other professional internships. During the course of the project, they experience firsthand the material consequences of their decisions, and when the project is completed, a very grateful segment of society applauds the interns for their efforts—an important component of the process.

"When public-service internship programs are structured appropriately, they can make advances in sustainability, materiality, technology, and artistic expression, all cornerstones of architectural knowledge."

Inside the office, interns are more vulnerable to the profit-driven, low-risk, liability-averse culture of firms, a culture that can impose distance from and insecurity with the tools of practice. The outside world, meanwhile, builds and affirms interns' skills and values when they are allowed to interact with it and master its complexities. When all practitioners see mentoring more as an ethical requirement and less as a voluntary act of charity, or when an authoritative accreditation of training environments emerges, the structural disincentives to nurturing successors will cease to be a problem. Until then, public-service internship programs appear to do a better job than IDP of making "your internship a meaningful experience by exposing you to many aspects of the profession so that you are prepared to practice architecture independently."

CARING FOR CLIENTS

True professionals must care for clients. As H. H. Richardson may or may not have said, the first job of an architect is to get the job. It's no secret (except perhaps to a very innocent intern) that the gateway to architectural practice is the client. Of course, architects must not only get clients; they must hold clients, and if they are going to produce great work, they ultimately must understand clients—and building users as well.

But professionals also have an ethical duty to understand their clients. They need to become well-acquainted with all their clients' interests in order to then place them squarely before their own. This "fiduciary" responsibility (the word shares a Latin root with the word "fidelity," i.e., faithfulness) does not arise out of the business-based relationship of payee to payer but out of the information-based relationship of expert to novice. Though clients wield the power of the paycheck, professionals wield the more dangerous power of knowledge. Novice clients cannot judge the actions of expert professionals and are therefore completely vulnerable to them. Professional ethics, therefore, requires professionals to refuse to use this power to prefer their own interests.

How do professionals learn to be "faithful" to clients in this way? Client contact is a start, and IDP does a good job of weaving the notion of client contact through many of its core competencies. But IDP's guidelines provide no guarantee that interns will ever discuss project preferences directly with the client so that they can responsively incorporate those preferences into their work. Nor do the guidelines guarantee that firm principals will step aside during highly critical meetings so that interns can "present [their own schematic] solutions to an owner/client for selection and approval."[16]

In the ancient democracy of Athens, citizens who were accused of crimes were required to defend themselves personally in court. However, defendants who were insecure about their own eloquence were encouraged to rely on a gifted friend or relative to speak for them. These early "advocates" were "forbidden by law to take pay for services rendered."[17] The advocate's friendship was to be selfless and true, creating a singular identity of the defender with the defendant, unmediated by any mercenary factors.

Obviously, society has moved far beyond such simple realities, but public-service internships recapture the ideals behind this ancient practice. First, and most pragmatically, public-service internships can guarantee intern contact with clients. Second, when the financial component of the relationship is removed, the focus shifts to serving the client's interests through the project design. The intern becomes a true advocate for and "friend" of the client and the architecture. Third, the client becomes a friend of architecture as well. The transformative effect that the process has on clients cannot be understated. A public-service internship program is the only exposure to the design process that certain client groups have ever experienced. In many neighborhoods, such programs may provide the only opportunity to inspire future architects and perhaps even cultivate a more diverse clientele for the profession.

Not only do public-service internship programs give interns a better chance of meeting a client to begin with; they facilitate a closer, more enriching relationship afterward. Unmediated client contact allows the design work to be more responsive, and the intern can directly experience how faithfulness to client preferences can be as productive as any other design strategy. Perhaps as a remnant of a studio education, many interns tend to believe that great architecture results from purely formal exercises. H. H. Richardson and subsequent "starchitects," however, know the truth: a great fiduciary relationship is a foundation for great architecture. Clients and their programs can yield masterpieces. But even if this were not the case, professionals would still be ethically bound to be fiduciaries of their clients, and public-service internships can provide a more direct road to understanding and embracing this role than IDP can.

"If interns are the designers, internships design the designers. What kinds of designers does the profession want to design?"

ADVANCING THE DISCIPLINE

True professionals must advance their discipline. The "dangerous" knowledge that professionals wield defines them as a group; without this knowledge, professionals would just be citizens. The scientific art of designing buildings is the unique tool that architects use to serve their clients and the public. Like professionals in other fields, architects have a duty to hone this tool, produce architectural knowledge, and advance architectural thinking.

As with mentoring, architects are the only people qualified to do this particular work. In a rapidly progressing society, maintaining and transmitting current approaches amounts to moving backward. Architects are ethically obliged to keep up with changes, explore new ideas, and invent new solutions.

If necessity is the mother of invention,[18] public-service internships may be the mother of necessity. Limited resources can steer internship projects toward simple, cheap, local, and reusable materials. Limited experience can steer projects toward highly creative solutions.

In the 2002 book *Rural Studio,* about Samuel Mockbee's public-service architecture practice, author Andrea Dean rightfully emphasizes Mockbee's interest in the education and service value of the work. But then come Timothy Hursley's photographs! There is no denying such formal ingenuity. Like alchemists, the designers have transformed hay bales, old tires, car parts, street signs, glass bottles, cardboard, and other trash into responsive client solutions that epitomize sustainability but that are also aesthetically "arresting"—a combination that inspires and advances the discipline of architecture.

Obviously, invention can occur even without necessity; see Gehry, Frank O. Yet some believe that even Gehry's work was more aesthetically challenging when he had less wherewithal at his disposal. The days of strand board and chain link, after all, inspired a generation of freer thinkers, architects who mimicked Gehry's inventiveness without mimicking his signature style—which is just the way Gehry says he likes it.[19]

The two-way nature of the client-designer agreement in pro bono projects can allow a freedom of exploration comparable to that conferred by a grand patron. Because both sides must benefit, if interns decide to research new materials or processes in their design work, they may not encounter the same resistance that a paying client might offer. However, avant-garde public-service projects have been criticized for "paternalism"[20]—imposing a design agenda on the poor and vulnerable. Perhaps this sentiment stems from false associations with the stigmatized megaprojects of High Modernism. The sensitively responsive and more modest custom projects of today can provide cutting-edge work that still makes clients proud.

But public-service internship programs have been criticized for their modest quality as well. After all, interns do not generally come away from such projects having revolutionized the curtain wall or the tuned mass damper. There are limitations to the kinds of technical knowledge that can be utilized when working so close to ground level. However, it is logical to assume that an intern accustomed to pushing the envelope with modest technologies may implement that creativity in a more complex or higher-tech scenario. The reverse, however, might not be true: working with sophisticated projects or technologies may or may not lead to creative thinking.

When public-service internship programs are structured appropriately, they can make advances in sustainability, materiality, technology, and artistic expression, all cornerstones of architectural knowledge. And these advances are not limited to the project at hand. The many constraints of public-service internships also produce a resourcefulness and creativity in the interns themselves that can continue to advance architectural knowledge through subsequent projects and entire careers. Public-service internships constitute a unique alternative for fulfilling the ethical obligation to advance the discipline.

"We could design our future architects to be leaders beyond the profession— to use the creativity unique to our profession to guide society toward a more humane, engaging, and beautiful inhabitation of the planet."

PUBLIC SERVICE INTERNSHIPS

Imagine, for a moment, the ideal human environment. It's full of great buildings and landscapes, and it's devoid of all the junky stuff. There is no more obvious profession to pursue goals like this than building and landscape architecture.

In an ideally structured profession, with comfortable wages and understanding contractors, rapid progress could be made. But even so, all the design work that needs to be done on planet Earth—just to provide humanity with decent shelter, not to mention other architectural needs—is not going to happen in our lifetime. We need interns.

If interns are the designers, internships design the designers. What kinds of designers does the profession want to design? As professionals, we are ethically obligated to nurture our future designers to achieve at least three goals, woven into one: serving the public interest by advancing the discipline through fiduciary work for clients. But architecture is a small, entrepreneurial, quirky profession (if it is one at all), and we might set our sights on other goals. We could design our future architects to be leaders beyond the profession—to use the creativity unique to our profession to guide society toward a more humane, engaging, and beautiful inhabitation of the planet. Public-service internships possess the ideal characteristics to help us fulfill our ethical obligations, and more.

VICTORIA BEACH is the sole architect to serve as a Faculty Fellow at Harvard's Center for Ethics and the Professions and now writes and speaks nationwide on topics in architectural ethics. Victoria is the winner of the 2008 AIA Young Architect Award and Principal of Arch-io [ár-kee-oh], an award-winning architecture, landscape, and furniture design practice based in Carmel, California, established in 1996. The same year, she founded Design Foundations, a nonprofit through which aspiring architects gave hundreds of thousands of dollars worth of pro bono services to under-served communities. Victoria earned her Bachelor of Arts in Political Philosophy and Economics from Yale University and Master of Architecture from Harvard Graduate School of Design.

THOMAS
FISHER

IN THE PUBLIC'S INTEREST:
CREATING
PUBLIC-
INTEREST
DESIGN
INTERNSHIPS

I come from a family of doctors whose experiences shaped my views about internship. I grew up listening to my relatives commiserate about their years as overworked residents. But when I was an architecture school student who struggled to find a job during the 1970s recession and who ended up taking an unpaid position with an architecture firm, I admired the residency programs that my family members had had available to them. They felt justified complaining about the long hours, great pressure, and relatively low pay of medical residents, but I faced all the same conditions in my first job in architecture. While I managed to avoid doing all-nighters in architecture school, I did, on occasion, have to work all night for that architecture firm because of the procrastination and poor time management of the pressure-cooker principal who headed our team.

I didn't necessarily mind those long hours; I learned a lot. But in hindsight, the fact that I did all that work for a profit-making firm while not getting paid even the legally required minimum wage seems to highlight the problem of internships in the architectural profession and the need for a more organized system. We have not done enough to ensure that students have a coherent transition from college to a career. The recent "Great Recession" has further revealed the dysfunction of the system, as large numbers of architecture school graduates have not found work in our field and thus cannot get the experience they need in order to get licensed as architects. They have become a lost generation who will likely leave the field of architecture and never return.

The loss of talented graduates is particularly pertinent to public-interest design. Graduates of accredited architecture programs, while suffering from low employment because of the economy, at least have a clear internship path; they can work in architecture firms or in a range of public, private, or nonprofit organizations related to architecture. The Intern Development Program (IDP) of the National Council of Architectural Registration Boards has also ensured that recent graduates have a more orderly and consistent experience than those of us who suffered through internships many decades ago. In theory, at least, the internship process should also work for those graduates intent on pursuing a career in public-interest design, because little in the IDP process precludes working on lower-cost projects for lower-income users.

Such work rarely happens in practice, however. Very few architectural firms engage in public-interest work. Some do pro bono projects, prompted in part by the advocacy of Public Architecture, whose "The 1%" program encourages architects to donate 1 percent of their time to communities or clients who have design needs but who lack the ability to pay. But the dominant model of architecture practice follows that of the medical profession, in which architects serve the individual needs of clients in much the same way that doctors deal with the particular medical needs of patients. Such custom service works fine for those who can afford it. However, this model excludes the billions of people on the planet who do not have the ability to pay, even though they often have the greatest need.

THE PUBLIC HEALTH OF ARCHITECTURE

Recognition of that need in the medical field led to the emergence of public health in the nineteenth century in the United States. This effort was initiated by a group of doctors and led by landscape architect Frederick Law Olmsted, who, during the Civil War, directed the Sanitary Commission that later became the American Red Cross. The public health profession arose to address the shared health needs of large numbers of people at once. Rather than focusing on individual patients or on curing a disease after it had already been contracted, public health seeks to prevent illness from occurring across larger swaths of the population, encompassing a broader number of other disciplines than medicine does, ranging from economics and public policy to anthropology and psychology.

The time has come for a public-health version of our field. Architecture and design have direct relevance to many of the most pressing public health problems in the world, whether they be obesity and diabetes linked to the overfed, sedentary lifestyles of people in the United States; zoonotic diseases transferring from animals to humans living in overcrowded slums; or the physical and emotional hazards facing families living in inadequate shelter with poor access to water or proper sanitation. Just as the global poor need preventive health more than the world's rich, who have the luxury of individualized care, so too do the billions of

"Just as the global poor need preventive health...so too do the billions of impoverished people on the planet need design assistance more than the affluent few who commission architects for individualized design."

impoverished people on the planet need design assistance more than the affluent few who commission architects for individualized design. Likewise, designers need the poor more than we do the rich, because design provides the greatest value when addressing the largest number of problems with the least means or the most constraints. Design is at its best when it does more with less.

PUBLIC-INTEREST EDUCATION

To create a public-health version of design, we should start with the schools. Educating public-interest designers has to include some aspects of a traditional architectural curriculum, such as courses in basic design, materials and methods of construction, and practice and technology. However, a public-interest track would also exclude some features of architectural education and would include others rarely taught there.

For example, public-interest design students would have little or no need to learn about high-rise construction, high-tech civil and mechanical engineering, or high-energy materials, which most of the world cannot afford and probably doesn't need anyway. Instead, such students would need to know about appropriate technology, indigenous buildings, and local materials in various cultures and climates. Having experience with basic construction methods and prototype development and fabrication would help, as would some knowledge of material science and industrial design, because many of the needs of impoverished communities involve not just structures but also infrastructure and products of various kinds. An understanding of anthropology, microeconomics, and foreign languages would also prove useful.

Ideally, such a curriculum would be situated within existing architecture and design schools, because many of the core skills needed for public-interest design reside with the faculties there. But the relationship between public health and medicine should serve as a warning of how difficult it might be to develop this curriculum. Although public health began in medicine, the field has its own distinct educational needs, so it eventually established its own schools and accredited curriculums, becoming a discipline in its own right among the medical fields.

For public-interest design to remain a vital part of architectural schools, it will require that the architectural profession relinquish the current one-size-fits-all, generalist approach to education, aimed at producing future employees for offices organized around the medical model. Instead, we need to see architectural education leading to multiple career paths with many different tracks; client-focused design would be one of these, and public-interest design would be another. Such an approach could have pedagogical benefits, because even now only about half of all graduates end up working in private architectural offices. There would be practical benefits too, given that the demand for traditional architectural services in the United States seems likely to grow more slowly in coming years than the need for design assistance in the developing world.

The creation of public-interest design as a field will also require a different relationship among faculty and practitioners in our schools. Public-interest design depends on research funding to develop prototypical, open-source solutions to people's shelter and sanitation needs—funding that typically goes to nonprofit research universities that guarantee the proper spending of those resources and reporting on their use. At the same time, public-

"In creating internship opportunities, we will help create the [public-interest design] field itself and all the myriad ways in which design can contribute to improving the lives of billions of people."

interest design will require the involvement of design practitioners to provide the personnel and project-management skills needed to ensure the proper implementation of the research and its translation into buildable structures and deployable infrastructure. That combination of research faculty and design practitioners already exists in most schools to varying degrees, although the two groups often remain disconnected in the curriculum, with the former focused on "support" courses and the latter on design studios. Public-interest design demands their integration, which will in turn create internship opportunities for students serving as research assistants in the universities and as paid interns in research-based design offices

PUBLIC-INTEREST PRACTICE

Such an education would shape the nature of public-interest practice. Like any new field, this one will require creativity on the part of its practitioners, because many of the funders and clients in this area have rarely worked with designers and thus may not see the need for our knowledge. But the public-health community seems ready to respond to a partnership with the design fields, as it has begun to discover what designers can contribute not just as technical experts, but also as problem solvers on a wide range of scales.

A bigger obstacle might be within the design community itself. The architectural profession has been so focused on the production of custom designs for fee-paying clients that the generation of low-cost prototypes that local communities can make or maintain with little expertise may prove too large a leap for many practitioners. That's fine, of course. The rise of public health did not spell the end of medicine, but rather an alternative practice for health professionals. Likewise, public-interest design will not reduce the need for architects in private practice; it will only expand the opportunities for design professionals and the scope of our services to include everyone on the planet.

Funding for public-interest design services will likely resemble that of public health, involving nonprofit foundations like the Bill and Melinda Gates Foundation and nongovernmental organizations (NGOs) like the World Bank or the World Health Organization, as well as governmental agencies like the National Institutes of Health. Clients might also include foreign countries and U.S. aid organizations working overseas. Private design firms may need to partner with universities to pursue much of this funding, because the development of locally appropriate, prototypical solutions involves research and testing as well as design and production.

These developments will require a change in orientation within architecture and design schools, as they, too, become more research-oriented than in the past. This prospect may seem daunting to some, but the need for public-interest design far outstrips the number of firms willing or able to provide such services. As the demand grows, so will the supply, especially as the demand for traditionally trained architectural graduates remains soft—possibly for a very long time—because of the triple whammy of the global recession, the overbuilding in many real-estate markets, and the increase in productivity brought on by building information modeling.

PUBLIC-INTEREST INTERNSHIPS

Until we have created a public-interest design curriculum and public-interest practices, where should a recent graduate interested in this as a career go to look for jobs? For those who want to work in impoverished communities, either in the United States or abroad, the Peace Corps and AmeriCorps remain excellent options. Both organizations offer incredible opportunities to work on service projects for people in need, providing leadership training and skill development as well as personal satisfaction. Many architecture graduates already know about and have participated in those public service organizations. That experience may not help graduates fulfill the requirements of IDP, but the Peace Corps and AmeriCorps do supply ample opportunities to learn the core skills of public-interest design, which can lead to permanent employment in organizations ranging from the federal government's Corporation for National and Community Service to the International Civil Service Commission of the United Nations.

Other NGOs also offer myriad internship experiences. These range from relatively small, architecturally focused organizations such as Design Corps and Architecture for Humanity to large NGOs such as the American Refugee Committee, Habitat for Humanity, and the American Red Cross. The Web has made it much easier to find public-service internships on sites like Idealist.org, created by Action Without Borders, which links to thirty-five thousand nonprofit and community organizations in 165 countries and which includes a Career Center that lists hundreds of internship opportunities.

This site and others like it give access to the demand side of the equation: which organizations have an existing need for interns. But those who want to pursue public-interest design may need to take more of a supply-side approach, creating opportunities that don't yet exist but soon will, given the extent of the need and the amount of work that needs doing.

"At its best, design often offers far more than what most people expect or even believe to be possible, which makes it particularly useful in situations where users have so few resources."

Many NGOs tend to focus on interns who have specific skills directly related to the service they provide: hunger-related organizations tend to hire graduates of food and nutrition programs, public-health organizations hire graduates of medical, nursing, and public health schools, and so on. Many NGOs serve people living in unsafe or unsanitary physical environments, and they see how those environments affect people's lives. However, NGOs sometimes overlook the physical-environment basis for some of the problems they seek to address. For example, a group working to help girls to stay in school in Africa—an effort reaping tremendous economic and demographic benefits, with profound social-justice implications—discovered that many teenage girls, especially in Muslim countries, drop out of school because the inadequate toilet facilities in the school buildings present an objectionable lack of privacy. The group realized that they could not keep girls in school in these countries without also upgrading school facilities.

These examples show the public-health community's growing recognition of design's value, but public-interest designers may still need to create their own internship opportunities. This may demand researching the organizations that most interest you, writing a query letter, and going for an interview that makes an argument for why the organization needs architectural expertise, even if it does not know or acknowledge it. Such letters need to get to the point quickly, because some organizations may have a degree of skepticism about a designer's value. As in any good, persuasive essay, the letter needs to start with a hook that compels the reader to want to learn more. In the case of the group working on girls' education in Africa, a letter that initially talks not about your credentials or your desire to help but instead about your ideas for how to provide better low-cost sanitary facilities in schools would go a long way toward piquing their interest and prompting an interview and possible employment with them.

Public-interest designers, in other words, need to have an entrepreneurial spirit. After all, the field, as such, hardly exists. In creating internship opportunities, we will help create the field itself and all the myriad ways in which design can contribute to improving the lives of billions of people. As designers, we should excel at creating a new profession. After all, our education equips us to imagine alternative futures, to connect seemingly unrelated phenomena, and to produce promising solutions to sometimes unnoticed needs. At its best, design often offers far more than what most people expect or even believe to be possible, which makes it particularly useful in situations where users have so few resources. However, communicating that value to NGOs, who may think that architects and designers cater only to the wealthiest 5 to 10 percent of the world's population, remains the greatest challenge—and opportunity—for public-interest designers.

A PUBLIC-INTEREST PROFESSION

All of which brings me back to my physician family members. While public-interest design remains in its infancy, it needs an organized residency program like that in medicine and a clear internship path like that of architecture and public health. Both the design profession and the design schools have a responsibility to make that happen, and we need to get started now, given the enormous need for improved living conditions for so many people. Too much remains at stake to allow public-interest design to languish as a well-meaning, donated activity of a few committed architects and designers. We need funding commensurate with need.

Over the last thirty-four years, the World Bank alone has spent $16 billion on shelter in ninety countries, or roughly $470 million annually. With design fees at, say, 5 percent of that figure, that would equal $23.5 million annually in research and development funding to devise better shelter—an amount of money sufficient to support those who see public-interest shelter design as a possible career. That amount of money, of course, pales in comparison to that spent on medicine and public health. The School of Public Health at the University of Minnesota does almost $100 million in research a year, so public-interest design has a long way to go. Research that produces successful results, however, often feeds itself. As has been the case for medicine and public health, funding for public-interest design will increase when the benefits of better shelter and sanitation become ever more evident to major public health organizations and agencies. With that increased funding will come opportunities for internships and fellowships of various kinds, and eventually a structure will emerge to coordinate the assignment of students and recent graduates to places where their skills will be of greatest use.

As designers, we should be able to design such a system—especially because we cannot continue along the path we are on. Public-interest design cannot remain an almost entirely pro bono activity, as it is now; design has incredible value for the billions of people who will benefit from its innovations, and its practitioners deserve compensation for their effort and expertise. Nor can it remain a largely piecemeal affair; as long as public-interest internships are catch as catch can, they will not attract the talent or the number of designers needed to meet the demand for public-interest design. Instead, we need to see the creation of a public-interest design profession as our first public-interest design problem: to do the greatest good for the greatest number of people at the lowest cost and with the fewest resources, as all good design should.

"Too much remains at stake to allow public-interest design to languish as a well-meaning, donated activity of a few committed architects and designers."

THOMAS FISHER is the dean of the College of Design at the University of Minnesota, a professor in its school of architecture, and past president of the Association of Collegiate Schools of Architecture. He has written 6 books, 36 chapters, and 130 articles over the last 11 years, many of which have addressed aspects of public-interest design.

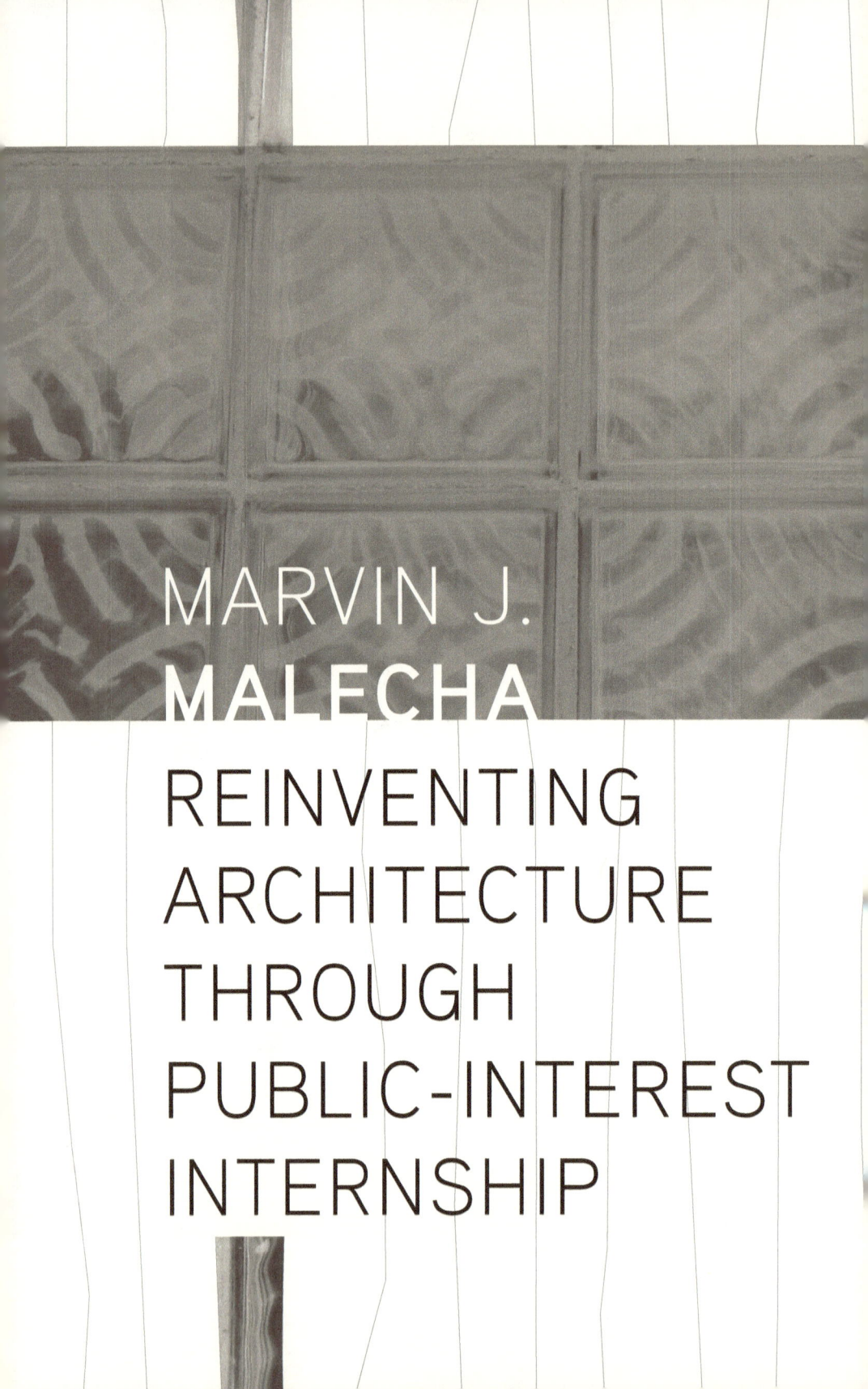

MARVIN J.
MALECHA

REINVENTING
ARCHITECTURE
THROUGH
PUBLIC-INTEREST
INTERNSHIP

BRIDGING THE DIVIDE BETWEEN THE NOVICE AND THE MASTER, BETWEEN THE PROFESSION AS IT IS AND WHAT IT WILL BECOME.

The experience of learning is the ultimate confirmation of the humanity of an individual. Learning involves engaging the world with an open mind and a willing spirit. It demands the freedom to venture and to accept risk and uncertainty. Learning is a complex mixture of success and failure, reflection and action. It requires both a wandering spirit and the purposeful determination to reach a goal. No two people navigate this journey in exactly the same way; some among us accumulate knowledge through a voracious appetite for reading, whereas others seek the motivation of a peer group to foster learning. Still others make a direct connection between learning and the work they do with their hands. Regardless, the learning endeavor is a mixture of all of these experiences in differing combinations, according to the inclination of the student.

Internship is one form that this mixture of experiences can take. The roots of experiential learning paths run deep in human history and are unquestionably related to apprenticeship, the mentor-mentee relationship, and the concepts of making the rounds in medicine and standing at the bar in law. In each of these variations, the learner is steeped in the discipline of a profession to learn its culture, ethical standards, and relevance to society. The medical doctor learns that the first principle of medicine is "first, do no harm." In the ancient Greek city of Epidaurus, the temple of Asclepius, god of healing, bore the following inscription: "Pure must be he who enters the fragrant temple." Similarly, every architectural student who has had the first professional practice class knows that the profession is licensed because of the health, safety, and welfare responsibilities with which the architect is entrusted. However, the novice's ability to shoulder these responsibilities cannot be adequately tested in the classroom. This is why immersion in practice must be part of the education of a doctor, lawyer, or architect. In the act of doing, the professional is tested in ways that cannot be replicated in the protected classroom environment.

In theory there is no difference between theory and practice. In practice there is.

—Yogi Berra

The internship experience is defined by exposure to the exigencies of practice. The skills learned in formal educational settings are tested by the situational challenges faced by working professionals. Internship gauges an individual's ability to act upon issues and concerns that arise in a real-time setting, which MIT professor Donald Schön calls "reflection in action." Interns learn these skills under the guidance of a professional who oversees the student's work. A master guides a novice to explore a culture of making and doing. Thus, the quality of the internship experience is dependent on the care taken by the person guiding the experience and the rigor with which oversight is conducted. In this way, internship is a form of apprenticeship with an important mentoring component. The culture of practice transmitted from professional to intern teaches the student a way of doing that encompasses professional ethics, necessary proficiencies, and a firsthand observation of the influence of the work of a designer. This experience is the bridge between theory and practice, master and novice.

"The culture of practice transmitted from professional to intern teaches the student a way of doing that encompasses professional ethics, necessary proficiencies, and a firsthand observation of the influence of the work of a designer."

For most of their history, architectural internships tended to be largely unmanaged experiences, but lessons from the medical profession have inspired considerable change toward a closely monitored process. Now the typical internship favors traditional experience and is mostly dependent on a managed process within a diverse architectural practice. However, this template exposes the vulnerabilities of a model that is dependent on a single vision of what the profession is. The American Institute of Architects has found itself in a similar quandary as the question of service to members is considered. Even the mantra of health, safety, and welfare of the public does not resolve the dilemma; the practitioner in a single-person office may affect public welfare just as much as an individual within a large organization. To address this issue, large-firm and small-firm roundtables have been established, complemented by a rich collection of knowledge communities focusing on varying building types and modes of practice.

As the recent recession has dramatically made clear, the role of the architect is evolving at a pace never before seen. New relationships are emerging from an integrated project-delivery process that has dramatically changed the services provided by the architect. A survey of architectural firms demonstrates that every commission, irrespective of a firm's size, is customized to fit unique financing, client definitions, public regulations, and construction processes. In addition, the organization of the architectural office has changed. The steep pyramid that was once common has been replaced by mergers, acquisitions, and project-management strategies that have resulted in less of a career path for middle management in large firms. Instead, firms now tend to be organized as a large group of individuals who work as contract employees tied to a specific project. One side effect of this change is a reduction in the availability of senior staff most capable of mentoring an intern. Also, because of the increase in contract employment, interns are less likely to plan for the internship experience to be completed in a single office. Interns expect to move and to be moved.

There is another change in practice that must be accounted for when the nature of professional preparation is considered. For centuries—perhaps millennia—we have measured the progress of architecture by the iconic artifacts we have inherited. We judge the importance of individuals within the profession by the structures they produce, and we memorialize these structures in glossy publications, cutting-edge websites, and other social media. Yet even as we focus on such exemplars, the very media that dominate our attention signal a significantly different way of seeing that must influence how the architect works. In one way, we are moving from simple signification to complex representation; in a different (but simultaneous) way, we are moving from artifact design to experience design. What this means to the architect is that an extreme focus on the structure ranks low on the scales of complexity and experiential focus. A building is certainly experiential, but our focus on the experience of a building has been largely self-referential, rather than deriving from the user's perspective.

The lesson from designers in related professions is that we are making an overall shift toward interaction design (implying continuing transformation induced by a complex group of users) and therefore toward service design. This is a radically transformed perspective on the purpose of design, and it demands a radically transformed posture from the architect. How will the profession meet this challenge of transforming perspectives and priorities? Perhaps an emerging phrase from business will point

"But we must now put our discipline's design-thinking skills into action on behalf of the public good through internship. In doing so, we have the opportunity to explore a new professional culture."

the way: cognitive surplus. Cognitive surplus implies the abundance of creativity and the natural tendency toward goodwill displayed by the creative personality. Cognitive surplus constitutes the binding element between academia, business, government, and financial institutions, allowing them to work separately and together to address the most pressing issues of our time. Cognitive surplus is the great advantage that can fuel another way of comprehending the design profession.

It is abundantly clear that there is significant opportunity in this period of increasingly diverse conceptualizations of the nature of practice and of the internship experience. For this reason, internship should include traditional experiences in firms of all sizes as well as nontraditional experiences in other venues. Internship experiences should be distinctly configured to the scale of the practice and the specific nature of the specialized practice, with an eye toward exploring new models of practice.

Traditionally, internship has been used to introduce the intern to the predominant culture of practice. It is generally thought of as a test of an individual's commitment to succeed in a chosen profession. However, with the advent of new information technologies, another possibility has emerged. It is not unusual for an intern who enters a professional setting to be the most proficient user of new information technologies that significantly affect the conduct of the profession. This has fostered an awareness that the intern in an office can actually be of great assistance in helping the practice enter otherwise unexplored realms—and without incurring significant costs. In such instances, the intern becomes a valued resource. This type of situation holds great possibilities for internship in the public interest and for redefinition of the profession as significantly invested in the benefit of society.

American universities have a well-documented history of involvement in the agricultural, manufacturing, and societal development of our nation. In 1862 Abraham Lincoln signed the Morrill Act, which created land-grant universities, setting in motion the greatest American contribution to the evolution of the university experience. The land-grant model was intended to support the vitality of the economic and cultural aspects of American life, and it was the logical expression of the thoughts of founding fathers such as John Adams, quoted here in a letter to his wife dated May 12, 1780: "I must study politicks and war so that my sons may have liberty to study mathematicks and philosophy, geography, natural history, naval architecture, navigation, commerce and agriculture, in order to give their children a right to study painting, poetry, musick, architecture, statuary, tapestry and porcelaine."

We have had the privilege to study architecture as John Adams envisioned. Now we have an obligation to invest our inheritance. The freedom to study architecture and other creative disciplines has revealed to us the amazing prize of design thinking. It is this prize that will sustain our nation as we address the most important issue before us: human health. But we must now put our discipline's design-thinking skills into action on behalf of the public good through internship. In doing so, we have the opportunity to explore a new professional culture. It is time to venture on a scale that can rapidly be increased to foster new modes of practice at a time when traditional practices are waning in importance. Internship can act as a bridge to an emerging profession as it helps us explore the role that architects and designers can play in addressing society's pressing health issues. Significant peer-reviewed studies have correlated quality of environment with quality of life. Work and life challenges including obesity, hypertension, material toxicity, and environmental air quality are only

> "The seed of the profession's evolution will be sown when its future leaders are inspired to conceptualize practice in new ways with a transformed purpose."

some of a long list of issues directly affected by the built environment. To address these issues effectively, a new culture of practice is required.

The lessons in service learning gained from the land-grant institution experience will inform these efforts. We must leave no doubt that we are committed to serving the public good. We must not frame public-interest internships merely as a strategy to better position the design professions or only as a way to enhance curricular experiences in the academy. Real-world issues must be addressed in a way that includes the many constituencies affected. The savior mentality has no place in this endeavor. The most creative approaches to difficult problems may be found in unexpected places and from unlikely people. These efforts must be exemplary in their rigorous approach, beginning with thorough inquiry that clearly establishes the issues to be addressed. Then the process to be undertaken must be documented, along with its ultimate outcomes, so that the success of the internship can be more fully assessed.

Over time, the accumulation of this documentation will constitute a knowledge base that will enrich the relationship between the academic experience and professional practice. Just as international experiences have been demonstrated to be essential in preparing design students to practice across borders, so too will it become evident that public-interest internships encourage students to question the accepted norms of conduct for the profession. The seed of the profession's evolution will be sown when its future leaders are inspired to conceptualize practice in new ways with a transformed purpose. The essence of the designer's motivation is to improve the human condition; this aspiration will be most fully realized when it operates in service of those most in need.

If there is any topic that is likely to provoke contention in this discussion, I believe it is the definition of *pro bono publico* work. Many believe that "for the public good" means "without compensation." In their conception, this work is to be done as part of the whole of professional services and as a moral obligation of the profession. Such an approach is unsustainable, and it will hinder efforts to transform traditional practice and the academy to better serve the public. Of course, there are times when serving the public interest requires freely given sweat equity; but at other times, such work can be sponsored by philanthropy. Certainly we would consider public health officials or elementary school teachers to be people who have devoted their lives to the public good, yet they are compensated for their work. Doing good need not entail a vow of poverty. The aspiration to serve the public good draws deeply upon the American spirit of entrepreneurship. Consider the advice of Thomas Edison as he reflected on his work as an inventor and entrepreneur: "My philosophy of life is work—bringing out the secrets of nature and applying them for the happiness of man. I know of no better service to render during the short time we are in this world. My main purpose in life is to make enough money to make ever more inventions. … The dove is my emblem. … I want to save and advance human life, not destroy it. … I am proud of the fact that I never invented weapons to kill."

These thoughts should inspire us to act with the confidence that stems from our certainty that the work we do is valuable. There is value in design thinking and the hard work of the iterative process. This value gives us the potential to make our lives as architects and designers more meaningful; it is the reason why we seek to ensure that the resources are available for us to continue our work.

Our vigorous exploration of the internship experience as the frontier of public-interest architecture supposes a model for the profession

"The essence of the designer's motivation is to improve the human condition; this aspiration will be most fully realized when it operates in service of those most in need."

that repositions the architect. This conception of the profession sees the architecture school as a school of public health, a conception that constellates issues as varied as ethical obligations, purposeful learning, reimagining traditional notions of the conduct of the architecture profession, and leveraging the university as the host for internship in the public interest. There is a strong case to be made for public-interest internships as essential preparation for all studies related to architecture.

As we serve the public interest through architecture, our discussion of beauty will be transformed. No longer can we conduct the architectural discourse as a consideration of artifacts. Great design moves people in their hearts and souls; it influences their quality of life and contributes to their physical and mental well-being. But this level of design skill cannot be taught only in the classroom. We must engage the needs of society directly with all of the discipline and rigor that architectural practice entails. As a result of this emphasis on the public good, we are clearly witnessing the transformation of the profession. Thomas Edison defined innovation as creativity merged with purposefulness. We are witnessing the purposefulness of efforts to serve the public good merged with the immense creative energy of a profession that is at its best when it nurtures new ways of living by imagining what does not yet exist. The best way to stimulate this transformation is internship directed toward the public good.

For public-interest internship to lead the profession, it will be necessary to foster an open attitude within the profession itself—and, perhaps more importantly, within the bodies that oversee licensure. Without such openness, the exploration of internship will not be realized in practice. Perhaps the best example of this kind of attitude is Auburn University's Rural Studio, founded by Sam Mockbee. The Rural Studio, conceptualized

"For public-interest internship to lead the profession, it will be necessary to foster an open attitude within the profession itself—and, perhaps more importantly, within the bodies that oversee licensure."

as an essential experience within an accredited architecture program, not only legitimized public-interest internship; it also structured students' experiences under the watchful eye of an accomplished professional. The Rural Studio model is built upon Auburn University's land-grant origins. It engages students in meaningful work as they learn valuable professional skills, including collaboration and comprehensive design. The students' inspiring work, serving Alabama's citizens with the greatest needs, has inspired the profession. Professor Mockbee gained international recognition for his work, and he was awarded the AIA Gold Medal. His example and the continuing work of his students—and now their students—have legitimized design/build projects on behalf of the public good in every school of architecture in the United States.

Similarly, another effort—The 1%—has challenged architectural practices to commit the equivalent of 1 percent of their billed time to serving the greater needs of their communities through the provision of much-needed design services. Perhaps the most important feature of this initiative is that it highlights the true breadth of services that an architect can provide. By opening the architectural office to new concepts of practice, new areas of service may be discovered. This strategy, when motivated by the will to do the right thing, will encourage the office to look to new areas and to expand the conception of the profession. These examples must be our models if we are to make progress.

Through internships directed in this manner, the student and the mentor alike face the most pressing issues of human well-being. The traditional confines of the academy and the professional office are expanded, and the leap to new models for business and practice can be imagined. The individuals who chronicle their experiences and observations during the internship process will lead the profession to a higher precipice of possibility. What is left for us in the profession is to find the courage to make the leap.

MARVIN J. MALECHA, FAIA, is the dean of the NC State University College of Design and an Association of Collegiate Schools of Architecture Distinguished Professor. He is an AIA/ACSA Topaz Laureate for excellence in architectural education. Dean Malecha is the recipient of the Architecture Research Centers Consortium James Haecker Award for Research and the Dale Prize for Excellence in Urban and Regional Planning Scholarship. He has served as President of the Association of Collegiate Schools of Architecture and the American Institute of Architects.

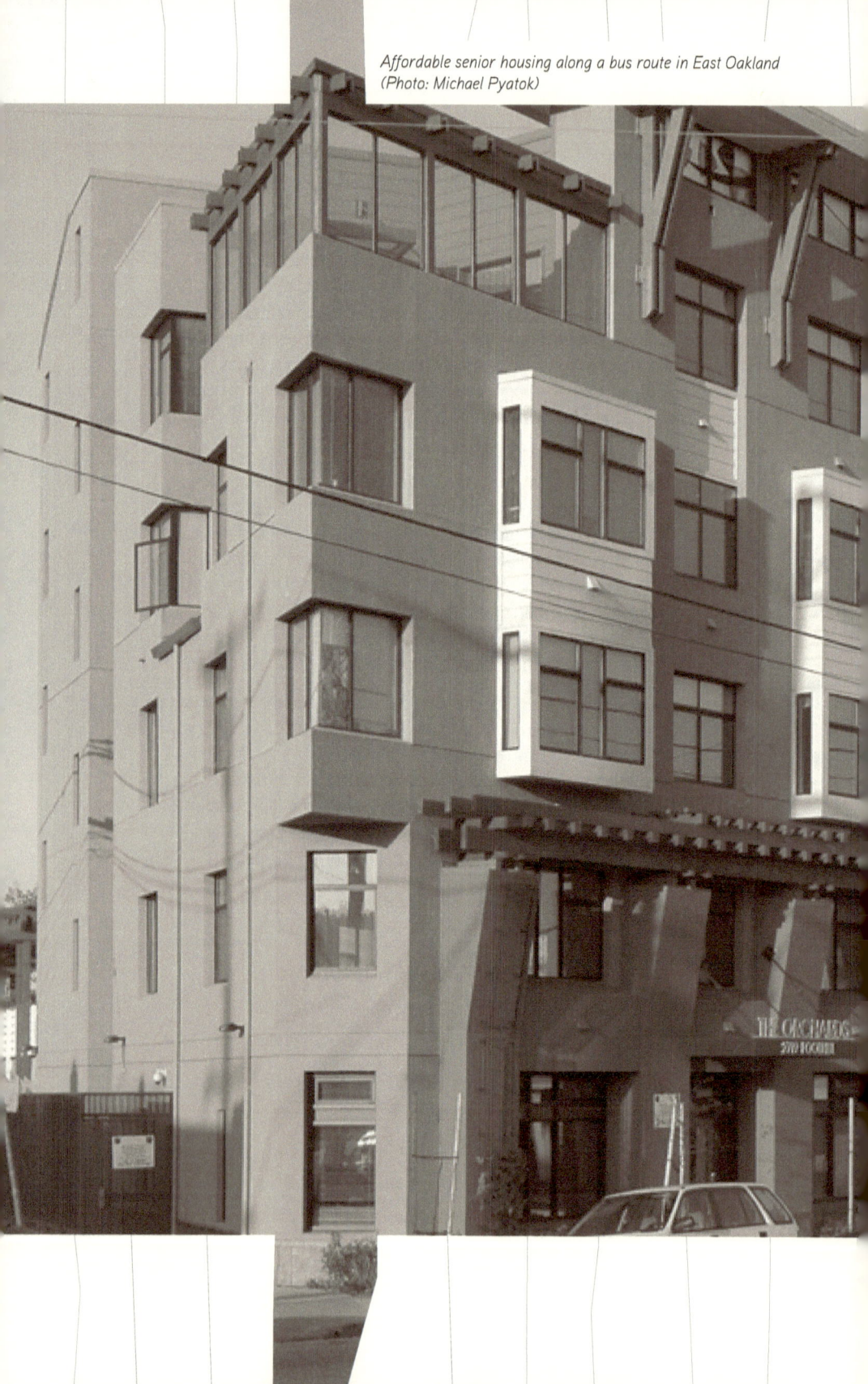

Affordable senior housing along a bus route in East Oakland (Photo: Michael Pyatok)

MICHAEL
PYATOK

WORKING IN THE MAINSTREAM, DESIGNING FOR THE PUBLIC

For at least the first two decades of my career, both as a practitioner and as a professor of design, I showed little tolerance for those designers serving for-profit clients in the "mainstream" design professions. I argued that, within a culture of consumption, their work was being forced to deceive, lure, mesmerize, and intimidate the general public into worshiping material goods and the places that promoted and sold them. I also felt that mainstream work was being used to make people feel insecure for not possessing such goods or living in such places, or for not understanding the supposedly complex and mystifying meanings and visual complexities of modern objects and places.

I argued that, within hierarchical class societies, the ruling class controlled culture by rewarding idealist epistemologies that prefer to invent from the top down, inspired by esoteric concepts invented a priori to direct engagement with the rough-and-tumble world of everyday people. This argument identified members of the avant-garde as the ultimate sellouts to the system of consumption for walking into the intellectual trap of radical individualism, pursuing fame through oddity and frivolous novelty, the cultural cornerstones of ceaseless consumption. This approach even invaded public-service efforts as exemplified by Sam Mockbee, whose students' work in the Rural Studio perplexed Mexican architects working in the barrios of Mexico City; they asked me, "How can your culture, and its design professions, be so confused and misguided?"

While I still believe there is much truth to this argument, proven each day by such catastrophes as the urban "renewal" project being developed

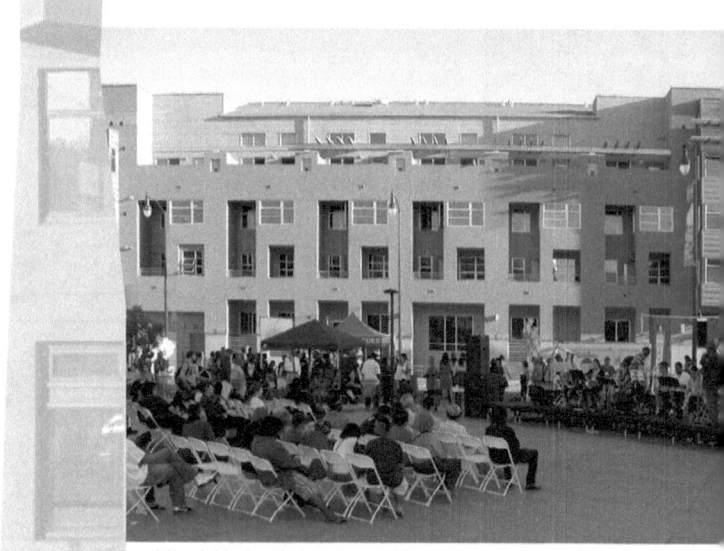

Affordable family housing and housing for formerly homeless singles above a childcare center in downtown Oakland (Photo: Michael Pyatok)

in Brooklyn's train yards at the hands of Frank Gehry and Forest City, there are also countless designers, buried in the bowels of corporate firms, who every day successfully beseech their clients, employers, and colleagues to stretch their interests beyond themselves to include the needs and aspirations of the general public and its fragile subset of lower-income households. Their work is far more arduous, more challenging, and, I would argue, at times more influential than that of those pursuing similar interests within settings whose mission and clients are explicitly supportive of and devoted to "public service." Often the scale of their work far exceeds the size of projects that are typical of community-design centers, so their impacts are greater. Their work can be quite difficult because they must convince both their employers and their clients of the value of more broadly defining responsibilities beyond profit margins, or at least that it is in their best long-term interest to satisfy the needs of more fragile populations within the orbit of their projects.

This is what I have learned in the third and fourth decades of my career as I have grown to know peers "across the aisle" working in conventional practices. So I offer these observations, not to put down the lack of experience or historical perspective of publicly minded newcomers who complain about a lack of opportunity in mainstream design professions, but to help others not to make the same mistake I did, i.e., writing off mainstream design practices as completely unsuitable for promoting the interests of the general public and lower-income communities.

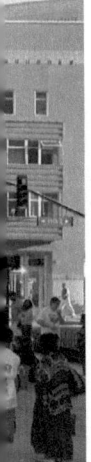

In this essay about internship opportunities I am intentionally using the general terms "design" and "designers," and not just "architecture" and "architects," because today more than ever, environments are being shaped by collaborations among many disciplines. An architect is but one player on a project's team and cannot be isolated from planners, landscape architects, civil engineers, interior designers, industrial designers, or mechanical engineers, just to name a few other pertinent roles. We are all "designers" attempting to improve the world around us, and we are nearly always all working together. While we still hold onto the myth that architects are the "coordinating" discipline, our efforts to integrate our work into surrounding human and natural ecosystems are complex and transdisciplinary. I believe it may be a bit arrogant on the part of architects to conceptualize this discussion about how to expand internships in "public service" as an isolated concern of ours.

I also believe it may be a sign of arrogance among "leftists/progressives" in design professions today to assert that "public service" is only being pursued by a small, specially trained, elite group

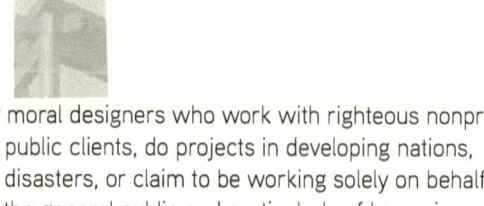

of exceptionally moral designers who work with righteous nonprofit institutions and public clients, do projects in developing nations, globe-trot after disasters, or claim to be working solely on behalf of the interests of the general public and particularly of lower-income communities. I argue that all designers, by definition, are working on behalf of the general public, including lower-income households, even when the designer is employed by private for-profit interests.

On the flip side, I also argue that those who believe they are solely working on behalf of the general public or lower-income communities through nonprofit and public clients are also at times pursuing narrow political or self-serving aims that are not in the best interests of the people they are serving. Such clients understandably must seek opportunities provided by government programs and funding sources that at times result in negative consequences for lower income communities. The HOPE VI program is still accused, and rightfully so, of displacing very-low-income households. Design-build studios often leave behind house designs in disenfranchised communities that are more reflective of the fashionable pursuits of students and their faculty than the needs of residents and their communities. The ultimate recipients of our services are usually not our paying clients. The paying clients, whether for profit or nonprofit, can often have motives not in the best interests of those whom we are ultimately trying to serve. Clients and their funding sources have political and financial goals that sometimes shape programs in ways that exploit the needs of the poor or paternalistically prolong their dependencies. The federal housing tax credit, a fundamental funding source for most affordable rental housing built in the United States today, helps corporations and wealthy individuals protect their wealth at rates far greater than their investments in affordable housing. The tax income lost because of this program could fund a much larger stock of affordable housing serving many more families.

OPPORTUNITIES IN THE MAINSTREAM

When I finished my graduate studies in 1967, there were virtually no design professors in the United States offering alternative models of teaching or practice through studios or seminars, promoting the social responsibility of design professionals, or talking about the impact of a class system and capitalism on the ideology of design practice. The Civil Rights movement, the Anti–Vietnam War movement, and the growing dissatisfaction with urban renewal were the larger forces giving shape to the questioning minds of young designers and planners at that time. A few books like Goodman's *After the Planners*, Jacobs's *The Death and Life of Great American Cities*, Turner's *Freedom to Build*, Abrams's

The City is the Frontier, and even Rudofsky's *Architecture without Architects* were discovered by designers searching on their own, not because there were faculty recommending them. Perhaps political awareness was keener in planning schools, such as Chester Hartman at the Harvard Graduate School of Design, but Robert Goodman provided a different vision of the profession as a whole in *After the Planners*.

Design schools showed little support for the Left, which is why we had to organize boycotts and shut the schools down. But that politically charged era spawned a generation of motivated young designers who wedged their way into the mainstream professions and into schools of design and planning as faculty, pushing for structural and attitudinal change. It was often a lonely, uphill battle, and many were denied tenure or lost their jobs, but slowly and surely curriculum changes occurred through the 1970s, and a small but growing number of progressive design faculty acquired tenure. By the late '70s and into the '80s they were even producing offspring entering the design professions or other academic positions. But most of the name schools of architecture remained impermeable to this stream of thinking, and even where such faculty and students had some presence in their departments, for the most part they remained a marginalized minority. But compared to a generation ago, the times have changed, because now there are even design and planning schools where the deans are solidly within the Left.

In 2010, by comparison, to find a younger generation of left-leaning designers complaining about the lack of public-service opportunity in

"The experience to be gained in mainstream offices with larger, more complex projects is essential for the full development of any design professional's skills, particularly those planning to work for most of their careers in public service and for low-income communities."

the fields of design and planning is somewhat laughable. But the complaint is based on the reality that there are indeed many more graduates coming out of the schools armed with progressive attitudes and models for practice and teaching than there were thirty years ago, because of the previous generation's efforts. The question is how this new wave of designers can best apply themselves within their respective fields.

There is no doubt that most design professionals earn significantly less than those in law and medicine, both often mentioned as professions that have devised successful models for "public service." Their fee structures more easily allow for pro bono work, and in the case of medicine, there are major public programs mandated by law for serving the interests and needs of lower-income individuals, such as Medicare and Medicaid.

But each day in practice, I am pleasantly surprised by the people I meet in for-profit design firms at all levels, from principals to junior staff, who, through their actions within and outside their firms, demonstrate a commitment to improving the lot of those usually less served by the design professions. Outside the office, they are members of boards of public-service-oriented organizations, where they provide the same level of expert advice as they do to their paying clients. During evenings and weekends, they are community organizers, tenant activists, or construction workers. Depending on their private lives, they are working as much as thirty to forty additional hours each week in these alternative, volunteer efforts. Even when serving their private, for-profit clients, they are engaged in constant client education campaigns,

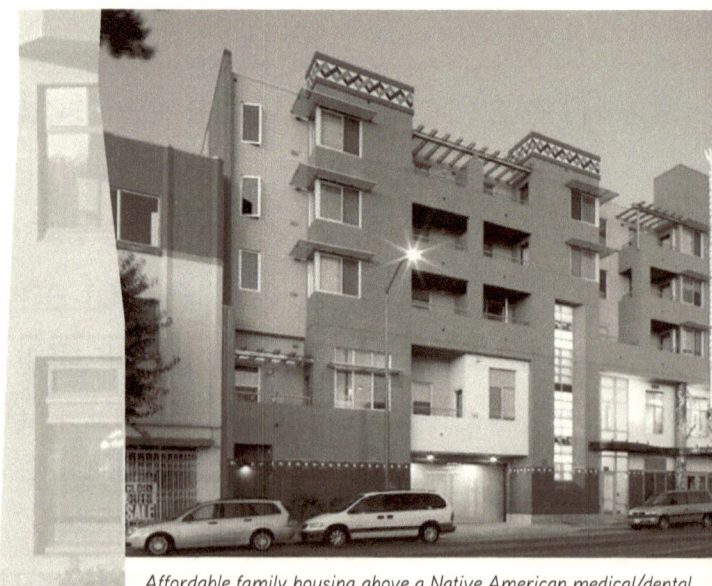

Affordable family housing above a Native American medical/dental clinic and community center in East Oakland (Photo: Frank Domin)

often necessarily subtle and diplomatic. These efforts are not just to steer clients into actions that are more "planet-friendly" and sustainable but also to take account of impacts on the public realm, sensitizing clients to their obligations beyond their property lines and pocketbooks. I have even met designers engaged in market-rate developments who have successfully convinced clients to include affordable housing when not obligated by law to do so.

As mentioned above, what is interesting about projects executed within mainstream corporate offices is that they are, more often than not, larger in scale and impact than projects undertaken by nonprofit community design centers. The scale of these projects and their technical complexities offer educational opportunities that are not readily available in the smaller projects of community-design centers. They teach complex organizational and project management skills, convey detailed complex technical knowledge, give practice in consultant coordination, and provide insights into the attitudes of those with whom we may not often agree. This latter knowledge is invaluable for future work that may place an intern in opposition to some of these people; the intern will benefit from having honed skills, from an insider's perspective, in how to converse, constructively debate, and ultimately negotiate with those who disagree with us on fundamental issues.

SHORTCOMINGS OF COMMUNITY-DESIGN CENTERS

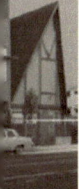

Unlike mainstream practice, much of the work of "alternative" careers seems to lie primarily in two phases of a project's life: (1) early conceptual design, including community participation and organizing, advocacy campaigns, design competitions, planning studies, policy formation, and writing; and (2) construction, usually on small-scale design-build projects. There is no doubt that the skills involved in the pre-design work of community organizing and political advocacy, facilitating community planning and design charrettes, are invaluable and crucial professional skills to acquire. But when all phases of development are engaged, a far broader and deeper knowledge base is needed than is typically acquired even after years of working in community-design settings. For example, Schematic Design—with its detailed attention to budgets, codes from several layers of government, and complex construction types—for a two-hundred-unit higher-density project is quite different from that for a twenty-unit lower-density project. Design Development, when the expertise of at least half a dozen other disciplines must be integrated, is also quite different, depending on whether the project is the construction of a whole new neighborhood of a thousand units or one small infill project.

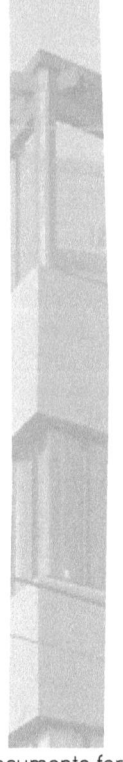

"I submit that there are many, many opportunities within mainstream design and planning offices for young interns to pursue their public-service goals."

Construction Documents for a mixed-use complex involving housing, retail, and medical facilities is far more demanding of precision, thoroughness, and technical knowledge than a one-story community center, child-care center, or open-air farmers' market. Construction Administration for urban projects at 100 dwelling units per acre demands a broader and deeper range of technical skills and a more demanding level of diplomacy to navigate the many accountability arguments during construction than would be required for low-density single-family or townhome developments.

With today's world of instant communications, responses to international disasters have become virtually instantaneous. Young people with few personal obligations are lured by the romance of international work, but they are blind to the potentially debilitating side effects of instant "charitable giving" on the populations being served. These short-term relief strategies may be a comfortable fit for adventurous youths with short attention spans who are unwilling or unable to remain for the necessary decades-long follow-through that comes only with sinking deep roots in a locale's people and culture. A steady diet of this type of instant-gratification work can stunt the growth of a design practitioner's patience and perseverance, traits that are needed for solid, long-lasting community development. Even two years in the Peace Corps is an improvement over a few months hopscotching between disasters or engaging with them virtually by designing over the Internet.

Notwithstanding all their good intentions and successes, the learning opportunities within community-design centers are for the most part somewhat limited. Some community-design staff have made lifelong commitments to the field, but their involvement with it is often limited to either front-end political and conceptual design work or back-end construction work on a small scale; thus, the senior staff may not offer the best training ground for young interns. The experience to be gained in mainstream offices with larger, more complex projects is essential for the full development of any design professional's skills, particularly those planning to work for most of their careers in public service and for low-income communities.

I think young interns should spend at least ten years working in mainstream offices, supplemented by their volunteer work during evenings and weekends, before joining community-design centers. Of course, they must make certain they have done some careful financial planning, because their incomes may diminish with the switch. But they will bring much more valuable talent, skill, and mature wherewithal to the tasks of the community-design centers during their tenure with them. The opposite approach—wanting to have change-the-world dream jobs in community-design centers or nonprofit corporations right out of school—jeopardizes the performance capability of community-design centers with an overabundance of inexperienced personnel, dependent on guidance from managers who themselves have had too many years of limited experience acquired solely within community-design centers.

CHANGING MAINSTREAM OFFICES FROM WITHIN

Not to stereotype and over-generalize, but I think twenty-somethings should come to understand the psyches of aging baby boomers, who are now mostly in control of mainstream design offices and schools of design. This is a generation that once believed it could change the world, and many still attempt to do so, harboring the belief that they are still young at heart and have the capacity to do it. In their youth they held full-time jobs while volunteering for almost another full-time job demonstrating against the Vietnam War and advocating for civil rights, women's rights, and tenants' rights, among other causes. I believe these aging mainstream designers can be, and generally are, very receptive to the enthusiasm, idealism, and energy of entry-level staff being produced by the schools, especially those who have attitudinally transcended a typical preoccupation with design and who come with a broader range of social and political interests, a proclivity for collaborative teamwork, and a respect for community involvement. If an intern demonstrates very strong design

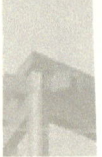

talents, above-average drawing and graphic simulation techniques, and an awareness of and respect for technical detail—the three most valued traditional office skills—the more likely it is that principals will listen to other issues the intern may want to raise within the office setting.

As the old adage from union organizing puts it, "Don't agonize, organize!" Along those lines, here are a few suggestions for young interns:

• If interns demonstrate to principals that they can organize constructively among themselves to suggest improvements in office procedures that not only improve their own educational opportunities but also the efficiency and effectiveness of an office, their suggestions will not fall on deaf ears. They will also improve their chances for raising other, more critical issues about environmental and social justice within the design professions in general and for specific projects within the office.

• Interns should recognize that their ability to earn the respect of principals is dependent upon two important representation/simulation skills: (1) exceptional hand-drawing skills that show not only quick, alluring rendering and visualizing capabilities but also sophisticated, technically informed form-making inventiveness; and (2) skills with computer programs, the latest being REVIT, which principals recognize is now the sine qua non of contemporary practice, and which they have no clue how to use. The success of their offices is literally in the hands of young interns skilled in these computer programs who can execute projects with a high degree of design quality and technical precision. Interns are of course still fully dependent on the experience, knowledge, and guidance of senior staff, but never before has execution of the work required this degree of mutual interdependence between generations. Senior staff used to be able to draw their own intentions; now they absolutely must depend on the computer abilities of junior staff. There now exists an unprecedented potential for mutually shared power within professional offices across generations.

• Armed with these skills and a willingness to organize among themselves as an identifiable force within a firm, interns can collectively assert their power in constructive ways to steer an office "from below." For example, rather than receiving bonuses, interns can ask that their annual share, matched by additional contributions from the firm, be put to various service-oriented uses, such as placing it in an educational fund that would finance their participation in conferences of their choice, even if with no apparent benefit to

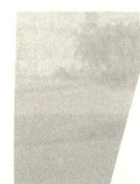

the firm; paying for time and expenses to work on construction projects related to improving homes and facilities within low-income communities; or assisting nonprofits with early feasibility studies.

• If interns volunteer their time to work on an office's marketing efforts, they could request that the office put aside the saved compensation, with a match from the office, to help interns engage in advocacy work for low-income community groups.

• Interns can organize weekly in-house office seminars, intentionally inviting speakers who will encourage the office's ownership and management to expand its sense of obligations to social causes through pro bono work, investment of profits in specific causes, or underwriting advocacy movements seeking improvements in lower-income communities, for example.

• If interns are being paid for their time to attend lunchtime seminars or presentations related to improving their technical knowledge, they can forgo that pay and ask that it be entered into a fund that interns can use to support advocacy or service work for communities in need.

• If an office's hierarchy seems too steep, with a remote top management, interns can organize social events during or after hours, either in the office or off-site, first inviting middle layers of management to join the interns. As the word spreads, principals may attend, and informal, warmer communication bridges can be built between generations and tiers of power, upon which can be built the trust and friendship necessary for making the reforms suggested above.

These are but a few ways that creative, energetic, idealistic interns can introduce their opinions and activities into the lives of mainstream offices where they work. Young design professionals, especially those in the pre-child-rearing years, have at least twenty to thirty additional hours available each week beyond those spent in an office, which can be applied to community-service work. This is what the Boomers had to do to oppose the Vietnam War or to solidify the rights of minorities, women, tenants, and others during the transformative years of the '60s. When interns' infectious commitments outside the office are linked to their office lives in ways like those suggested above, they will not experience such a dramatic split in their lives. The office culture will benefit, and the individual's life will not be so schizophrenic. If anything, interns would be developing the stamina to do what will be needed if and when the time comes to open their own offices, an endeavor that will certainly require them to work eighty-hour weeks, perhaps for many years.

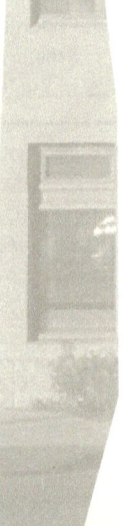

In conclusion, I submit that there are many, many opportunities within mainstream design and planning offices for young interns to pursue their public-service goals. Every project—not only those specifically targeted to the needs of lower-income communities, but also those ostensibly intended for the middle and upper classes—has common spaces that will be shared by the general public and will thus require an attitude of public service. This covers just about every project imaginable. They all will have corridors or plazas, alleys or totlots, sidewalks or driveways, bicycle paths, fire stairs, parks, lounges, lobbies, or other places to simply sit and wait. Meeting the needs of people who will use these spaces is not a mundane task, it is not a task in the service of private profit, it is a task requiring a most heightened awareness of the universal human condition. A sensitized awareness of how these designed places will serve people across the economic spectrum can only enrich the built environment and provide opportunities to demonstrate the universality of human tendencies, regardless of economic status.

It takes at least thirty years to create an experienced designer: ten years to become a mere novice; ten more to become a midlevel professional who still may make some serious misjudgments; and another ten years to become a confident (and thus more likely to be modest) professional who will still make some misjudgments. In addition, it takes another ten years to know enough to warn others of all the pitfalls to avoid, which they most likely will still encounter regardless of the warnings. My recommendation to young interns is to simultaneously be in tenth gear at all times, but remain patient; to be stubbornly idealistic but humbly understanding of others' predicaments; to be self-motivated yet always ready to work collectively. Consider waiting to work for community-design centers until acquiring at least five, and ideally ten, years of experience in mainstream offices. In a developed nation such as ours, a young, well-educated, well-fed professional should never say that there is not enough opportunity to engage in public service.

"My recommendation to young interns is … to be stubbornly idealistic but humbly understanding of others' predicaments; to be self-motivated yet always ready to work collectively."

MICHAEL PYATOK, FAIA, has been an architect and professor of architectural design for forty-two years. Since opening his own office in 1984, he has designed more than thirty-five thousand units of affordable housing for lower-income households in the United States and abroad, and he has developed participatory design methods to facilitate community involvement throughout the design process. He is professor emeritus at the University of Washington.

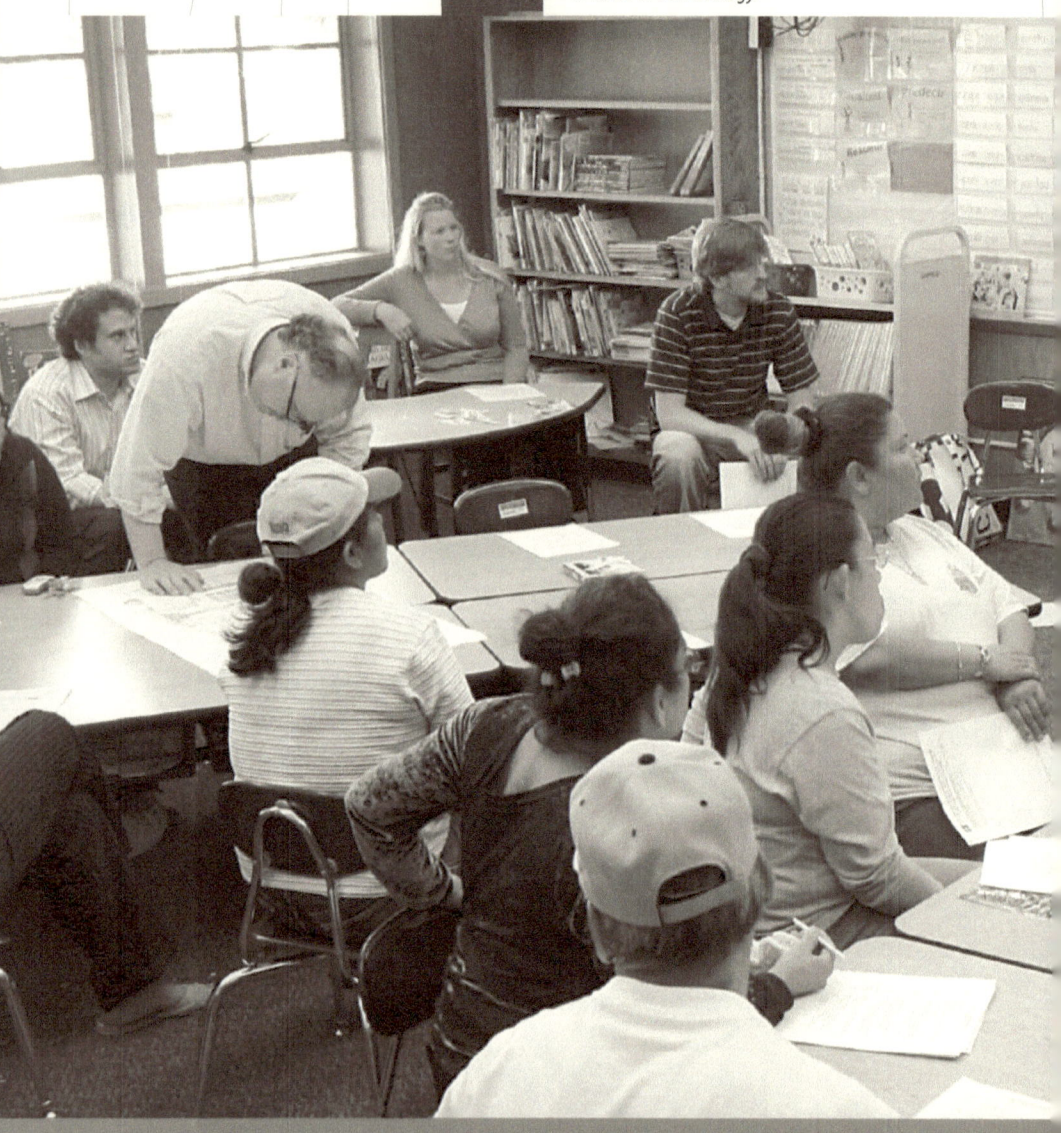

The author leads a community workshop in the Lower San Antonio District of Oakland, California. (Photo: Urban Ecology)

JESS
ZIMBABWE

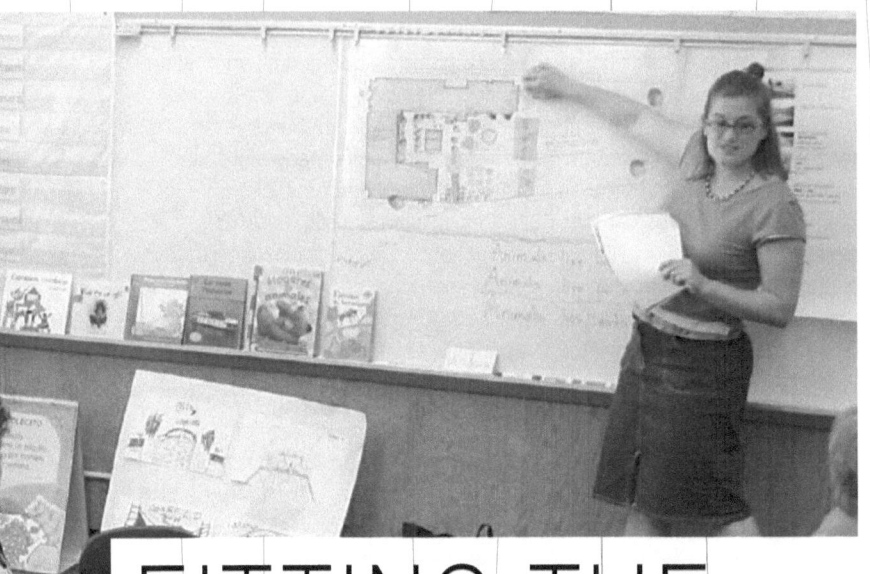

FITTING THE SQUARE PEG OF A SERVICE-ORIENTED INTERNSHIP INTO THE ROUND HOLE OF IDP

COMMUNITY SERVICE: DONATING BLOOD?

ARE Forum is a popular online message board frequented by architectural interns and licensure candidates of various stripes. The forum—which had over sixty thousand members and more than seven hundred thousand posts as of June 2011—dedicates one of its many message boards to the subject of the Intern Development Program (IDP) of the National Council of Architectural Registration Boards (NCARB). On this board, interns ask each other questions about such matters as convincing their supervisors to allow them to work on areas that they need IDP credit in, finding and working with IDP mentors, and using tools like the Emerging Professional's Companion Web site.

In September 2005, an intern posted the following message in the ARE Forum IDP message board: "I am doing my employment verification for ncarb and am trying to find out what they mean by performing professional and community service. I'm guessing volunteer work but can anyone give me an idea as to what ncarb might or might not accept as community service?" Among the most helpful responses to the original post was that of another intern who wrote, "Several times I put one-hour for donating blood and they accepted that. If giving blood is not community service, what is?" (The ARE Forum discussion thread on community service in IDP can be found at http://www.areforum.org/forums/showthread.php?t=88440.)

My first reaction upon reading this thread was to be incredibly disappointed in my professional peers, for both their lack of creativity in choosing a community-service activity and for a pervasive sense of trying to "pull one over on NCARB" that permeated the discussion thread. On second thought, however, I realized that NCARB itself states that "community service does not have to be limited to architecturally related activities for you to receive these benefits." (See http://www.ncarb. org/Experience-Through-Internships/Meeting-NCARB-Experience-Requirements/Professional-and-Community-Service.aspx.)

Because NCARB defines a "community service" category of work experience in IDP, the implication is that all other work experience in IDP is *not* community service. The challenges of completing IDP during a service-oriented architectural internship are the result of NCARB's inflexible refusal to sanction any form of internship other than the most traditional ones. NCARB's lack of imagination means that any intern who does not have an internship based on a template taken from the internship pattern book will have to learn how to subvert—or at least work around—the IDP system. For the moderately motivated intern, working around the system might be as simple as coming up with the idea to donate blood, get IDP credit for it, and then discuss your donation and ensuing credit with your peers on a message board. But emerging architects who are more deeply committed to public service will be forced to be more independent and entrepreneurial, simultaneously learning the professional competencies of an architectural internship and working to demonstrate that mastery to an institution that is only now beginning to grasp the complexities of the daily lives of service-oriented interns.

To NCARB's credit, in the most recent rounds of revisions to IDP—some issued as recently as October 2010—the organization has acknowledged and remedied some of the most egregious obstacles that the program presents. But the fact remains that IDP is fundamentally attempting to quantify an architectural intern's learning, and most public service-oriented interns will need to employ creativity in making the system meet their needs.

A NONTRADITIONAL PATH

The Enterprise Rose Architectural Fellowship funds an early-career architect to work deeply in communities for three years. The fellowship has paired young architects with local community housing and development agencies to help them create affordable housing and other facilities for low-income Americans since 2000. There are now thirty-five current and alumni fellows. I was fortunate to serve as an Enterprise Rose Architectural Fellow from 2003 to 2006. I worked at a nonprofit community-design and planning organization called Urban Ecology, and my primary project was to design and develop the Eastside Community Cultural Center in the low-income, largely minority San Antonio district of east Oakland, California. The center gives neighborhood youth opportunities for education and cultural enrichment that can divert them from crime and gang activity. These programs had previously been scattered across several locations in facilities that weren't designed for artistic, educational, or cultural pursuits. In order to make the project happen, I found myself wearing many hats not typically associated with an architectural fellowship. The client needed architectural support, to be sure, but they also needed fundraising, real-estate development, and program development as well. In the end, with a lot of partners in the project, we cobbled together eighteen separate sources of funding from state and local programs.

This amazing project taught me some very technical competencies in architecture, along with dozens of other skills in community organizing, real-estate development, public agency negotiations, and contractor relations. When Urban Ecology held community meetings in the San Antonio district, we had as many as eight different language tables to engage the diversity of the community that lived there.

For much of the same period when I was working for Urban Ecology, I was also serving as an elected associate director for the California chapter of the American Institute of Architects (AIA). The state's two associate directors (one each for northern and southern California) represent all associate (unlicensed) members of the AIA. At the California AIA, there was significant discussion about the terminology that architectural interns could and should use to describe themselves and their work. Every month, the California Architects Board newsletter contained a listing of "enforcement actions," and every quarter, this section included write-ups on people who represented themselves as architects when they did not have a license to practice architecture. Invariably, the board charged them with fees and other penalties. From what I read in these quarterly reminders and the discussions we had on the AIA California board of directors, I knew that licensed architects (or at least their leaders) felt strongly about using the term "architect" *only* to describe a licensed architect.

And yet, after each Saturday AIA California board meeting, I returned to work in San Antonio and met with the artists at Eastside Arts Alliance, or the director of the neighborhood clinic, or some other community leader whom we were working with to provide design services. At first, I tried to explain in a technically correct way that I had a master's degree in architecture and several years of work experience in architecture, but I was not a licensed architect. Finally, when responding to the blank stares of a group of Hmong immigrants at a community design meeting, I gave in: "I'm an architect," I said, and the translator restated my sentence. Nods of understanding swept across the group. At that moment, I realized that my experience in this community was so far afield from what the AIA board members in California or the NCARB record evaluators could imagine that I was occasionally going to have to bend the rules to make it work.

There are three IDP regulations that are most likely to present a challenge to someone pursuing a service-oriented internship: (1) a prohibition on short-term and part-time work experiences; (2) a prohibition on unpaid work experiences; and (3) a requirement of "direct supervision" of your work. I experienced obstacles related to each of these regulations during my Enterprise Rose Architectural Fellowship. Though NCARB has become more responsive to nontraditional situations with the reforms adopted for IDP 2.0, the system is still flawed for most nontraditional licensure candidates.

SHORT-TERM AND PART-TIME WORK EXPERIENCES

> To receive IDP credit you must typically work at least 35 hours per week for a minimum period of 10 consecutive weeks, or at least 20 hours per week for a minimum period of six consecutive months. (Rule taken from the NCARB IDP Work Settings page: http://ncarb.org/en/Experience-Through-Internships/Meeting-NCARB-Experience-Requirements/Work-Settings.aspx.)

People choose part-time jobs for a variety of reasons, often because part-time work offers the only way workers can balance competing job and family demands. Taking care of children or elderly parents is nearly impossible when employed in a job that requires a commitment of thirty-five or more hours per week. Women are more often responsible for this kind of family care, so it is not surprising that they account for approximately two-thirds of the part-time workforce. (See http://www.bls.gov/cps/wlf-table20-2006.pdf.) Unfortunately, choosing part-time employment comes at a considerable cost for these workers, primarily in the form of lower wages, lack of health and pension benefits, and diminished opportunities for advancement. The architecture profession is no different than other industries in this regard.

To add insult to the injuries of reduced pay and benefits, during my years of internship part-time architectural interns were excluded from earning IDP credit along with their full-time peers. No allowance was made for part-time interns to earn prorated part-time IDP credit. In response to the economic downturn that began in 2008, the guidelines promulgated in October 2010 removed the references to minimum weekly hours required, which seemingly will allow future licensure candidates to earn IDP credit for the hours they work, even if they work less than a traditional work week. I applaud NCARB's recent removal of the prohibition on prorated IDP credit for part-time work, but I fear that the driving force behind the change was current economic conditions, not a drive to ensure that an architectural internship is open to people in a wide variety of circumstances, including those who need to work part-time even when the economy is booming.

UNPAID WORK EXPERIENCES

> To earn training hours for the Intern Development Program (IDP) you must be employed (for pay) in a work setting recognized by your registration board and NCARB. (Rule taken from the NCARB IDP Work Settings page: http://ncarb.org/en/Experience-Through-Internships/Meeting-NCARB-Experience-Requirements/Work-Settings.aspx.)

I completely understand NCARB's resistance to allowing interns to receive IDP credit for unpaid work. With the U.S. economy in recession, businesses of all types are looking for ways to reduce expenses. In an architecture firm, payroll is the largest single expense by far. One popular strategy for reducing payroll costs is to seek out free labor in the form of interns. But it is clear that, generally speaking, an intern is not a volunteer. The U.S. Department of Labor defines a volunteer as someone who "provides services to a nonprofit organization or public agency for charitable or humanitarian reasons." An intern working at a for-profit firm does not fit this definition, and NCARB is correct for not wanting unscrupulous firms to define work as a "learning experience" in order to avoid paying IDP interns for their labor.

But excluding all unpaid experience from IDP credit prevents interns from learning valuable technical skills while providing services to charitable organizations. NCARB's October update of the IDP Guidelines reflects a new policy of allowing up to forty core hours of IDP credit for "volunteer service in support of a pre-approved charitable organization outside of a recognized work setting or academic requirement." This new policy seems to address my concerns that service-oriented interns are forced to unnaturally bifurcate their efforts into those they do out of commitment and those they can earn IDP credit for.

However, at press time for this essay, NCARB had approved only six organizations as settings for volunteer work that can earn IDP credit, because the policy is so new. While I am confident that NCARB will come to approve a number of organizations, it's difficult to believe that NCARB will be able to successfully and efficiently approve many of the hundreds of such organizations that exist in this country (excluding hundreds more doing good work abroad)

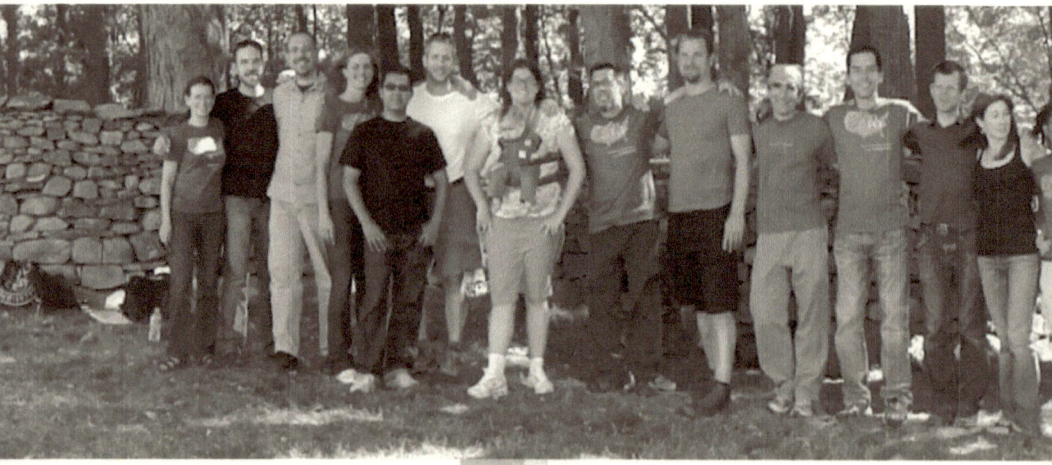

"This amazing project taught me some very technical competencies in architecture, along with dozens of other skills in community organizing, real-estate development, public agency negotiations, and contractor relations."

when NCARB cannot even review an intern's Experience Verification Reports as they are submitted; instead, NCARB waits to review an intern's file until the intern is close to completing IDP altogether. I hope that I'm wrong here and that in a few months, interns will be able to access a populated database of volunteer opportunities that are approved by NCARB, so that they can find an opportunity in their area and in a field they are interested in.

DIRECT SUPERVISION

This is the IDP requirement that nearly tripped me up. Every IDP Experience Verification Report I completed contained a section for my supervisor's signature; at the top of that section of the form, it stated: "This portion of the form must be completed by the applicant's DAILY SUPERVISOR at the referenced organization." (Those two words are actually in all caps on the form.)

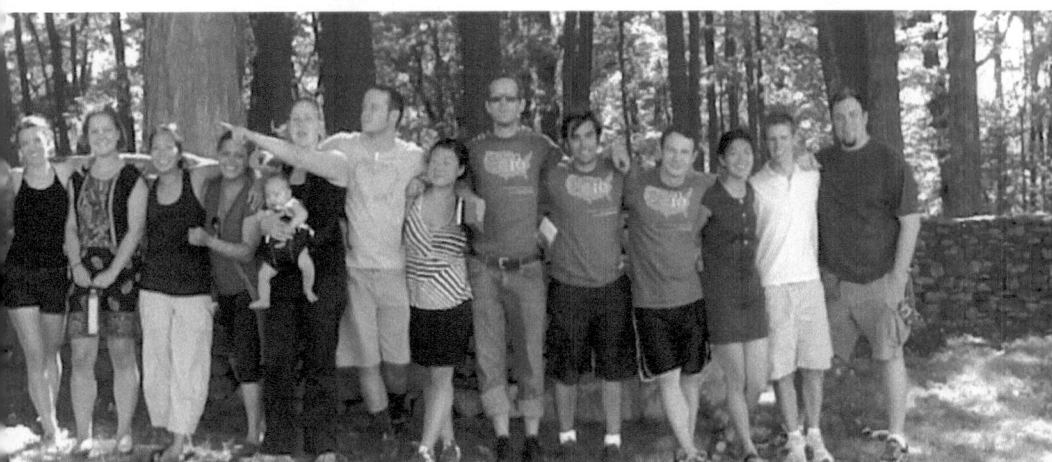

The Enterprise Architectural Fellows at a retreat in Mountainville, New York
(Photo: Trinity Simons)

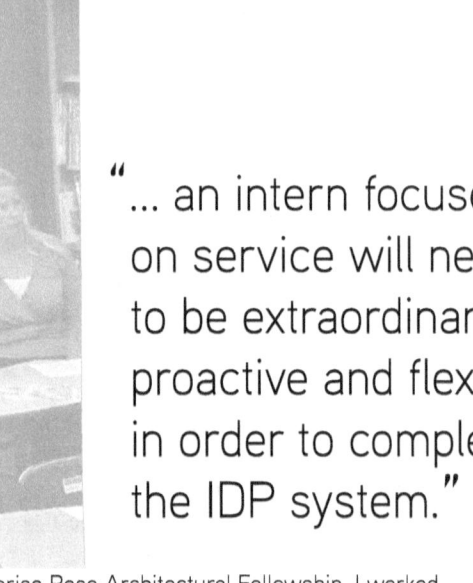

> " ... an intern focused on service will need to be extraordinarily proactive and flexible in order to complete the IDP system."

During my three-year Enterprise Rose Architectural Fellowship, I worked two days a week in the office of the private practice of my IDP supervisor, and I worked three days a week in the offices of the nonprofit organization I worked for or out in the field at community, client, or construction meetings. My supervisor and I were in contact every day, but sometimes only through phone, e-mail, or the exchange of documents for review or edits.

Being somewhat of a natural nonconformist, I easily accepted this situation as equivalent in spirit—if not in letter—to the architectural internship situation that NCARB was imagining I would have, and I dutifully submitted my experience earned in this scenario. I didn't pause much to consider the fact that my supervisor wasn't employed by the same organization that I was or that we weren't in the same office every day. Initially, NCARB indicated no concerns with this situation, accepting many Experience Verification Reports from me that were signed by my supervisor, an employee of his own firm. For more than three years while I was recording these IDP credits, they appeared in my online IDP record as being earned while I was working at the nonprofit organization. When I neared the completion of IDP, with 5.25 units of work experience left to go, NCARB apparently looked into my file in more detail and then rescinded all of the credits I'd earned in this manner. They then asked my IDP supervisor, the architect of record on my primary project during my Rose Fellowship, to explain how he was able to supervise me during this work. Fortunately, he did send a letter, and NCARB acknowledged that he had the appropriate oversight, so the credits were restored, but this rule of IDP is a challenge to many nontraditional architectural interns.

I was not the only Rose Fellow who had a working arrangement that involved being in the architect of record's office only some days a week. In fact, that arrangement is recommended by the fellowship organizers as a way to keep a young architect engaged with the community and nonprofit organization while providing sufficient technical and design oversight for the project.

In the revisions that comprise IDP 2.0, the definition of the term "direct supervision" changed:

> "Direct supervision" of interns shall occur either through personal contact or through a mix of personal contact and remote communication (e.g. e-mail, online markups, webinars, internet) such that the IDP supervisor has control over the work of the intern and has sufficient professional knowledge of the supervised work so that the IDP supervisor can determine that the intern understands and is performing his or her work experience within the professional standard of care.

> To earn training hours in workplace settings described in the *IDP Guidelines*, the intern must work under the direct supervision of an IDP supervisor. The supervisor shall verify the training activities of the intern and foster a professional relationship that is grounded in a direct professional association between the intern and the supervisor. (This change is discussed in the November 2009 issue of *IDP E-news*: http://www.ncarb.org/idp/enews/2009/november/index.html.)

This change was instituted largely to reflect the more complex way that supervision occurs, when, for example, an intern might be reporting to a project manager in a different office of the same firm, but the change also makes the working arrangement of my Enterprise Rose Fellowship explicitly allowable under the IDP 2.0 guidelines. NCARB seems to have reached the conclusion that sometimes, IDP supervisors and interns are related through something other than the traditional employer/employee relationship, and they have made IDP flexible enough to reflect that.

"NCARB—and, indeed, the entire architecture profession—should recognize that no single training path can impart the complex set of skills that architecture demands."

DATA AND RECORD KEEPING

Not incidentally, all of my obstacles in conforming my non-traditional internship to the IDP system were made more difficult by the fact that all of the paperwork burden of IDP falls on the intern (not the employer) and that NCARB's IDP division has difficulty keeping up with the demanding paperwork reviews and approvals that seem necessary in a system so heavily based on documentation. If NCARB had asked questions about my supervision situation following the first Experience Verification Report I submitted during my Rose Fellowship, I could have cleared up the situation then and possibly could have even made changes to the daily working situation to respond to NCARB's concerns. But because my submitted paperwork was simply logged into my file without comment, I had no idea that the supervision situation would even be an issue until years later, when NCARB reviewed my file.

Most comically, at one point during a long correspondence with NCARB, I had not received a response to a letter that I'd sent several months before. When I then received an envelope with an NCARB return address, I thought it might be the letter I was awaiting. Instead, it was an invoice from NCARB for my annual $50 record maintenance fee. (To be fair, when I wrote to check on the status of my ignored letter, NCARB did reverse the charges for that year's annual fee.)

Though NCARB has made many excellent and much-needed changes to the IDP system even in the few years since I began the program, the fundamental fact remains that the multifaceted aptitudes that make one an "architect" are too complex to capture in any single recording system.

NCARB has tried in recent IDP revisions to expand the options that are available within the IDP path, but still, an intern focused on service will need to be extraordinarily proactive and flexible in order to complete the IDP system.

NCARB—and, indeed, the entire architecture profession—should recognize that no single training path can impart the complex set of skills that architecture demands.

IDP should be a recommended path to an architecture license rather than the mandatory path. One obvious advantage of this change would be that the administrative load of logging interns' hours would be lessened—for interns, for employers, and for NCARB staff. By describing what should happen during an ideal internship, IDP may encourage some employers to provide a high-quality training environment, but it certainly does not move the entire profession to that end. As attested by my experience and the experience of dozens of other service-oriented interns who did IDP before the most recent changes were adopted, it is possible to achieve a substantive internship experience without IDP—and if you're tenacious, you can get IDP credit for it too.

JESS ZIMBABWE is the founding executive director of the Urban Land Institute's Daniel Rose Center for Public Leadership in Land Use. Previously she was the Director of the Mayors' Institute on City Design and an Enterprise Rose Architectural Fellow at Urban Ecology in Oakland, California. She is a licensed architect.

ANDREW
CARUSO

THIS ISN'T YOUR
FATHER'S PROTEST:

LEVERAGING
A NEW
GENERATION
OF (DESIGN)
ACTIVISTS

The sounds of clinking glasses and hustling waiters filled the room on a warm summer evening. The alumni association of my university had arranged its annual meet-and-greet for the Washington, DC, metropolitan area in a swanky downtown design firm. As I leaned against a column, I noticed a young man with a colorful name badge on his left lapel. We had both committed the faux pas of arriving early, so I walked over and introduced myself.

John, a fellow alumnus, was in his early thirties and quickly began recalling times past in architecture school. While there was no overlap in our actual enrollment, there were certainly familiar memories, common experiences, and shared laughs.

And then I asked the dreaded question: "So what did you do after graduation?"

"I was in the Reserve Officer Training Corps (ROTC)," John said, "so I set out with the Navy right after school and spent six years completing my tour of service."

"And after the Navy? With what firm did you start practicing?"

"I wish," he said. "A lot happens in six years. I met a wonderful woman and married. We just had our first child last year. I'm in commercial real estate now," he said with a smile, anticipating my questioning look. "Although architecture was my passion—and I would have given anything to be an architect—I didn't fit back into the profession."

"Why not?"

"There was no way my family could survive if I had to be an architectural intern," he said matter-of-factly. "But I think every day about how I wanted to change the world as an architect."

I felt as if I had been hit between the eyes with a brick.

From coast to coast, I've talked with thousands of people connected in some way to the design professions, from aspiring high school students to retiring legends, but it was in this singular exchange that I saw the true limitation of our profession. How is it that John, an accomplished design school graduate with far more training in public service than his peers, could not find a home in the design industry?

In that instant, my heart sank for the future of our profession.

> "First, new generations of designers are imbued with a sense of activism, a need to serve a larger good through their professional pursuits."

ACTIVISM: PURPOSE FOR A NEW GENERATION

John's story is poignant but not uncommon. While my experiences in our profession have given me a unique perspective on a number of topics, two facts remain remarkably clear. First, new generations of designers are imbued with a sense of activism, a need to serve a larger good through their professional pursuits. Perhaps this is a reaction to coming of professional age alongside global climate change, technological access to a vivid understanding of global living conditions, or the legacy of parenting by a generation who found their identity in civil disobedience. Regardless, the new generation of designers is decidedly an activist generation, albeit in a different form.

Second, the design professions lack the capacities, mechanisms, and opportunities to engage these bright minds in relevant and meaningful ways. These are minds that view design as both a means for and method of social activism and societal engagement.

NEW FORMS OF PROTEST

Activism is an enduring truth of humanity: an innate call to serve a greater good. There is, however, a shift underway, a nuance to one's personal investment in change. Does the condition of anonymity forsake activism within contemporary culture? In one sense, activism is powerfully rooted in and shaped by the person or persons seeking change. The alignment of many individual missions into a collective want is what triggers a catalytic voice within society. Historic examples of activism are, most commonly, not anonymous. Instead, they are purposefully human, drawing power from the graphically personal manifestation of faces and bodies caught in the tension of an issue.

While there will always be a place for provocative action, I observe a contemporary society that finds less leverage in the type of confrontational expression of the 1960s and 1970s. Social media and technology present the opportunity for a silent, faceless activism: a watchdog or whistle-blower mentality whereby a single person can topple a large organization behind the veil of a screen name and the click of a button. Citizen journalists expose social injustices to a global audience by way of cell phone uploads. Students mobilize against environmental injustice through simultaneous Facebook posts. The picket line is replaced by a media blog. Are these not all activist enterprises?

In its own way, a new generation has distinguished between "protest" as a reactionary endeavor and "activism" as a synthetic one. Evidenced by a general trend away from overt political expression and toward a generative, entrepreneurial approach to issues of social justice, early-career designers leverage technology, access to information, and a grassroots (perhaps virtual) coalition of peers as the main components of a new activist toolkit.

What are the implications of such shifts on the ability to mobilize a new generation of activists? Traditional displays of activism are about the need for ritual as much as they are about the issue in debate. Through activism and protest as ritualistic displays of collective emotion, society undergoes a cleansing, healing process. Perhaps then we can begin to understand opportunities for directed public service in the form of internships as a new form of ritualized activism.

BUT WHERE ARE THE DESIGNERS?

When I was in design school, my university challenged me to prepare a public-policy analysis as the institution's nominee for a public-service fellowship. The first red flag: In the penultimate year of my degree, this was the first time I had been asked to interface with the systems of public policy as a designer, and the invitation had come on behalf of a community outside of the school of architecture. Second red flag: During my research, I asked a group of my faculty how they influence local and regional policy as architects. They stared at me quizzically. One said, "Architecture cannot solve social problems." Perhaps he meant to say that architecture alone could not solve social problems; but it surely affects them.

As designers, we don't say often enough that the spaces we build are representative of our social policies, our values, and our conviction for justice. It is not just the power of our pen, but our presence in the political milieu that will define our profession's ability to affect change. How do we grow this type of design professional unless we give emerging talent the opportunity to launch a design career in service to the public? Contemporary students come of age as designers in a profession that often underestimates and undercommunicates the power of design to make visionary change actionable.

THE CURRENT INTERNSHIP MODEL: SUCCESS OR FAILURE?
Does the traditional internship model work? No. At least not to the capacity it should.

Public service is often understood as the domain of volunteers. The term conjures images of selfless commitment and personal sacrifice. Indeed, volunteering is a valuable and celebrated part of a civically engaged community. In a somewhat nostalgic and romanticized way, we celebrate those who step away from a rewarding, successful career in an effort to "give back" to the communities that have given them the opportunity to grow throughout their professional lives.

Volunteering is tremendously important, but it must not be the only form of civic engagement. Building a culture of effective public service is not just about giving back after (or in addition to) a rich career. The key difference consistently overlooked is that emerging designers need the ability to begin their career in service to the public. The two operative words are "begin," meaning public service serves as the entrance to a professional trajectory; and "career," meaning that the life-long pursuit of public service is sustaining, rewarding, and viable. To limit public service to volunteer efforts is to fundamentally undermine its potential.

There are significant structural barriers to beginning a design career in public service, however. Those who seek hands-on early-career training in public service find only a small network of not-for-profits, fellowships, and other civically oriented design-build enterprises. These opportunities greet newcomers with open arms, but the limited capacity to embrace only a handful of new graduates and early-career professionals each year.

Moreover, for the lucky few who do find a start in public service, such opportunities are likely to come at significant personal cost. The delayed ability to start or support a family, the staggering burden of student loans, and the postponement of establishing a financially secure future are all sacrifices that some may be unwilling or unable to make. And so disappears some of the most brilliant and passionate talent in our industry.

What effective system of civic engagement would require participants to make significant life sacrifices in order to help their neighbor? How can these activities be successful if they are exclusionary—if they only allow those wealthy enough, connected enough, or educated enough to participate? Moreover, organizations and individuals consistently exploit the nobleness of volunteerism to evade real investment—financial, temporal, or political—in a cause. If this is to be the construct for public service architectural internships, it is an unsustainable model.

POINTING FINGERS

From academia through internship and into practice, we all have a role in creating change. Naturally, it is important that graduates enter the fertile beginnings of their careers armed with the right tools to be effective civic contributors in whatever line of work they pursue. In 2008, the American Institute of Architecture Students authored *Issue Brief on Architectural Education* (available at www.aias.org) that identified nine emergent trends in architectural education that will define the future of the profession. Among these, students and graduates across the country identified social responsibility and the development of professional and multidisciplinary capacities (such as leadership, entrepreneurship, and multi-disciplinary collaboration) as priorities.

These specific areas are crucial to developing designers prepared to engage the public good. Some programs are pursuing these issues with rigor, such as AIAS Freedom by Design, Architecture for Humanity, DesignCorps, Public Architecture, Studio 804, and the Rural Studio; from these organizations comes an architecture of activism. Yet such initiatives are the unique surprise, not the norm. Architectural curricula have yet to formalize a learning path that includes the theory and practice of leadership, principles of collaboration, and public-policy skills.

Most often, professional capacities are assumed to be the result of contemporary architectural education. When asked to provide evidence of teaching methodologies that instill these capacities, faculty quickly point to "group work" in the studio. Has group work trained graduates to be proactive civil servants? Has it prepared them to bend the ear of a local congressman, or better yet, run for office?

It would be unfair to suggest that academe should shoulder the burden of developing the world's future civic leaders alone. Armed with the right tools, the profession becomes the arena in which early-career designers should shape and hone—i.e., "practice"—their craft in service to the greater good. Chief among the challenges for internship are two: first, to provide adequate capacity for minds and hands to engage these pursuits; and second, to demonstrate by example the value and centrality of these issues to the ethical and professional practice of design.

HIGH OR LOW, THE ROAD IS NOT EASY

How do we get where we need to be? Finding alignment between the for-profit mission and the not-for-profit initiative would make it possible to increase the profession's capacity to provide meaningful public service. Pro bono design is often seen as the bridge between these two missions, and it may be one answer, but it is not the only one. Serving a community that cannot afford design services does not necessarily mean that such services must be offered gratis; assuming so limits the potential of these for-profit/not-for-profit partnerships. When firms do not have to do the work for free but are simply compensated through a mechanism other than their client, they will have a greater capacity to do similar work. Everybody wins. Thus, designers must be as creative with how they fund and deploy their ideas as with the design of the ideas themselves.

"Contemporary students come of age as designers in a profession that often underestimates and undercommunicates the power of design to make visionary change actionable."

What else prevents innovative partnerships and programs from taking root? Among them are compensation and benefit issues, training and professional development needs, employment duration requirements, the cost of lost talent and embodied knowledge, recruitment expenses, time commitments for supervision and oversight, and insurance and liability concerns. All of these factors are key challenges to innovation of new models for professional internships. If proposals are to be viable, they must accommodate the realities of these issues. An argument for "doing the right thing" must consider not only the recipient of the proposed services but also the good of the company and those to whom it is responsible. Service proposals must be enriched by the business case.

CAPACITY BUILDING:
FINDING ROOM FOR INNOVATION AND CHANGE

Cooperatives, practicum programs, and practice academy models in architectural education (in which students engage in academic and professional settings simultaneously) continue to present incredible opportunities for an integrated educational experience. Yet, how will these innovative teaching models grow in light of the limited financial and physical capacity of firms to take on a growing number of temporary internship positions? The profession is ill-equipped to accommodate such a change.

Never could the issue of finite capacity have been more apparent than during the economic tumble of 2008. As the economy spiraled downward, a new generation of design professionals—some in firms for multiple years, others just graduating and planning their first steps into the industry—found no opportunity to exercise their skills. Yet, through it all, public need for design services grew. How do we enhance the capacity of a profession to raise a new generation of leaders while simultaneously meeting a growing demand for our services? Herein lies a significant opportunity, but its answers likely exist beyond the boundaries of the traditional model of architectural design services.

INTERNSHIP: A TINY WINDOW

What are the implications of these forces on architectural internship? First, we must acknowledge that the vernacular of our profession has perhaps inappropriately used the term "internship" to narrowly describe the initial years of one's career in practice as a design professional. It is a term out of sync with other industries and laden with significant baggage.

For the sake of argument, consider the early-career design professional who chooses a path that leverages design thinking into process-oriented solutions rather than product-oriented ones. One might consider community-design centers, public-design education programs, or environmental policy initiatives as likely targets for these graduates, but we must remember that these opportunities are currently limited. However, efforts to extend design thinking across industries that do not traditionally partner with or recruit architecture and design talent are key to growing such opportunities.

Additionally, these individuals must not be shunned by their peers. Too often designers who work outside of architecture are spoken of as having fallen out of the fold; they are beyond the limits of a profession that attempts to hold its boundaries sacrosanct. Yet these individuals are affecting positive change for the public as designers. For what better ambassadors could our industry ask?

Now, let's explore the impact on "internship" if we are considering graduates who enter a professional service design firm in pursuit of their license to practice architecture. Is it the role of the Intern Development Program (IDP) to teach graduates how to serve the public? Absolutely not.

Ethical public service should not merely be the by-product of a learning experience, whether in school or in practice. All clients deserve competent, safe, and complete professional services. While this fact underscores the importance of licensure and therefore the importance of completing the IDP program, one must not conflate public service with a teaching opportunity simply because those who are learning cost less.

One must also recognize the limitations of the IDP program. It is one of many components in a professional development sequence aimed at preserving the health, safety, and welfare of the public through supervised professional experience—nothing more, nothing less. The profession needs to let this be the only goal for IDP, in order for the program to be successful. IDP should not be a vehicle for any particular agenda, and frankly, it isn't important enough to be so. However, the IDP program should recognize public-service design as a legitimate part of one's professional development. To that end, the program has made considerable strides to recognize a greater array of experiences as eligible for credit toward licensure.

"Why are issues of the built environment not correlated with global activist movements against disease, poverty, and hunger?"

WITHOUT CHANGE, A FINITE HORIZON

If we return to the idea of directed public service as a new, ritualized manifestation of activism, we can see that architecture and design disciplines need different systems to affect change. As benchmarks, opportunities like AmeriCorps and the Peace Corps structure and mobilize large numbers of civically oriented people toward measurable results with remarkable success. But while components of these programs engage design acumen, a comparable program has yet to be created that leverages the value of design in identifying and solving social issues of our time. Is it because the power of architecture (at least as architects and designers might understand it) is not accessible to the layperson? Is it because manipulating the built environment is a lengthy and complex process? Why are issues of the built environment not correlated with global activist movements against disease, poverty, and hunger? Surely the built environment plays a role in shaping, sheltering, and supporting these efforts.

To be truly effective, new programs must strategically ritualize contemporary activism and modify traditional methods of engagement to leverage a new activist toolkit. Developing creative yet realistic partnerships with for-profit organizations and effectively engaging systems of policy and government will yield increased capacity for a wealth of viable, long-term career opportunities in public service. Measureable results must demonstrate the relevance of the design industry far beyond its borders.

Ultimately, the mark of ritualized activism is the creation of an authentic movement for change that allows multimodal connection of participants via the systems and technologies of a new era. Through this momentum, the voices of many become one, and the challenges of the past become opportunities for innovation in the future.

ANDREW CARUSO, ASSOC. AIA, LEED AP, CDT, is head of intern development and academic outreach for Gensler, one of the world's largest multidisciplinary design firms, with more than thirty-five locations across the globe. He has held seats on the boards of directors of three of the five governing organizations of architecture in the United States, and he served as the fifty-first national president of the American Institute of Architecture Students.

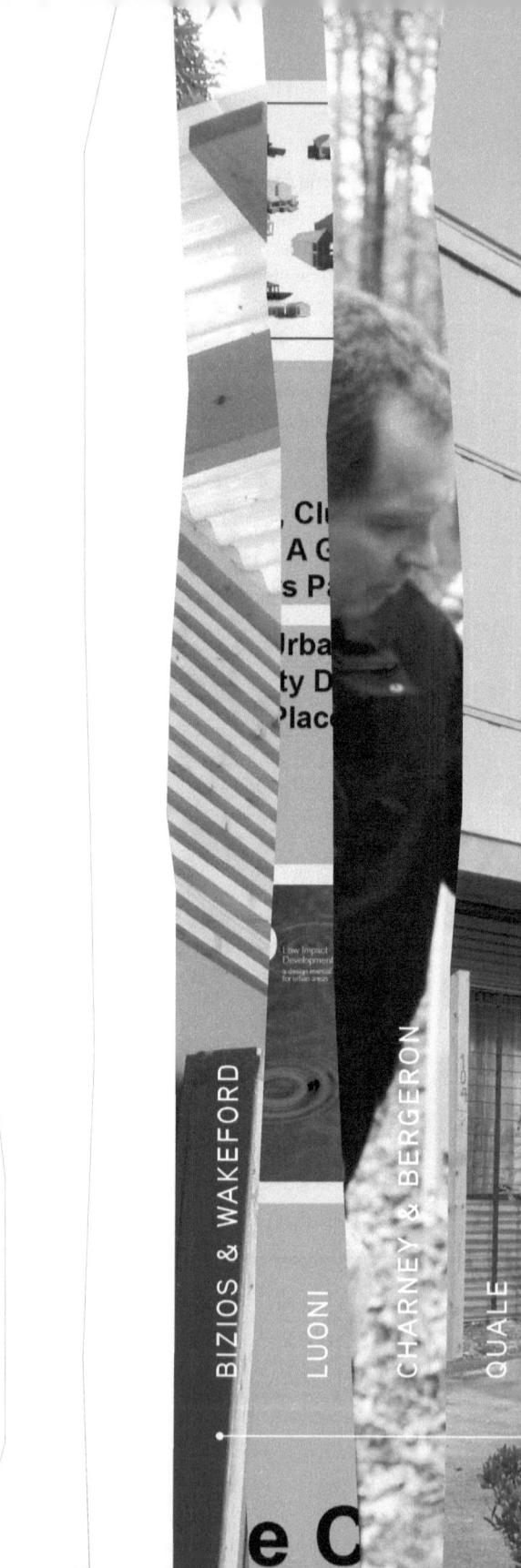

, Cl
A G
s Pa

Irba
ty D
Place

Low Impact
Development
a design manual
for urban areas

BIZIOS & WAKEFORD

LUONI

CHARNEY & BERGERON

QUALE

e C

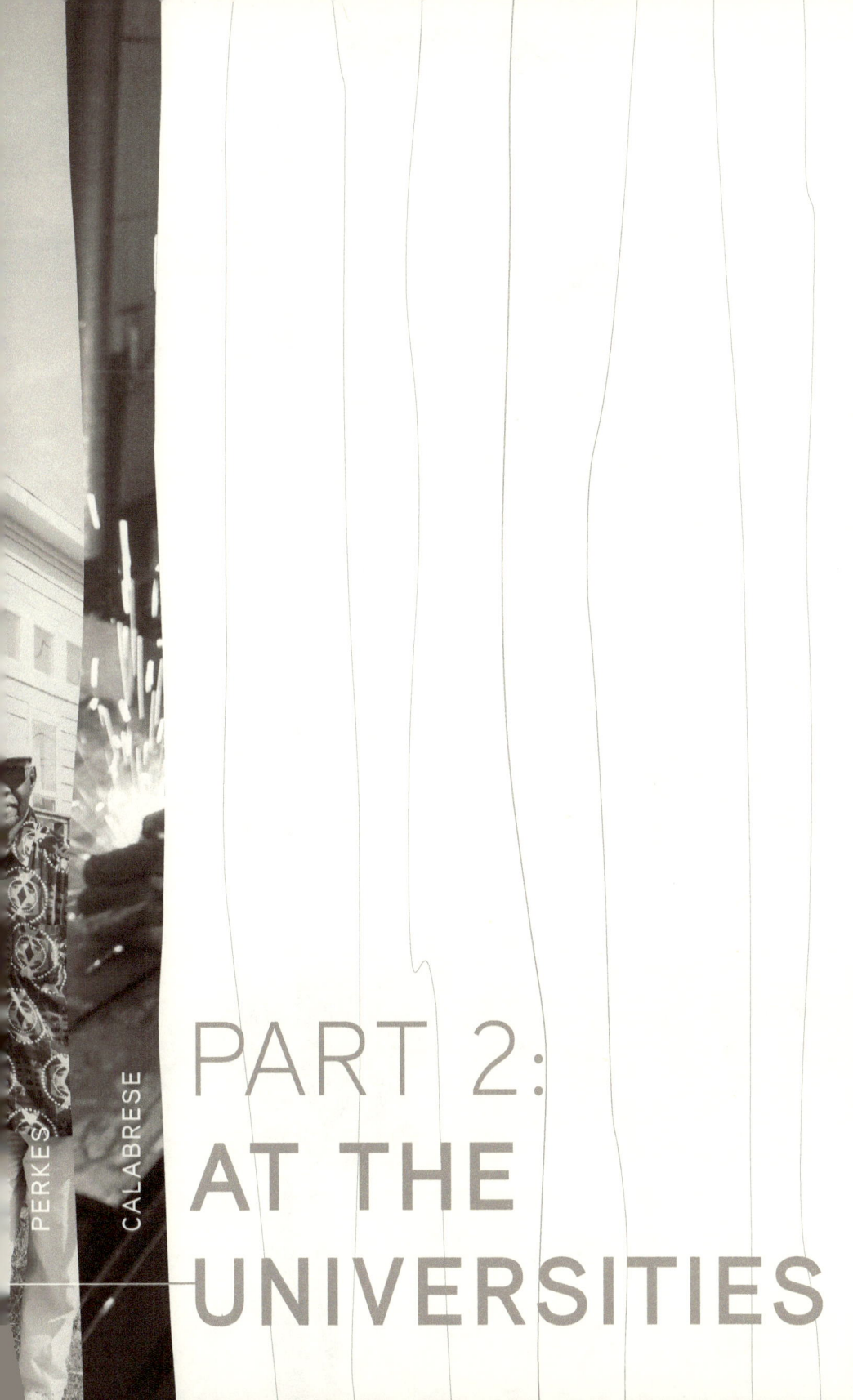

PERKES

CALABRESE

PART 2:
AT THE
UNIVERSITIES

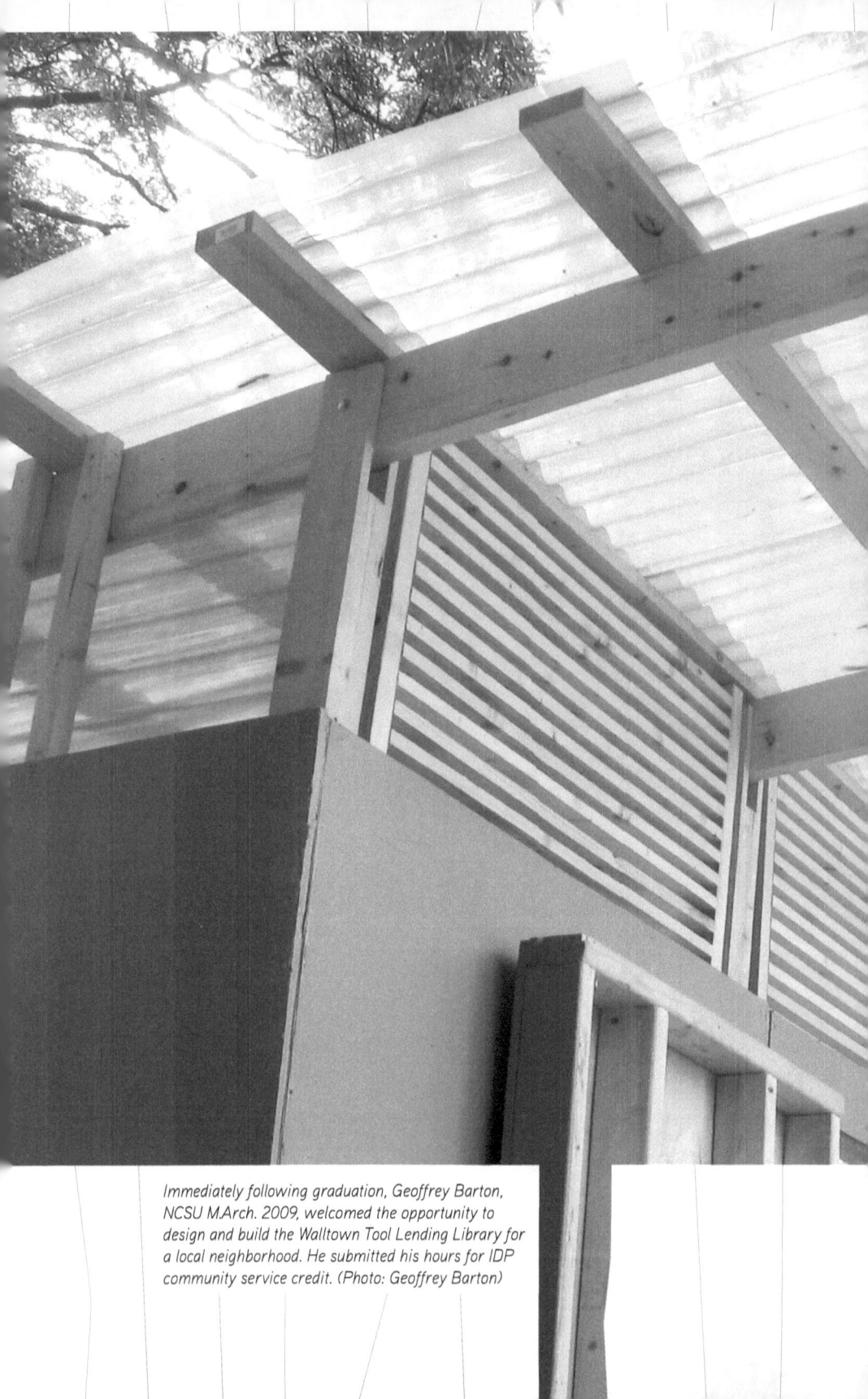

Immediately following graduation, Geoffrey Barton, NCSU M.Arch. 2009, welcomed the opportunity to design and build the Walltown Tool Lending Library for a local neighborhood. He submitted his hours for IDP community service credit. (Photo: Geoffrey Barton)

GEORGIA **BIZIOS** & KATIE **WAKEFORD**

UNIVERSITY-BASED INTERNSHIPS IN PUBLIC-INTEREST ARCHITECTURE

Universities are leaders in innovation, education, and increasingly in community engagement, making them ideal laboratories for testing new models of public-interest internship. Universities are in a unique position to establish such internships. Many schools already have active extension endeavors and consider it part of their mission to share resources with their communities while providing students with real-world learning. Sponsoring public-interest interns is a logical outgrowth of those priorities. Universities are well-positioned to seek funding and leverage faculty expertise and qualifications for supervision of public-interest interns.

As part of our work with North Carolina State University's Home Environments Design Initiative, we have been developing opportunities for architecture students to study and gain experience in their profession through service-learning projects. Students have been involved through seminar, studio, and independent study courses as well as through research assistantships during summers and academic semesters. Expanding on these methods, we have experimented with giving students and recent graduates of NC State's School of Architecture the opportunity to work on service grants and earn Intern Development Program (IDP) credits just as an intern would do when working in a traditional architectural practice. This model has given interns the equivalent of five years' worth of nonprofit work experience. The interns contribute significantly to the initiative's community-partnership projects, and they experience a supportive, rewarding transition from academia to the professional world. It is our strongly held belief that the experience that interns gain in these positions will have a powerful positive effect on their careers, the profession, and our communities.

The model has great potential, but a minefield of challenges. Examples are emerging at various universities. Learning from these existing efforts by inventorying the issues and implications for the stakeholders will be useful in proliferating and advancing public-interest internship programs.

ARCHITECTURE IN THE PUBLIC INTEREST
In the United States, the discipline of architecture has a history of providing community design as a public service. The political activism of the sixties found fertile ground in architecture, leading the American Institute of Architects to establish the Urban Design Assistance Team and the Rural Design Assistance Team programs that sent professional teams to work on-site in a charrette mode to develop design proposals for community-revitalization projects. A number of design schools also established outreach programs to provide architectural services to communities and organizations in need. Such projects usually involved master planning, urban renewal, and adaptive reuse of existing buildings.

In a recent overview of service-learning in architectural education, Anthony Schuman observes that in the 1980s architecture began to renege on its commitments to social engagement, retreating instead into theoretical debates over postmodernism and deconstruction, and focusing on explorations of digitally generated design.[1] Now that the tide is once again turning toward a socially and politically conscious practice of architecture, Schuman and others encourage design schools to teach students a broader understanding of the discipline and to train them in the skills required for community engagement.

Public service objectives combined with the hands-on nature of architectural training has led to the increase and popularity of design-build programs, which involve students in the act of making by allowing them to participate in the construction of a structure they have designed. Design-build projects typically have a public-service component because the built structure is usually intended for community use or is sponsored by a nonprofit, and the community of users is often involved in the design process. But where does the student go from there? What are university programs doing to nurture the enthusiasm and grow the skills seeded by those popular studios?

In *Building Community*, a report exploring new directions for architectural education and practice, Ernest Boyer and Lee Mitgang conclude that communities both want and need architectural services, and universities and students are eager to participate in service projects; but the climates of many architectural education programs are not sufficiently supportive of these efforts.[2] A review of the literature, and of our own experience, clearly indicates that outreach in architecture curricula is sporadic, not systemic. When we consider the magnitude of the need for community service and the benefit that service-learning experiences can provide, the importance of making a public-service ethic pervasive in our schools becomes apparent. We believe that fostering university-based public-interest internship programs could be an important part of these efforts.

STRENGTHENING EXISTING UNIVERSITY SERVICE PROGRAMS
Our suggestions for a model of university-based internship in public interest are based in part upon our firsthand experiences with the difficulties and limitations of service projects within the architecture curriculum. We see these internships complementing academic experiences and providing solutions to issues inherent in university outreach efforts undertaken by faculty and students as part of the regular academic curriculum.

"It is our strongly held belief that the experience that interns gain in these positions will have a powerful positive effect on their careers, the profession, and our communities."

Such internships will not replace student engagement in service projects; they will instead facilitate project delivery and the transition of new graduates to practice. For instance, academic schedules do not easily accommodate the workload demands and inconsistent flow of community-service projects. Client meetings and deadlines may fall during exams, concurrent with studio-project deadlines, or during vacations. Interns, unlike students, are not regimented by the academic calendar. Similar to working professionals, interns can control their schedules to accommodate appointments and project deadlines. The participation of interns can liberate projects from the constraints of the semester or quarter systems.

Students involved in service projects can experience high stress levels because they are often trying to manage many diverse responsibilities in addition to their engagement efforts. For example, community-service projects often require travel, necessitating absences from other classes. It can be difficult to balance the demands of studio and seminar work with the requirements of a research assistant position. By contrast, interns are free of the obligations to coursework and able to focus on the outreach project.

The teamwork requirements of community-design projects can be problematic for students, who may be ill-prepared to work in a group. The demands of service projects may exaggerate the challenges of working as a team, and conflicts can result. For interns, however, there are no grades to pressure the drive for individuality. Interns work with professors and students in collegial relationships and have opportunities to experience and even promote teamwork as a productive and professional mode of design practice.

For faculty, outreach projects require more time commitment and emotional involvement than any other teaching assignment, including studio courses. The students involved are constantly challenged as designers, community organizers, and team members, and they require prompt, consistent support from an experienced faculty member. Due to these unusually high demands, there is a high faculty burnout rate in service-teaching in architecture. Interns might offer architecture faculty a reprieve from this intensity. Presumably, an intern would require a reduced level of supervision and might even bear some of the burden of student oversight, previously shouldered by faculty advisors alone. While students have a reasonable expectation to receive extensive support from a professor, as graduates, interns can be expected to work more independently. Finally, faculty may get more personal reward from projects involving

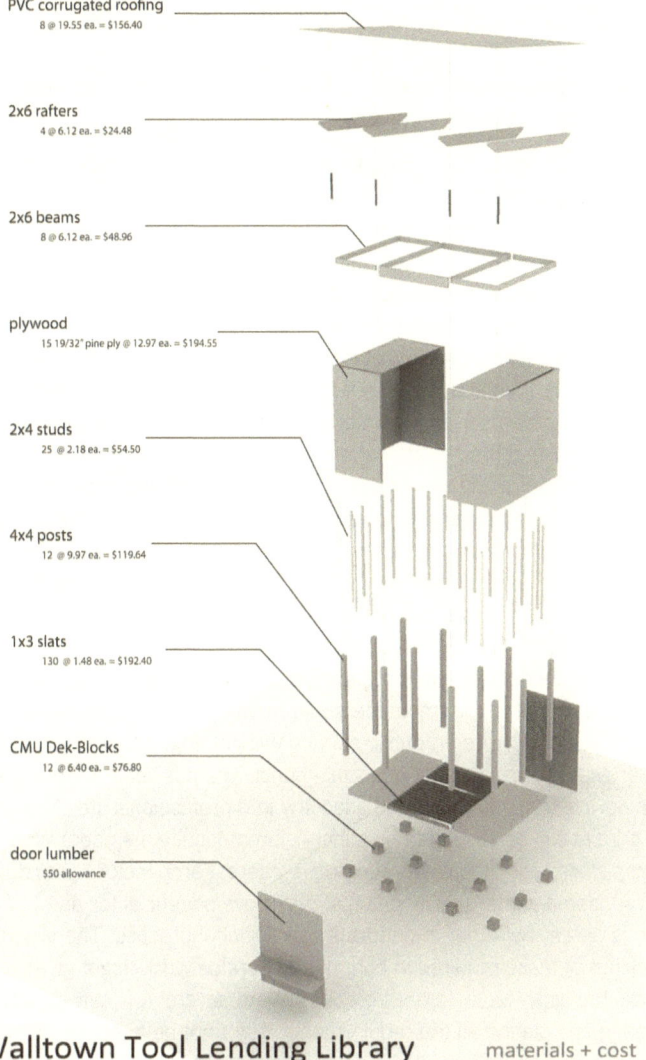

PVC corrugated roofing
8 @ 19.55 ea. = $156.40

2x6 rafters
4 @ 6.12 ea. = $24.48

2x6 beams
8 @ 6.12 ea. = $48.96

plywood
15 19/32" pine ply @ 12.97 ea. = $194.55

2x4 studs
25 @ 2.18 ea. = $54.50

4x4 posts
12 @ 9.97 ea. = $119.64

1x3 slats
130 @ 1.48 ea. = $192.40

CMU Dek-Blocks
12 @ 6.40 ea. = $76.80

door lumber
$50 allowance

Walltown Tool Lending Library   materials + cost

Barton used this drawing as a tool for the cost estimating. The differences between a studio proposal and a real world project became quickly apparent. Overlooking nails in the rendering proved to be a challenge to the small project's budget. (Rendering: Geoffrey Barton)

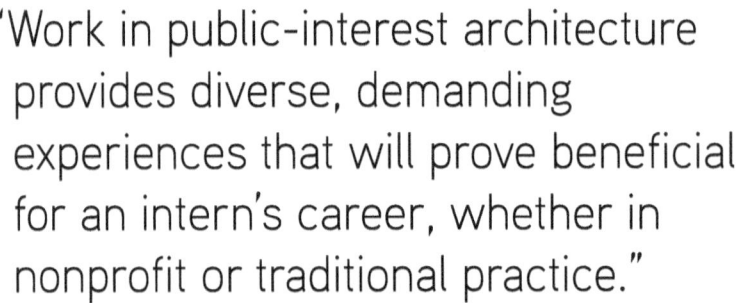

"Work in public-interest architecture provides diverse, demanding experiences that will prove beneficial for an intern's career, whether in nonprofit or traditional practice."

interns as the projects move more smoothly and can be potentially larger in scope or reach completion more quickly and effectively.

It is difficult to evaluate the results of service-learning projects at the end of an academic semester. As is the case in practice, design is only one aspect of the work performed; student appraisals must include the value of other acquired skills. Also, this teaching is tutorial in nature and can involve only a few students at a time, and despite the close interactions—or perhaps because of them—it is sometimes difficult to grade the work produced and the knowledge gained. Assessment of intern work is basically evaluation of job performance and requires less time and emphasis than traditional pedagogy. A professor and an intern can relate more as professional collaborators, and their relationship can be less focused on testing, reviewing, and grading. An intern working with a professor can give top priority to project delivery, whereas a student's educational needs might sometimes trump project goals.

STAKEHOLDER INVENTORY AND
ASSESSMENT OF IMPLICATIONS

For interns, these new types of jobs will offer challenging projects, vital design training, and enormous personal rewards. Interns looking for jobs that place a high value on public service will get engaging assignments that provide a strong sense of social impact. The positions will provide a supportive transition from the academy into professional life. Accruing IDP credits will be facilitated by supervision of faculty members who are registered architects. Work in public-interest architecture provides diverse, demanding experiences that will prove beneficial for an intern's career, whether in nonprofit or traditional practice. The broad spectrum of tasks required in community-service work might give interns the opportunity to earn credits toward several IDP categories, although completing all the requirements might not be possible.

Like other public-interest internship opportunities highlighted in this volume, the skills acquired in university-based positions may differ from those conferred by traditional architectural positions. For instance, these projects emphasize participatory design skills. Participatory design requires cultural and social sensitivity and the ability to listen well and communicate effectively, both verbally and visually, with a variety of constituents. Asset-based development strategies are extremely beneficial for designers working in underserved communities. The process of inventorying the strengths of stakeholders is a way of gathering resources and establishing a project's context. This process is typically not taught in the architectural studio because it is not easily replicated in the academic setting; rather, it is best experienced in practice.

Public-interest interns must learn to adjust to the pace and tenor of community work. Projects often proceed according to stuttering schedules dependent upon funding cycles, volunteer boards, and nonprofit partners who are spread too thin. Interns who work in this field develop the patience and persistence to accommodate schedule changes and relinquish expectations about when a project will be completed. They also gain valuable experience with fundraising and grant writing, critical components of public-service work. Interns write proposals for partnerships with nonprofits or participate in "brick and mortar" fundraising. The sobering realities of seeking money to execute a project will often encourage interns to develop an entrepreneurial mindset and financial savvy.

Interns who do public-interest work also learn to acknowledge their limitations. For example, familiarity with nonprofit management, finance, and real-estate development would be advantageous, but it would be unreasonable to expect any one intern to be proficient across all those areas. The complexities of project delivery require professional collaborations. Bankers and politicians are teammates, not adversaries. Negotiation and compromise are strategic tools. Design proposals improve as a result of community feedback, budget realities, and holistic project evaluation. This kind of teamwork is not emphasized by architectural education, where young designers usually labor alone and must defend siloed proposals, but community work demands integrative skills and multidisciplinary solutions.

For faculty, interns will provide welcome support in research, scholarship, and service, much like postdocs in other disciplines. As mentioned previously, this could result in greater satisfaction and stronger project results due to the greater sophistication, competence, and time availability offered by interns as compared with student research

assistants. The public-interest internship system will act as a mechanism for keeping faculty engaged with communities and practice. Faculty scholarship on engagement will be enriched by intern involvement. It must be noted that supervision of interns will add workload and may be difficult to balance with regular teaching obligations. This cost can be ameliorated by the above benefits. Finally, faculty may be required to assume some responsibility for fundraising in support of the intern position, but interns could provide assistance with grant applications to fund project expenses, intern salaries, and faculty release time.

For university administrators, a commitment to outreach and service is becoming increasingly important. Interns can be a critical element of this engagement agenda. The relationships forged between the academic institution and partnering organizations yield reciprocal benefits. Community engagement provides valuable opportunities for research and education, while dissemination of new knowledge and achievements leads to a robust public discourse. Strong active service and outreach projects are public relations assets that are beneficial for student recruitment and for courting the financial support of alumni and philanthropists.

Universities are encouraging faculty to connect the classroom with the community, and faculty are recognizing the enrichment such activities can bring to the curriculum: real-world application of theoretical concepts deepens understanding of the linkage between conceptualization and implementation. Architectural design, by its very nature, strives to meet client needs, which makes it the perfect venue for learning about a discipline while performing a service for the community. Architectural programs that take leadership roles in community engagement can become significant players in universities' efforts to achieve the extension aspects of their mission. Sponsoring public-interest internships will further demonstrate this commitment.

Architecture departments have been criticized for dropping inexperienced students on the doorstep of the profession. These internships will ensure that universities address this criticism and continue to contribute to the education of young professionals after graduation. In-house interns can also act as on-the-ground mentors for students with regard to such matters as the IDP process, for example. Fundraising for intern salaries may be an administrative responsibility, and some may question whether interns are competing with enrolled students for support. The payoff is the enrichment of the overall program and the service provided to both the discipline and the community.

As with the schools, there is a significant public relations benefit to the profession from turning attention toward public service through support of these internship positions. Architects and firms will have opportunities to connect with universities by partnering in the program. An influx of young architects skilled in community engagement and collaboration with nonprofits will bring an important new focus and client base to the profession and will encourage the emergence of public service as a legitimate architectural career track.

At present, some professionals might perceive this work by universities as competition. Typically, however, the type and scope of projects that university-based interns would undertake are not desirable to architectural firms, either because of the clients' insufficient funds or their lack of clarity regarding what is needed. Many nonprofits, for example, turn to universities for the predesign or conceptual design work needed in advance of fundraising and hiring design professionals.

Communities learn and grow as a result of their engagement with the resources of a university, and interns can be instrumental in this engagement. Before a single structure is framed, the client community involved in a university partnership is exposed to the design process, which teaches them what architects do and how architecture can benefit them. Interns become teachers, sharing their knowledge and skills. The creativity and enthusiasm of interns are valuable capital to harness and apply in our communities.

Internships often influence the direction a student will take in professional life. If only a few public-interest architectural interns embark on a career path dedicated to meeting community needs, we will have reaped a significant benefit. If the rest maintain a public-service ethic as they establish themselves in traditional practice, the ripples will expand, and the architecture profession will serve a wider audience and will more effectively contribute to the public good.

YES WE CAN

This model of university-based internship in public service is both simple and feasible. It requires one or two interested licensed faculty, some service grants or gifts for intern compensation, and a few service projects with communities or nonprofits interested in collaboration with the university. Such a program requires commitment and support from the administrators at the department, college, and university levels, but it can be implemented within the existing legal and organizational frameworks.

A modest start, with one or two interns for six months or a year, is both doable and significant. It is important to note that the funds sought for such internships must be sufficient to provide salary and benefits at close to market rates so that interns do not suffer economic hardship and so that these positions have the potential to become prestigious, coveted opportunities that can attract and recruit exceptional talent to work within the university community. It is also advisable to give supervising faculty some release time to ensure the success of the program.

In 2005, Marvin Malecha published a monograph proposing a bridge between the academy and professional practice.[3] He suggests that some schools could become integrated into the profession by taking on additional roles and developing internship experiences. On the other hand, some offices might organize themselves as "practice academies," functioning as learning organizations transforming both the internship culture and the practice environment. We see great promise in the concept of practice academies working with universities, and we propose the public-interest internship as one model of how this concept might be realized.

Neighborhood kids Wayne and Quintin were enthusiastic assistants, potential job site hazards, and critical community liaisons for Barton's internship experience. (Photo: Geoffrey Barton)

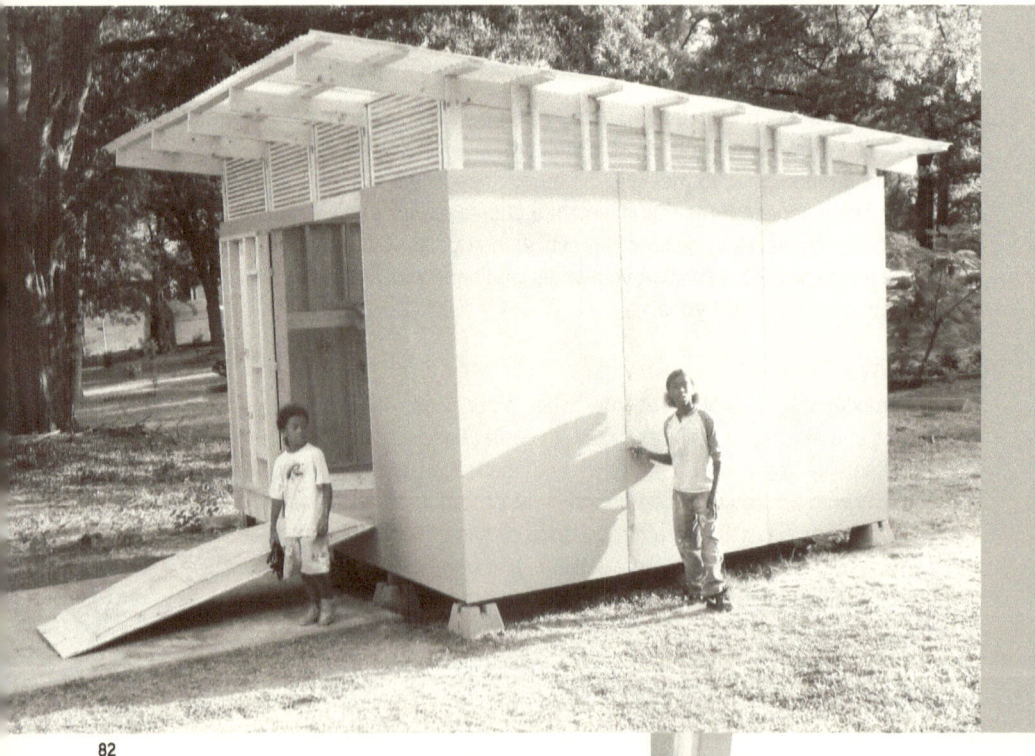

We are confident that university-based public-interest internships, and the other programs they might inspire, have the power to profoundly change the architectural profession and our communities and to provide many professionals with meaningful, rewarding careers. They will help the architectural discipline create the culture of service called for by Boyer and Mitgang.[4] Now it is time to test the theories and assess the proposals by creating and implementing pilot programs. Hypothetical debate is an insufficient way to discover best practices and build a knowledge base.

We think the time is right for this new model. If each accredited school of architecture were to employ two interns supervised by one registered faculty per year, that would be equivalent to a firm of more than two hundred people working under the supervision of more than one hundred experienced professionals, all in the service of our nation's communities. Cities, towns, and neighborhoods faced with issues of substandard housing, suburban sprawl, dwindling public open space, and toxic buildings will have a new army of designers to assist them. Inevitably, university initiatives will inspire public-interest internships outside the academy. The conspicuous breach in the training of citizen architects will be closed by developing new outreach internship positions. We will bridge the gap. The prospect of such accomplishments gives us hope.

GEORGIA BIZIOS, FAIA, is an ACSA Distinguished Professor in the College of Design at North Carolina State University in Raleigh. In 2004, she founded the Home Environments Design Initiative with the mission to initiate, facilitate, and coordinate scholarship, research, and outreach in quality design for home environments. In addition to teaching, Bizios has focused her practice on residential architecture and has sought to mentor and supervise architecture interns.

KATIE WAKEFORD is coeditor of *Expanding Architecture: Design as Activism* (New York: Metropolis Books, 2008), a collection of essays on design in the service of the greater public good. Wakeford is an intern architect with the NC State University School of Architecture's Home Environments Design Initiative and a LEED Accredited Professional.

Retail Strategies

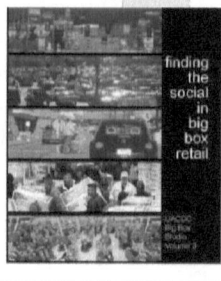
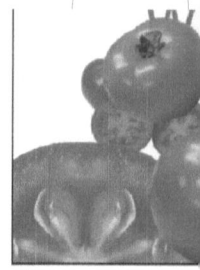

Campus Hydroscapes: Watershed as a Planning Platform

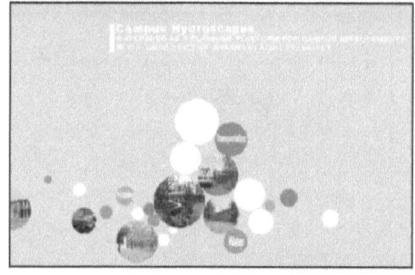
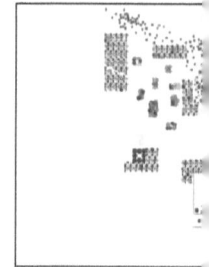

Porchscapes: An Affordable LEED for Neighborhood Development

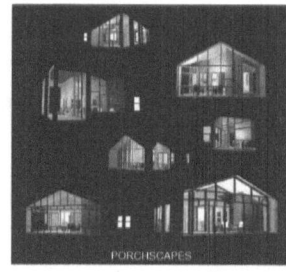
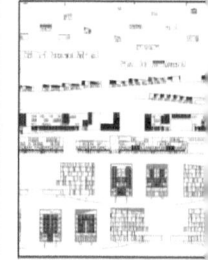

Monticello: Place-Based Plans and Codes for an Arkansas Delta Community

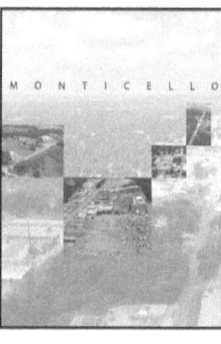

Visioning Rail Transit in Northwest Arkansas: Lifestyles and Ecologies

NWA Rail Transit Primer

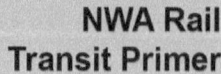
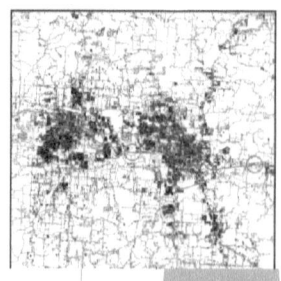
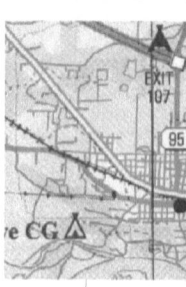

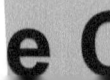

e C

STEPHEN
LUONI

WORKING FOR THE MARKET VS. WORKING IN THE PUBLIC SECTOR

Professional internship in the public sector requires a profession fully embedded in public policy processes. Professions, neither entirely market-driven nor government-based, are unique cultures of work that uphold a special public interest in the delivery of services. By definition, professions triangulate policy making, governance, and work in the public interest through an institutional ecology that includes schools, research institutes, professional settings where teaching takes place, outreach centers, policy institutes, and internship. While licensure is required to ensure the public's safety, health, and welfare in the course of executing work, licensure alone is not a substantive rationale for internalizing the public interest.

Unlike the professions of medicine, law, teaching, and engineering, architecture is still essentially a collection of private practices structured around service delivery in the commercial market. Design culture in architecture, landscape architecture, and urban design functions within an underdeveloped institutional structure, lacking the third-party organizations that bridge academia, public policy, and practice—the hallmark of a vital professional sphere. While it is inaccurate to presume that private design practice lacks regard for the public interest—because professionals generally theorize and internalize conceptions of the public good in everyday projects—design virtually never participates in structuring the public realm. Ironic, since architecture, as sociologist Robert Gutman has observed, "is today one of those few fields that keeps alive the utopian tradition of social thought."[1] Nevertheless, the structural gap between the design professions' sociocultural aspirations and the dominance of their service delivery by a market economy invariably precludes the formation of internship pathways via nonmarket sectors.

Lessons may be learned from medicine's transformation into a profession once its scattered field of healers organized to address public health concerns beyond the scale of individual care. As public health evolved from a sanitation matter rooted in engineering to a medical framework grounded in bacteriology and epidemiology, medicine developed enduring institutions—i.e., the teaching hospital, public-sector internship, and the research/policy institute—that continue to sustain its centrality as a public resource.[2] Likewise, the enlargement of design's efficacy in public sector processes will require a similar evolution in its institutional structure.

The University of Arkansas Community Design Center (UACDC) offers one model for institutionalizing design in the public sector, including opportunities for public-service internship. Akin to the teaching hospital, UACDC functions as a teaching office delivering professional design and planning services, but within a framework that augments capacity in public agencies, communities, and nonprofits, all of which routinely shape the

"Nevertheless, the structural gap between the design professions' sociocultural aspirations and the dominance of their service delivery by a market economy invariably precludes the formation of internship pathways via nonmarket sectors."

built environment. While the public sector shapes the physical context and regulatory environment in which design practices function, it does so almost entirely without the participation of the design community. This lack of influence makes it nearly impossible for the design professions to reproduce nonmarket values consistently championed throughout their schools and practices. The following discussion of UACDC addresses this linkage between institutional structure and service delivery that facilitates public-sector involvement and ensures the viability of a public-service internship.

NONMARKET VENUES: FROM PHILANTHROPY TO THE PUBLIC SECTOR

Discussions about nonmarket venues for service delivery in the design disciplines often conflate public-sector processes with philanthropy. Some of the higher-profile efforts to deliver design services outside of the market model feature "activist" practices to serve the other 90 percent of the population whose design needs are neglected by the market.[3] These practices, mostly university-based, recognize a remedial role for design in the wake of market failures, serving distressed clients primarily through design-build projects that meet essential needs. Both the work methods and project outcomes by these practices are highly expressive of their entrepreneurial capacities to circumvent obstacles and deliver professional products for underserved populations. Their work is highly regarded and rightfully celebrated.

However, discussions of service to the underserved 90 percent are rarely devoted to transformational engagement with public-sector institutions that shape the built environment and thus determine the social, economic, and ecological livability of communities—core concerns of design. In this context, discussion of the public interest is cast within the limits of the discrete project, a scale of design that carries only so much critical and transformational weight. Instead, philanthropic activity should be seen as the first stage in capacity building, because its expressive capacities play a powerful niche role in setting larger civic agendas. Projects alone rarely mobilize structural change, especially when they lack prototypical functioning, pattern language, and public-sector impact. Structural problems require structural solutions.

In other words, the concept of "service to the other 90 percent" includes some real blind spots, because philanthropy's service footprint is far narrower on a unit basis than comparable design activity that serves the market. Philanthropy is no less capital intensive when factoring in the hidden costs of subsidized labor, donated material, institutional participation, and embodied intellectual work. One major difference between philanthropy and the market sector is revenue streaming; otherwise, the amount of service provided by each design sector proportional to the total built environment is

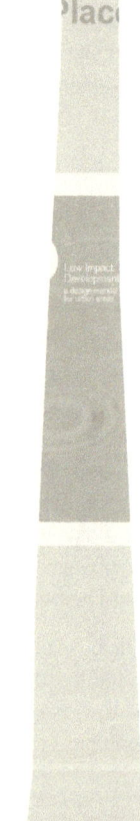

"Thus, shifting nonprofit design activity away from conceptions of philanthropy to that of public-sector participation is the only way to sustain meaningful scales of public-service internship in design."

"It's not just the poor who are underserved; there's an even larger middle with unmet design needs, suggesting that design should engage civil economies of scale."

fairly comparable. Yet the question remains: how might design truly service the other 90 percent? Is it simply a matter of expanding access to goods and services, which is often the outcome of philanthropy? Author Michael Edwards challenges the nonprofit sector's tendency to focus on the poor's capacity to be new consumers when he asks "whether increased individual participation in markets is sufficient to transform society. The answer is clearly no. Extending access to useful goods and services benefits poor people as both producers and consumers, and it is only possible to achieve large-scale progress in this way by utilizing the power of the market. But that is the beginning of the journey toward social transformation, not the end, and it leaves everything else virtually untouched. ...Creating markets is not synonymous with solving social problems."[4]

It's not just the poor who are underserved; there's an even larger middle with unmet design needs, suggesting that design should engage civil economies of scale. Those needs include more equitable transportation systems, land-use patterns that support urban lifestyle options, and livable communities with clean air, good water quality, and healthy ecosystems. Perhaps the tipping point for mainstreaming public service in the design professions lies in the prospect of place making or context production (as opposed to project production), which depends upon partnerships with the public sector in infrastructure development, planning, policy, and code development. Here, design intelligence becomes part of governance processes in managing resources, cities, and ecosystems toward more sustainable ends with greater returns on public sector investments. Competent design and management of human habitat—what Jane Jacobs calls "problems in organized complexity"—require continuous design input. Thus, shifting nonprofit design activity away from conceptions of philanthropy to that of public sector participation is the only way to sustain meaningful scales of public-service internship in design.

THE POTENTIAL OF COMMUNITY DESIGN CENTERS

UACDC's mission is to advance creative development in Arkansas through education, research, and design solutions that enhance the physical environment. As an outreach center of the Fay Jones School of Architecture, UACDC is developing a repertoire of recombinant place-building design methodologies applicable to community development issues in Arkansas with currency beyond the state. UACDC design solutions introduce a triple bottom line, integrating social and environmental measures with economic development. The center works multilaterally with clients, collaborators, and government agencies to build learning networks that facilitate creative development, triangulating public policy, best management practices, and design. Emphasizing the city as ecology, these place-building design models include work in watershed urbanism, transit-oriented development, green streets, shared street design, big-box urbanism, low-impact development, urban forestry, context-sensitive highway design, and smart-growth planning. An urban agriculture model, important for compressing sprawling food supply chains while improving access to nutrition, is under development.

"Interns are constantly challenged to combine critical and instrumental thinking in developing new planning prototypes that yield affordable, plausible solutions."

These building blocks, or "recombinant ecologies," for the everyday public realm address each of the three environmental-social landscape types designated by ecologist Mark Brown: "Protected Wild Systems used for watershed control and life support; Extractive Yield Systems such as agriculture, forestry, mining, and aquaculture that provide products for the economy; and Interface Systems (urban) that are self-organizing with society."[5] By solving for biological and urban dynamics simultaneously, UACDC's applied design scholarship explores how community infrastructure can deliver new combinations of ecological and urban services.

UACDC is an off-campus center with a full-time staff of five design and planning professionals, three of whom teach. Combinations of design-studio

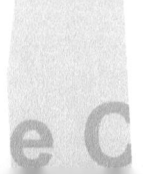

students, work-study students in architecture and landscape architecture, independent-studies students, summer interns, and full-time interns also staff the center. Sixty percent of UACDC's $550,000 annual operations budget (including salaries and benefits) comes from the university, while the remaining 40 percent is sought through project fees and grants. The administration of the University of Arkansas at Fayetteville is unique in recognizing both the academic value and the social impact of applied scholarship in community development. The state, however, is a different story; it is marked historically by an underdeveloped public-policy sector and weak local planning traditions. Consequently, design and planning costs are not typically scheduled in public sector or private business plans (they have the lowly status of commodity pricing), making it difficult to obtain funding for the center and the general design community. Advocacy for good design and planning then constitutes a considerable portion of the center's work. Keeping in mind that Arkansas has the nation's third-lowest median household income, good design is fundamental to building sustained economic development and livable communities. Despite entrenched challenges to building a more supportive environment for design, UACDC has emerged as a statewide leader in sustainable planning and design.

UACDC champions latent environmental development issues whose stewardship requires advocacy and design innovation. For instance, to socially optimize regional transportation systems, UACDC initiated a study to develop light rail in Northwest Arkansas (NWA), and proposed expansion of Little Rock's tourist streetcar system to serve urban commuters in Central Arkansas. Subsequently, two of the four major cities in Northwest Arkansas adopted transit-supportive land-use codes, anticipating a lower-energy future in need of public transit. Meanwhile, with regard to the pressing issue of urban stormwater management and its impact on regional watershed health, UACDC has produced a best-practices manual on design for low-impact development, commissioned by the U.S. Environmental Protection Agency and the Arkansas Natural Resources Commission. The 230-page manual illustrates lessons learned from UACDC's two low-impact development neighborhood projects, the only two planned in Arkansas. UACDC has been working with the City of Fayetteville to legalize low-impact development as an entitled, by-right development code and to mainstream implementation of low-impact development technologies in urban development.

Obviously, work formats and divisions of labor at UACDC do not fully approximate the profile of experiences required by the Intern Development Program (IDP) of the National Council of Architectural Registration Boards. IDP is designed to work within market-oriented service delivery leading to the construction of a building. Because UACDC is not routinely involved in delivering comprehensive architectural services, our interns only partially fulfill their IDP requirements at the center. Interns occasionally participate in the preparation of construction documents and contract administration, which constitutes two-thirds of IDP training requirements. Employment at UACDC is essentially an alternative career path to conventional architectural practice, requiring staff to routinely work through multidisciplinary problems in architecture, landscape architecture, urban design, planning, and ecological engineering. Work processes routinely require the integration of research, design, advocacy, and communication skill sets, often challenging existing codes with new design prototypes. Interns are consistently challenged to combine critical and instrumental thinking in developing new planning prototypes that yield affordable, plausible solutions. The center's work environment, which houses staff and students at large tables in an open studio, operates less like a cubicled office and more in the spirit of a "skunkworks" shop, a term that refers to a loosely structured, agile development group specifically tasked with the innovation and testing of new solutions. For this reason, the more enterprising students are offered internships, because they thrive in this seemingly unstructured, porous work environment where most graduates with conventional conceptions about practice would be uncomfortable.

Internship at UACDC differs from the normative internship experience in private practice because of continuous market rationalizations of labor in the profession. Whereas UACDC agglomerates units of work across various knowledge sets in lateral decision making, work patterns in the professional firm tend to subdivide work segments (and knowledge) into an ever-increasing specialization of autonomous services—with lasting socioeconomic implications. Thirty years ago, Gutman called this trend the "dequalification of labor," a process wherein work is segmented "into smaller and more limited tasks requiring less sophisticated training and expertise."[6] Dequalification in professional work is certainly a factor behind the widespread complaint over the proletarianization of interns as "CAD jockeys" doing routine drafting work.[7] Early work experience that lacks robustness not only undermines the objectives of a structured internship; it also stunts the profession's capacity to produce a successor generation of practitioners equipped to exercise comprehensive and enterprising professional judgment.

While Gutman made his observations on the parcelization of work within the context of the traditional firm's pyramidal work flow—from designer to production staff to consultant to contractor—an updated model by Paolo Tombesi recasts the ecology of design production

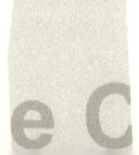

altogether. Now design responsibilities are dispersed among autonomous technical actors or "economic subjects other than purely professional firms thriving on horizontal economies of scale for technical tasks developed in collaboration with or on behalf of project-based firms."[8] This redistribution of professional labor, from the comprehensive professional firm to a global periphery of specialized and well-networked vendors, is restructuring internship. Tombesi predicts that as opportunity for advancement within the traditional firm wanes, more interns will likely acquire valuable expertise and interfacing skills within the realm of these external, autonomous technical actors. This new constellation of service delivery communities includes public-sector units like UACDC, which stand apart from the traditional professional firm. Public-sector prospects, however, hinge on whether community-design centers can harness the upside of these rationalization processes to create scaled alliances with public-agency cultures. Urban development, housing, and environmental resource management agencies, the likely consumers of design services, will have to be convinced that good design and planning are not narrow aesthetic enterprises, but rather management and development resources that add value beyond the scope of the discrete project.

Unlike the professional firm, where the request for proposals drives the project—a "pull" relationship generated by client demand—at UACDC the research proactively "pushes" the project, driven by supply from the designer. UACDC interns engage a very different form of professional agency, recombining work methodologies among the various design and engineering disciplines in one shop, a work approach more intrinsic to urban design (than architectural work). Subsequently, a majority of UACDC's full-time staff, who are technically interns, hold project-management responsibilities, sharing teaching duties and public advocacy tasks in project development. Working horizontally, all staff members are engaged in project definition, research and policy, coordination of collaborating disciplines, prototyping, schematic design, design development, and publication production. Most will eventually become involved in public speaking, including client contact, community meetings, and advocacy work.

An especially important focus of UACDC's work involves communication of complex planning issues structuring the built environment. Drawings serve a didactic function, particularly in sustaining public conversations on smart growth approaches that affect resource allocations in infrastructure and land-use development. The entire staff is involved in the graphic design and generation of content for UACDC publications. For instance, our book, *Low Impact Development: a design manual for urban areas,* now in its second printing, is widely used by governmental and nonprofit interests in advancing new forms of green infrastructure. Horizontal work arrangements between interns and staff who hold architectural licensure and LEED accreditation demand that interns demonstrate equivalent initiative in generating discourse, research, and design approaches. Indeed, interns operate entrepreneurially to assist in devising interdisciplinary project frameworks. Productivity is measured more by the influence of their inputs—the processes, capacities, relationships, and values developed to shape the public sphere—than by unit of construction output used to measure productivity in the market. Such expectations do not suggest that internship is free agency, which can be a problem at nonprofits without a culture of managed service delivery. But it does increase the probability that interns will exercise a more integrative application of their design and analytic skills than what is usually facilitated in market-based internship.

Meanwhile, IDP—which is likely headed for big changes—has not anticipated ongoing market transformations, let alone the claim of public-sector service on internship. While IDP is structured around the acquisition of core production competencies necessary for traditional architectural practice, there remains an unreconciled schism between the pathway to licensure and options for public-sector work. Unlike the American legal profession and architecture associations in most nations, where candidates are eligible for licensure upon graduation, the licensure process here does not leave much room for internship alternatives to market-based practice. This may be why some interns elect to work at UACDC once they have satisfied their credit requirements for construction documentation and contract administration.

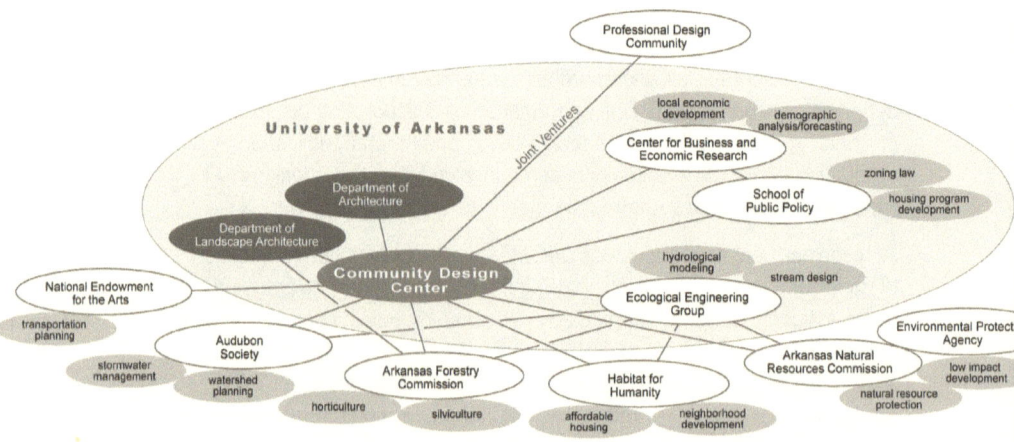

Partners Diagram (Graphic: University of Arkansas Community Design Center)

It remains to be seen whether UACDC can form sustained alliances with Arkansas' public sector to provide design and planning services in the public interest. The center's ability to develop transactional service relationships with communities is challenged by the fact that 95 percent of the state's cities have populations below fifteen thousand, and state government lacks cabinet-level administration in housing, urban development, and transportation (with the exception of highway development). Most of the center's external funding has come from federal sources representing national public interests in design, such as the National Endowment for the Arts, and in environmental resource management, such as the Environmental Protection Agency. Most of the center's work (akin to philanthropy dynamics discussed earlier) remains at the level of demonstration, useful for its expressive capacity to stage transformative action by local decision makers in the public sector. But as Edwards reminds us, philanthropy should be provisional: "a support system, not a control system"[9] for releasing broad-based social energies. Philanthropy can nurture an underdeveloped civil society's capacity for follow-through, but philanthropy is not a viable substitute for the public realm. It's an extended process, and the good news for now is that UACDC interns are well-compensated full-time state employees who receive matching retirement investitures, vacation, sick leave, medical benefits, and all of the rights of a public-sector employee.

STEPHEN LUONI is director of the University of Arkansas Community Design Center, where he is the Steven L. Anderson Chair in Architecture and Urban Studies. Luoni has a B.S. in architecture from Ohio State University and an M.Arch. from Yale University.

LEN **CHARNEY** & GABE **BERGERON**

ENGAGED, PURPOSEFUL LEARNING THROUGH COMMUNITY DESIGN

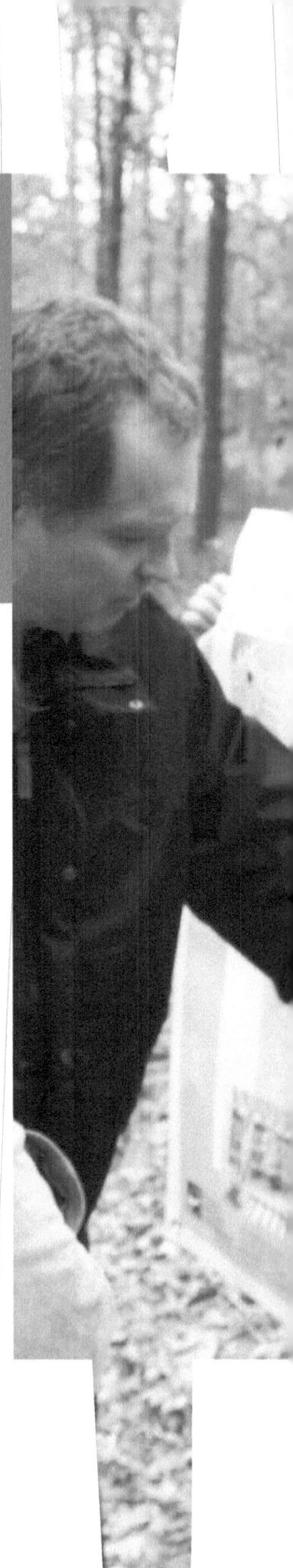

Site Meeting, Ecotopian Project at Community Green, Sandwich, Massachusetts (Photo: Len Charney)

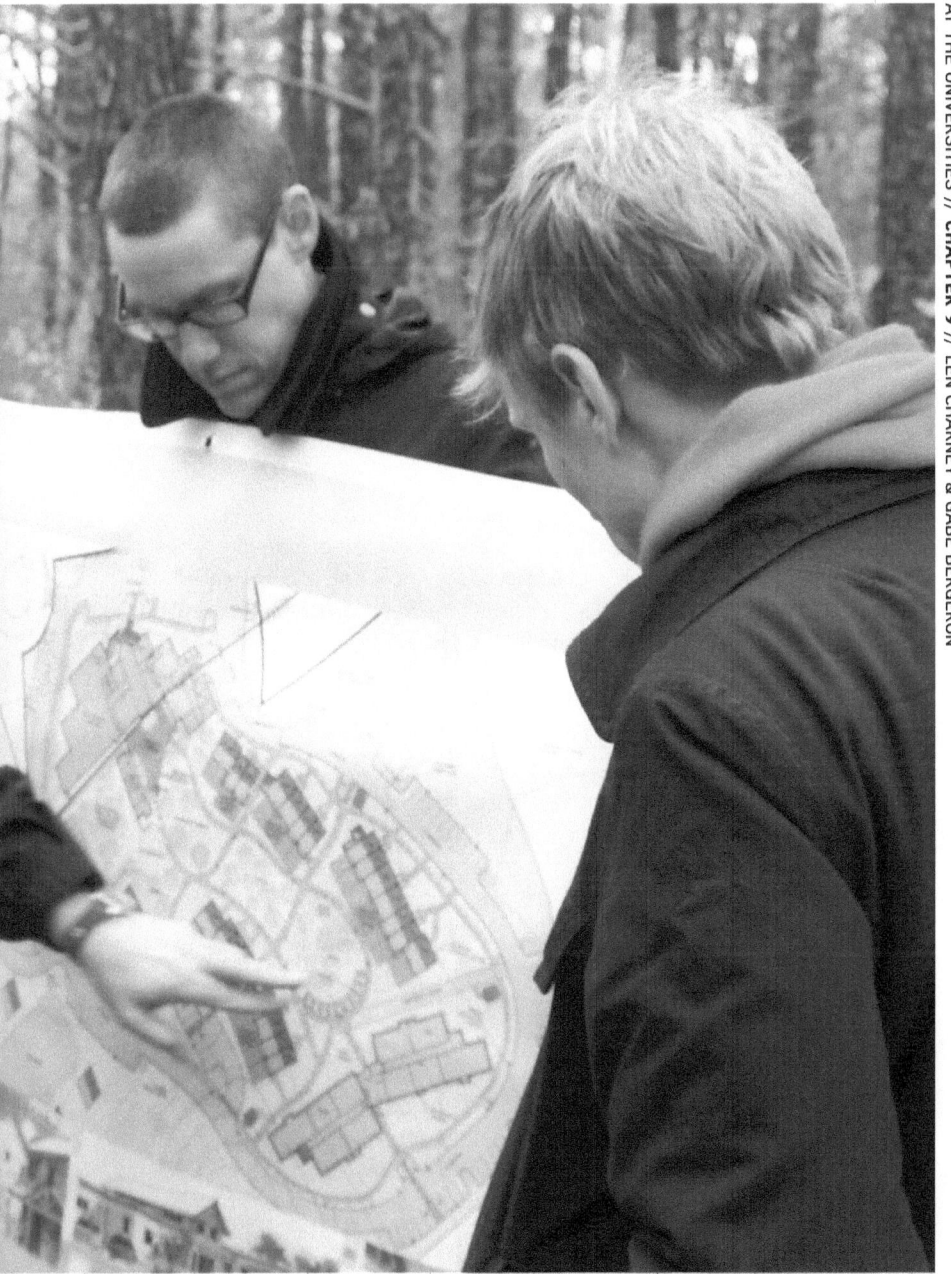

This time, like all other times, is a very good
one, if we know what to do with it.

—Ralph Waldo Emerson

No profession has been immune to wrenching change over the past decade.
Technological progress, a crashing economy, fears of environmental
degradation, global competition, and a range of industry-specific factors
have confounded those who struggle to practice in the face of factors
over which they have little control. At the same time, these changes
have also confronted educators in programs charged to prepare the next
generation of leaders within these industries. The design professions
are in the midst of addressing these dilemmas, and so are the field's
educational institutions, including Boston Architectural College (BAC).

This essay describes a series of recent community-based projects
conducted at the BAC, but when placed in the context of asking how best to
prepare the next generation of spatial designers, it also challenges design
educators and practitioners to reconsider their own assumptions about
what it will take for the design professions to evolve, maintain relevance in a
changing world, and flourish.

CRISIS PRESENTS OPPORTUNITY
FOR REFLECTION AND CHANGE
A legacy of learning through the sponsorship of community service
projects at the BAC dates back to the 1970s, with the launch of community-
design center studios. Each semester for the last thirty-three years,
teams of advanced-level students have participated in more than 350
planning, design, and design-build projects focusing on neighborhoods
throughout metropolitan Boston. These ventures have fostered an
awareness of social responsibility, reminded designers of their obligation
to provide comprehensive design services to underserved members of
the community, and underscored the rewards of meeting this obligation.

Against this historical backdrop, fast-forward to 2009, when design
professionals throughout Boston found themselves in the stranglehold of
the current recession. The architecture and engineering industry in Boston
was decimated, with more than 90 percent of design firms experiencing
layoffs or pay cuts, and half of the city's firms operating at a loss.[1]

This situation presented a particular problem for BAC students, who have
historically worked in approved, supervised settings to earn requisite
degree credits in accordance with the college's signature concurrent

"... the process transcended basic skill-gathering to become a fully integrated, connective experience featuring a real client, a supportive community, and rigorous design process, complete with deliverables connected to fundraising."

model of design education. Acquiring knowledge and skills through experience has been a critical cornerstone at the BAC throughout its 122-year history, where learning through doing is believed to be the best approach to becoming a critical thinker and accomplished designer. Accordingly, students at the BAC are engaged in professional practice during the day and take academic classes in the evening.

During the height of the current recession, the number of BAC students unable to find employment in credit-bearing, design-related positions jumped more than 12 percent. While many students managed to sustain themselves working in nondesign positions, they were increasingly stymied in their attempts to synchronize academic and practice-based learning. In addition to having difficulty earning the minimum threshold of credits to advance in their degree studies, students were hard pressed to gain necessary technical skills and competency.

In response, the BAC's Practice Department, charged with administering and assessing all experiential learning at the college, developed the Gateway Initiative, which gave students the option to earn credits and learn in 4 discrete, structured, faculty-supervised areas: (1) educational partnerships with community-based organizations, secondary schools, and municipal agencies working on ventures that encompassed planning, preliminary design, and small-scale design-build endeavors; (2) involvement in sponsored design competitions with students forming "mock firm" teams, whose success was measured as much by their ability to reflectively communicate (both graphically and orally) the iterative development of their work as by producing excellent design; (3) completion of modest independent or freelance projects under close instructional guidance from practice faculty; and (4) research and travel that furthered their professional growth and development. While these activities were specifically shaped to helped stem the tide for students needing practice-based credit, few could have anticipated the insights and self-discovery that resulted.

STRUCTURING COMMUNITY
SERVICE-LEARNING OPPORTUNITIES

Once community-design opportunities were introduced, interest in community design projects both within and beyond the BAC campus grew exponentially. While projects were initially secured through networking with various government agencies and grassroots organizations, word spread quickly that the BAC was interested in expanding its capacity to engage with municipal and nonprofit groups on a specific project basis. Student teams with three to five members were organized in a vertical manner, with graduate and younger undergraduate students teamed together; additionally, projects were often conducted in an interdisciplinary manner, with architecture, landscape architecture, interior design, and degree studies joined on the same project whenever possible. Most participants dedicated an average of fifteen to twenty hours per week, with one scheduled all-team meeting held at either the BAC or at the supervising faculty member's office. They often came together in smaller subgroups to focus on specific tasks, with results brought back to the entire group for further discussion and to ensure consensus. While most community projects were designed to run an entire semester, many assumed a life of their own as either the breadth of work expanded or additional time was spent generating polished presentations for a more public exchange of ideas.

CRITICAL CURRICULAR DISCUSSION

The broad, comprehensive nature of work undertaken by our students has led the BAC to rethink how experientially based learning requirements should be defined and assessed. Metrics for awarding practice degree credit have always adhered to both prescriptive minimums of time students are expected to spend in approved design-related settings and to standards or gauges of excellence to evaluate the acquisition of critical professional skills. However, observing experiences in the Gateway Initiative, it has become evident that the value of the concentrated experience gained through community-design work directly supervised by the BAC warrants a shift in emphasis in the basis for awarding credit, away from measuring time spent and toward measurement of learning outcomes.

Our results also support the development of a unified academic and practice curriculum, with instructional goals and outcomes more closely aligned and monitored. The previous ad hoc, inconsistent synthesis between a student's daytime employment and evening classroom instruction is being carefully scrutinized. This is particularly applicable when considering younger undergraduate students, who find it increasingly difficult to secure entry-level design-related employment as the entire design profession undergoes its own dramatic metamorphosis and ratchets up expectations about the roles and responsibilities of student interns. Quite simply, there needs to be a stronger connection between how students learn and what they learn, rather than simply assuming that students will be able to quickly, naturally adapt and be useful contributors in their first professional assignments.

THREE CASE STUDIES

The problems of real-world practice do not present themselves to practitioners as well-formed structures. Indeed, they tend not to present themselves as problems at all but as messy, indeterminate situations.

—Donald Schön, *The Reflective Practitioner*

The following snapshots from three representative community projects bring to life the work that BAC students, faculty, and practitioners have been absorbed with and learning from together.

CASE STUDY 1: THE WILLIAM CARTER SCHOOL
Comprehensive Learning through Community Interaction

The Carter School is a K-12 facility for students with severe disabilities. With the guidance of BAC faculty, a team of students developed an interactive design process for a new aquatic-center addition to an existing building. Through site visits, observations, and participatory workshops, the team formed a design that is highly responsive to the specific needs of students, parents, and staff.

The BAC team experienced a level of engagement beyond the typical classroom or office setting. They joined students in their classrooms and at remote pool facilities, interacting and observing the process of assisted pool use in order to gain firsthand understanding. They met with parents and staff, conducting participatory design workshops to consider program needs. Through this process they learned about the care and accessibility requirements for the children, and they gained critical insights into the conceptual qualities of the project that ultimately served to inspire and strengthen the educational experience, as well as the Carter School community.

This participatory process, combined with reflective interaction at

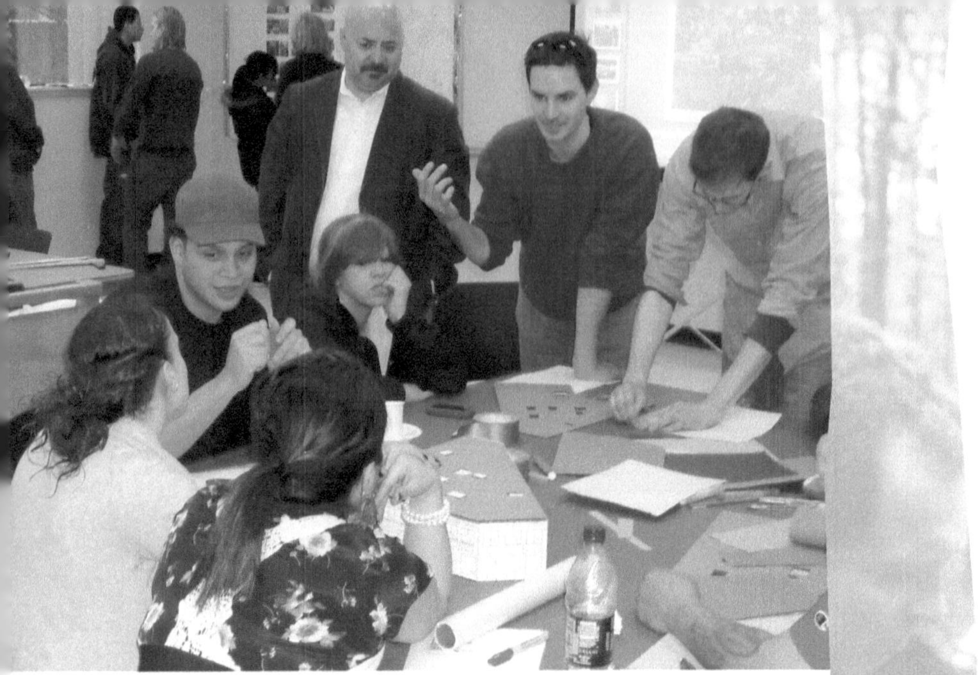

The Roca Community Center (Photo: Gabe Bergeron)

the BAC, far exceeded the normal criteria for a design project of this type; it provided the team with skills in critical thinking and lifelong learning to better prepare them as future design professionals. Moreover, the process transcended basic skill-gathering to become a fully integrated, connective experience featuring a real client, a supportive community, and rigorous design process, complete with deliverables connected to fundraising. All these elements came together to give the students an understanding of the real reach and responsibility of design.

CASE STUDY 2: THE ROCA COMMUNITY CENTER
A Research Approach to Design Thinking

The ROCA Community Center, an intensely used facility in Chelsea, Massachusetts, provides a wide range of youths with job training and mentoring programs. BAC students were asked to formulate an approach to "green" the existing building. The client's request led the students to creatively define the framework of their investigation. This process allowed research and problem definition to blend inseparably, ultimately creating an opportunity for the students to gain strengths in creative problem solving. The team's efforts included the preparation of an informational video to educate the entire ROCA community about the building, along with suggestions for potential energy performance and waste reduction. The team went on to conduct an interactive workshop where design ideas were generated for a green roof, and alignments between ROCA programs and green initiatives were identified. This further led the students to focus on assisting the community center to identify and pursue appropriate future grants.

The team of students incubated their ideas under the supervision of a BAC faculty member at his own office, structured to encompass a nonprofit organization devoted to developing links between the urban environment and surrounding ecosystems. This arrangement enabled students to gain a more thorough understanding of sustainability, connecting research and systems documentation with technical architectural skills and exhaustive client/community interaction.

CASE STUDY 3: THE ECOTOPIAN PROJECT
A Sustainable House Helps Bridge the Gap between Academics and Practice

The Ecotopian Project represents an innovative format for students at the BAC. The project relied on the BAC's advanced leadership studios, which gave students who were further along in the program a chance to practice leadership with teams of first- and second-year students. This combined group was charged with developing imaginative designs for a sustainable single-family staff residence for the Housing Assistance Corporation on Cape Cod in their post-homeless enterprise development, Community Green. The client selected a single design at the end of the spring 2010 studio class, which was further developed under the supervision of BAC faculty during the summer months. The goal is for students to produce construction documents and remain involved with the home's eventual construction, which is slated to begin in the spring of 2011.

Each team, comprising both leadership- and foundation-level students, strived to define a discrete firm identity and establish individual roles and responsibilities based on members' individual interests and skills. Schedules, working methodologies, collaboration methods, and project deliverables were facilitated by team leaders, who were in turn coached by BAC faculty. The process was infused with reading assignments, design exercises, and the purposeful creation of collaborative inquiry.

This format provides a new integrated approach to professional training and education, in which the research and pedagogy of the studio experience are connected to professional instruction in a symbiotic, mutually supportive manner. Students are engaging the questions of design inseparably from questions of how to best work together and develop ideas as a professional team. The format contains opportunities for students to conduct research and analysis, factor in relevant context considerations, conceptualize and develop iterative designs, communicate and negotiate with clients, and embrace architectural theory in an integral, interconnected manner.

OBSERVATIONS AND LESSONS

Observations about the quality of learning and mentorship have emerged from this experience. Viewed holistically, they suggest changes and improvements to the college's concurrent educational framework; in addition, they raise important questions about the existing calibration of skills and competencies prescribed within the Internship Development Program (IDP) of the National Council of Architectural Registration Boards.

Intentional reflective learning. Full-project involvement with community-based initiatives gives students the opportunity to understand and articulate how individual tasks are interwoven to complete projects involving actual clients. Their participation in design-based endeavors outside a classroom setting supports the concepts of reflective practice put forth by Donald Schön, educator and critical thinker. In his seminal 1983 book *The Reflective Practitioner*, Schön argues that professional education should focus less on the acquisition of a specific set of technical skills, bound to quickly become obsolete, and more on an ability to reflect on and respond to real-life situations.

Collaboration expertise. These endeavors, often interdisciplinary in nature, facilitate greater communication and understanding between students assigned to project teams, resulting in a higher level of collaboration. Students very noticeably assume ownership over their own learning, are more accountable for their actions, and challenge one another to produce their very best work.

Expanded mentorship and stronger educational partnerships with practitioners. This series of community ventures, primarily involving independent student efforts, is guided and supervised by BAC practice faculty in a more hands-off manner, representing an energized approach to teaching, mentoring, and genuine apprenticeship—characteristics that have unfortunately decreased in many students' intern experiences. Simultaneously, the same enhanced habits of mind that result from involvement on project teams encourages students to openly and honestly assert themselves at their daytime employment positions within firms. They are learning how and when to speak up and request support from veteran practitioners.

Community projects serve as an ideal "triadic" learning model—bringing together students, faculty, and administrators, as well as veteran practitioners—to form functional educational partnerships that guide and instruct emerging design professionals. The experience of coordinating community project activities with practicing professionals—many of whom are either BAC alumni or who teach our students in their evening classes—has helped the BAC move closer to developing strategies that are aligned with the "Teaching Firm" or "Intern Friendly" program agenda of the American Institute of Architects (AIA). According to the AIA, these structured initiatives "provide benchmarks for support and commitment to interns on their path to licensure," in harmony with the AIA's program objectives, and "provide a foundation for a firm culture that values continuous teaching, learning, mentoring, creativity, and innovation."[2]

Comprehensive learning instead of accounting for hours. One criticism of the typical internship-to-licensure experience is that there is too much emphasis on accounting and too little emphasis on comprehension and thoughtful reflection. In many office settings, interns qualify to take registration exams by completing an array of assignments (often in a disaggregated manner) as project support staff, neatly slotting their time into prescribed core competencies and training requirements. Students who gain a comprehensive understanding of all phases of community-based projects hold a distinct advantage in this regard.

Replicable model for learning design. This new combination of experiences encompasses a replicable learning model that can readily be effectively adapted to work within structured, more conventional classroom settings, helping students develop sets of technical and interpersonal skills that prepare them for the vicissitudes of actual projects.

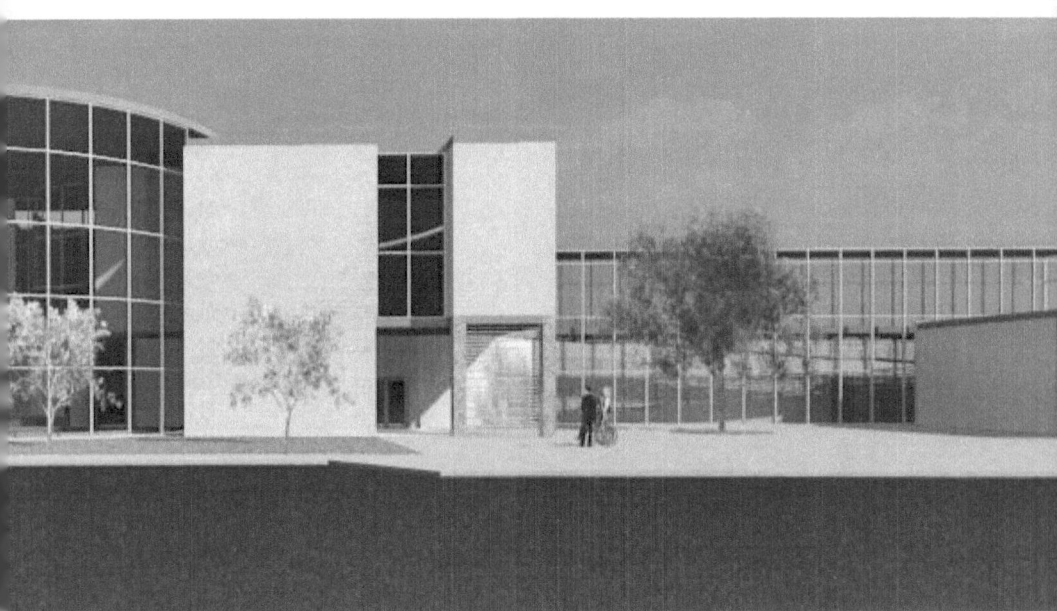

The Carter School (Rendering: Students Maya Tal, B.Arch. and Fredwin Molina, B.Arch.)

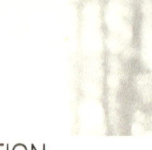

ACCEPTING THE CHALLENGE OF COLLABORATION BETWEEN PRACTICE AND THE ACADEMY

The increased prevalence of community-based design at the BAC was born out of a legacy of service-learning, and this change has more recently been accelerated because of the necessity to create additional credit-worthy learning opportunities for students at a time when real employment has dwindled. The unprecedented outcomes suggest a new way to view the training of design professionals in today's rapidly changing, increasingly complex project settings.

The clear result of these changes is a more thorough educational experience, engaging both tacit and explicit learning and leading to a new generation of design professionals who will be prepared to serve as creative thinkers and problem solvers in an ever-changing global society.

The Ecotopian Project (Rendering: Student team — Brien Baker, M.Arch.; Declan Keefe, B.Arch.; Arlen Stawasz, B.Arch.; Maya Tal, B.Arch.; Levi Tofias, M.Arch.; Holly Arnold, M.Arch.; Mika Gilmore, B.I.D.)

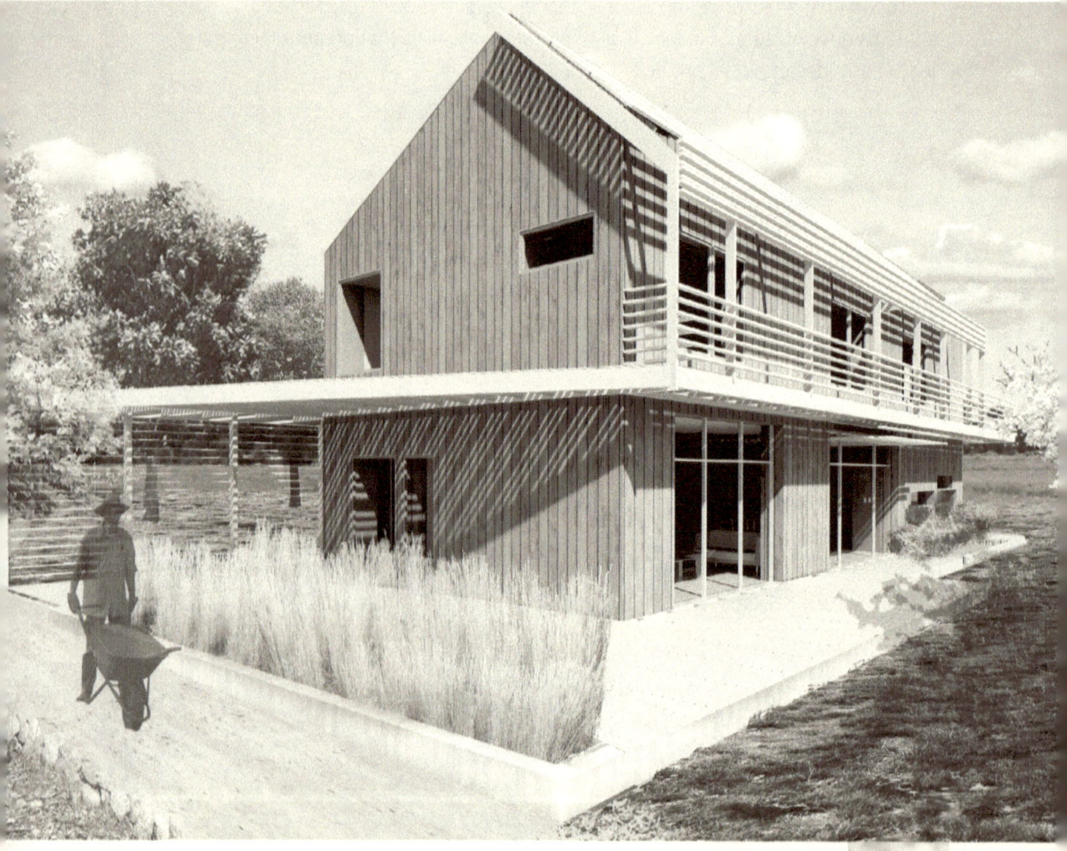

Engaging design through a community process provides a stronger sense of context and professionalism in a manner that is more relevant to the real needs and issues of the practice environment and that is more closely aligned with the integrated approaches to project delivery that are slowly being adapted across the entire architecture industry. The segmented accounting of hours represented by the IDP system, while helpful in calibrating experience in an office setting, falls short of the need to interrelate ideas and the even greater need to frame and reframe design problems in collaboration with all project stakeholders.

LEN CHARNEY, Head of Practice, Boston Architectural College, received his Master of Architecture degree from MIT. His career has focused on three diverse areas: education and career development; design and construction management; and community planning and real estate development. In 2006, he received a 3-year AIA grant to create a Practice Academy at the BAC, and in 2009 his leadership contributed to the BAC's receiving an NCARB Prize for Creative Integration of Practice and Education in the Academy.

GABE BERGERON is a Boston Architectural Center alumnus, graduating as the valedictorian of the Masters of Architecture program in 2005. He began studies at the BAC after 5 years of working in architecture firms in Denver, CO. Throughout his career, he has had a dominant interest in the social considerations of design and planning, culminating in a thesis on participatory design and experience in community design firms in Boston. His efforts as the director of the Gateway Initiative have greatly expanded the community-based design focus of the BAC.

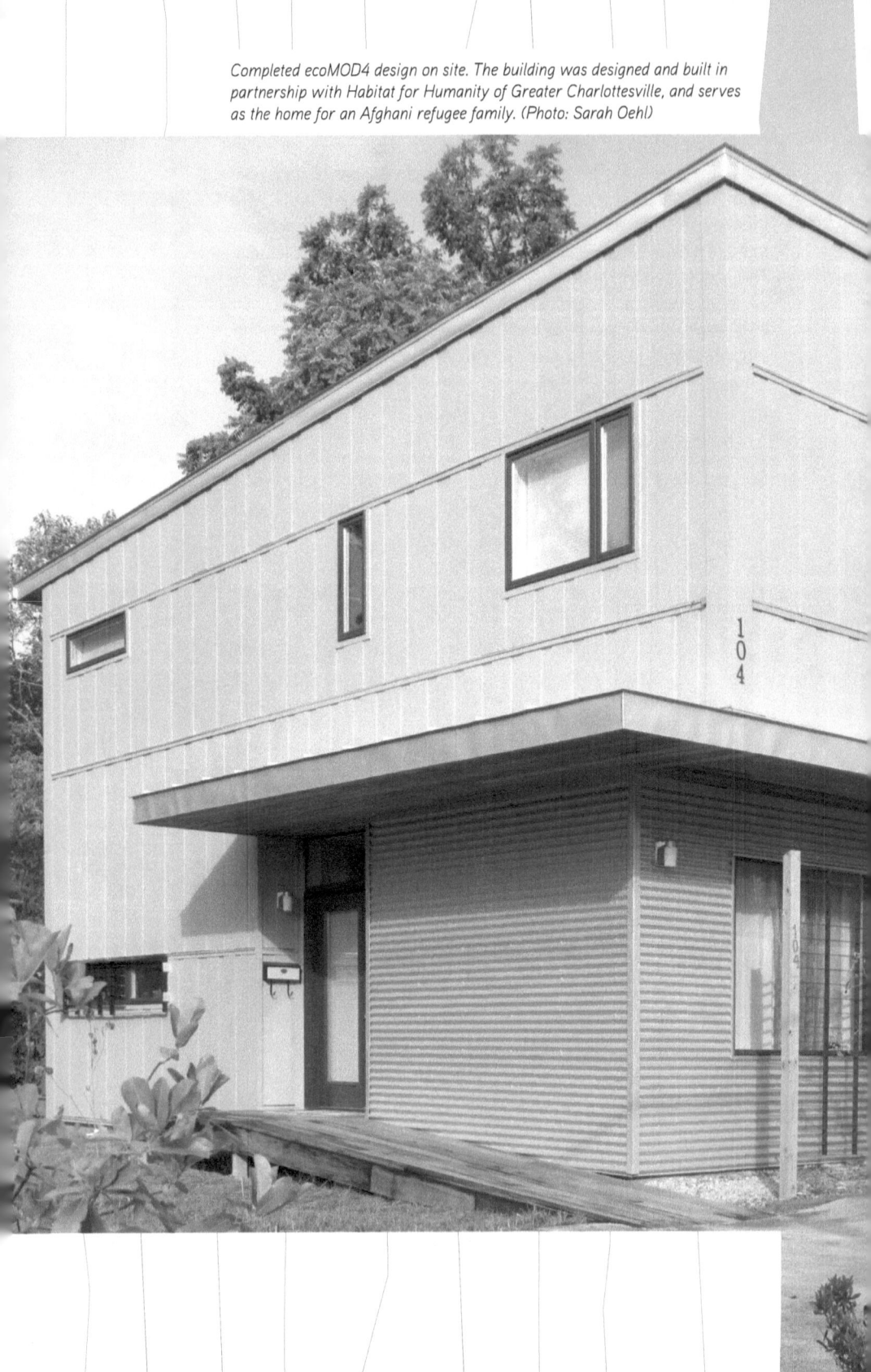

Completed ecoMOD4 design on site. The building was designed and built in partnership with Habitat for Humanity of Greater Charlottesville, and serves as the home for an Afghani refugee family. (Photo: Sarah Oehl)

JOHN
QUALE

THE CHALLENGES OF PUBLIC SERVICE AT A PUBLIC UNIVERSITY

Every man is under the natural duty of contributing to the necessities of the society; and this is all the laws should enforce on him.

—Thomas Jefferson, letter to Francis Gilmer, 1816

I look to the diffusion of light and education as the resource to be relied on for ameliorating the condition, promoting the virtue, and advancing the happiness of man.

—Thomas Jefferson, letter to C. C. Blatchly, 1822

Since Thomas Jefferson founded the University of Virginia, public service has been a core principle of the institution. Jefferson's vision of an educated citizenry that is prepared to address the important challenges of society has continued to expand and evolve in the twenty-first century. For example, the university recently started the Jefferson Public Citizens program, a well-supported fellowship initiative to encourage student-led teams to work directly with nonprofits on service projects that also have a clear and compelling academic deliverable. Students receive summer funding, training on how to work with nonprofits, and direct support and advice from administrators and faculty. Training for students in the program is largely focused on helping them see beyond their preconceived ideas about the topics they want to pursue, and on helping them listen carefully to their partner organizations so the team can work on the issues clearly identified by the leaders or clients of the organizations.

SERVICE-LEARNING INTERNSHIPS IN THE DESIGN DISCIPLINES

The School of Architecture (SARC) at the University of Virginia (UVA) encompasses four departments: architecture, landscape architecture, architectural history, and urban and environmental planning. Architecture and landscape architecture have had a long-term commitment to remaining current within their disciplines while simultaneously emphasizing the long-term impact their work has on society, the economy, and the environment. For decades these programs have been defined by their commitment to sustainable design and financially viable urban and rural development, and their interest in providing design services to communities that cannot afford them. Recent examples include the ecoMOD Project, focused on creating sustainable affordable housing for nonprofits; the Learning Barge, an environmental learning center on a barge in the Elizabeth River; and reCOVER, focused on providing design solutions in the context of post-disaster and developing-world settings. Each of these involve multidisciplinary collaboration among all four disciplines in the school as well as other schools, such as engineering, education, and business. They have each received funding from the university to support their activities, including support from the Jefferson Public Citizens program. These and other initiatives are often fully integrated into the curriculum of the school, to ensure that students have a rigorous, thoughtfully considered educational experience. Projects such as these allow faculty to effectively blend teaching and research, and provide students the opportunity to receive credits toward their internship leading to professional licensure.

Since 2004, the ecoMOD Project at UVA has created sustainable, prefabricated housing units for affordable-housing organizations. Interdisciplinary teams of students collaborate on the design and construction of these homes, and evaluate the homes' performance, environmental impact, and livability after they are occupied. Participants include students and faculty from architecture, engineering, landscape architecture, planning, and architectural history/historic preservation.

The project is intended to both provide a public service to affordable-housing organizations and to integrate that experience into the curriculum of the university. Client/partners for ecoMOD projects have included Piedmont Housing Alliance, Habitat for Humanity of Greater Charlottesville, Habitat for Humanity of the Mississippi Gulf Coast, the Jefferson Area Board for Aging, and People Incorporated of Virginia. Typically the teams spend a year designing and building prototype housing units that are immediately occupied by affordable-housing clients. A distinguishing characteristic of ecoMOD is the integration of the evaluation phase for each housing unit. Although the nature of the evaluation process varies according to funding, location, willingness of the occupants, and the research interests of individual students, the evaluation seminar courses are typically focused on energy performance, human comfort, overall environmental impact, and affordability or constructability beyond the prototype.

The student teams truly take responsibility for the scope of their work and demonstrate meaningful leadership within the project as they work on the design, construction, and evaluation phases. Unlike many design-build projects, the student work is not limited to narrow design and construction tasks. Design and financial decisions are made by the students, within constraints established by the faculty and client partners. We want this approach to lead to a richer experience that more closely mimics the challenges they will face in the professional world.

For the architecture students who have just completed their undergraduate or graduate degree before the summer of construction, ecoMOD also provides an opportunity for them to gain practical experience that counts toward their architectural internship. The students requesting that their participation be verified and documented with the National Council of Architectural Registration Boards are generally the more professionally oriented ones and are looking for credits in the public service or university-based research project work setting categories.

During three of the first four ecoMOD projects (ecoMOD1, 2004–6; ecoMOD3, 2006–8; and ecoMOD4, 2008–10), students working through the summer construction phase received a fellowship ranging from $1,800 to $4,000, depending on the student's time commitment, with the top range provided to students who worked full-time for the entire summer. This is an enormous fundraising challenge, requiring as much as $60,000 to support the large teams. With the recent economic downturn, the fundraising for ecoMOD4 fellowships was particularly challenging, and we were not able to fully support all the students who wanted to participate. The project is dependent upon the willingness of students to work for a low wage—less than minimum wage if divided up hourly. Some students continue their commitment into the fall when the construction phase inevitably extends beyond the expected completion date. So far this has happened for every ecoMOD project—due to circumstances beyond the control of the project—and is an experience that is pretty typical in the "real" world. Occasionally, we have been able to

A collaborative deep dive session for the ecoMOD4 interdisciplinary team of architecture, engineering, landscape architecture, planning, and business students (Photo: ecoMOD4 team)

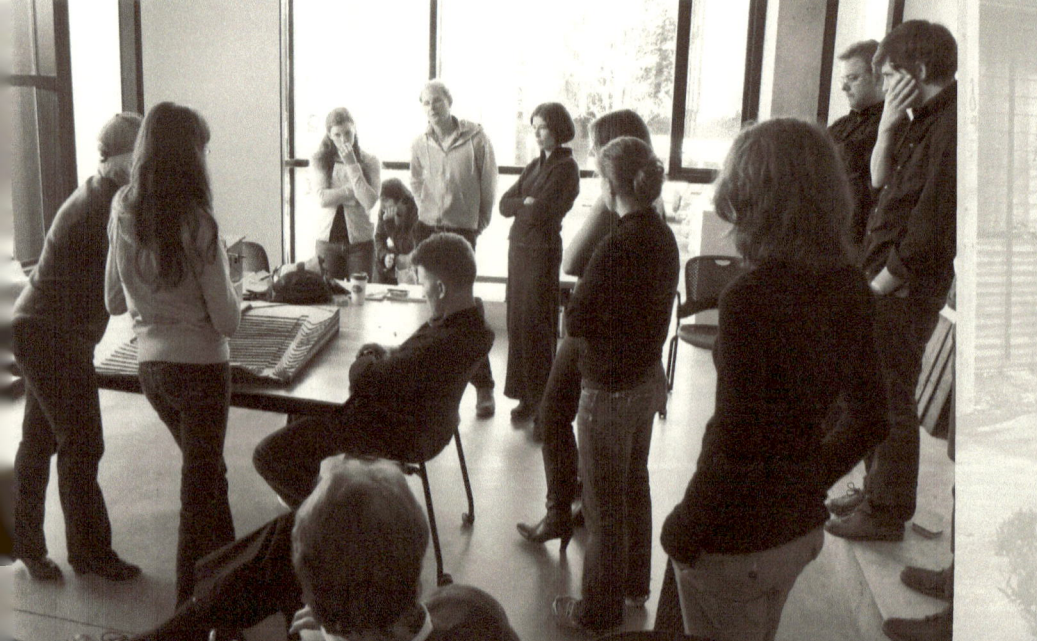

find some additional support for students who stay around to complete the project, yet this is never easy to secure at the end of the process.

Because roughly 85 percent of the summer construction fellowship students have just completed their degrees, financial support is essential for them. In the architecture school this high percentage of recent graduates occurs because ecoMOD is always offered as an "option studio" limited to fourth-year undergraduates and graduate students in the final or penultimate year. In the engineering school, while ecoMOD courses are technically open to students at any point in their curriculum, the courses are usually populated by third- or fourth-year undergraduates or graduate students. The summer construction teams have consistently been students coming directly out of the studios or engineering class, which gives the project a level of continuity from "design" into "build" that has been extremely important. Occasionally the construction team is expanded by volunteers or students receiving summer academic credit through independent study. With the economic difficulties of 2008–10, it has become essential for us to rethink the financial aspects of the project, and the experience of the independent-study students has offered a solution for us to expand upon.

The new models we are pursuing for upcoming ecoMOD projects are to (1) limit projects to the academic year so that students receive credit and don't need fellowships; (2) pursue projects that allow students to be paid directly by nonprofit or local government partners; and (3) offer a summer-long workshop for returning students to receive academic credit, supported by a small team of recent graduates who will receive fellowships. By working in one or more of these three modes, the fundraising requirements are substantially reduced.

ecoMOD2, completed between 2006 and 2008, was the first ecoMOD project for which we attempted to limit activities to the academic year. The project involved working in partnership with Habitat for Humanity of the Mississippi Gulf Coast to create a single-family home for a family displaced by Hurricane Katrina. Due to scheduling considerations, the design time was limited to one semester, unlike the usual two semesters, so I did the schematic design of the project myself; but by the end of the design process, the ecoMOD2 team clearly owned the design. The construction phase started in the last two months of the semester, and soon after graduation, the team shipped a flat-pack panelized design to Gautier, Mississippi, for assembly. Several members of the team spent two weeks in Mississippi to help assemble the project with Habitat volunteers, but foundation and utility construction delays limited the productivity of that first trip. Without any funding, several team members made additional trips to work with Habitat volunteers to finish the home over the next twenty months. This was made possible by the many options for free housing in tent cities for volunteers in the region at the time. Yet the chaos of the construction industry in the post-Katrina era meant the house sat untouched for months at a time. So while the project offered a unique opportunity for students to contribute to a post-disaster relief process, in the end it constitutes a difficult model to replicate in future projects.

The fall 2010 semester offered the second example of an ecoMOD project limited to the academic year. Named ecoMOD XS (for "extra small"), the project team consisted of architecture and engineering students working in studio and the engineering class to develop prototype housing-unit designs for accessory dwelling units (ADUs). The target audience is people who want to age in place. The ecoMOD XS team did not build any of the five designs they created, but the construction drawings will be made available to the public on the ecoMOD website and via distribution to affordable-housing providers. Like most ecoMOD designs, the XS ADU designs aim for zero energy use and reduced environmental impact overall. The intent is to give homeowners and communities ways to create ADUs that encourage multigenerational living. ecoMOD is partnering in this project with the Jefferson Area Board for Aging, a Charlottesville-based nonprofit that provides services for the aging population in the area.

The second model we are pursuing within ecoMOD is the provision of internships that are funded directly through nonprofit organizations or local governments. Starting in 2009, the ecoMOD project expanded to include a parallel initiative called ecoREMOD. A partnership with the City of Charlottesville, the Local Energy Alliance Program (LEAP), and Alloy Workshop, a for-profit design, construction, and graphic design company, ecoREMOD involves the renovation of a 1920s bungalow to demonstrate that sustainable upgrades are compatible with rigorous historic preservation. ecoMOD first pursued the integration of sustainable design and historic preservation with ecoMOD3, completed in 2007, in which a historic house from the 1860s was combined with a new 398-square-foot ADU behind the historic house. The ADU eventually achieved LEED for Homes Platinum certification.

ecoREMOD has been less well-integrated into the university curriculum; there has not been a design studio focused on it, although students have received independent-study credit for working on it, and some have come from the regular ecoMOD engineering course. The design and research team is small and has mostly been funded by the university; or, in the case of the lead ecoREMOD designer/project manager, paid as an intern working directly for the City of Charlottesville. Because of the complexity of historic preservation work, the students are only participating in a small part of the construction process, and the renovated home will become the home for LEAP, making the project substantially different from a standard ecoMOD project.

The final method we are exploring is the summer workshop. In the spring and summer of 2011, ecoMOD5 became the first project to use this model. The Falmouth Field School, a project of the architectural history department's Historic Preservation Program, has been providing historic preservation research and renovation assistance to Falmouth, Jamaica, for several years; but recently the need has become more urgent. A major cruise line company chose the port in Falmouth as a new destination and has begun constructing a new tourist wharf. While this will bring economic development to the city, it is also likely to increase development pressure on homeowners with older homes that lack modern conveniences. Already threatened are a group of wood-frame homes built by a free black community from the eighteenth and nineteenth centuries. Many of these homes do not have useful kitchens or indoor bathrooms, and slowly they are being torn down and replaced with generic concrete homes that have modern conveniences. ecoMOD5 consists of a small kitchen and bathroom addition behind one of these homes, which has already been historically documented by the Falmouth Field School. A Jamaican university is partnering with UVA on the project, and our hope is that the design may provide the impetus for a new local business in Jamaica to provide more options for local homeowners.

Student participants receive credit during the academic year as the design is developed, and any returning students receive credit during the summer Field School. Recent graduates from the spring semester design phase and who want to help build the design during the summer are eligible for a fellowship to offset travel and housing costs. Although it is not possible to offer a fellowship to all who want to participate, this strategy does allow for some degree of continuity, which is important because it is likely that several of the other students who receive credit for the Field School will not have been involved in the design phase.

Students building the ecoMOD4 home off-site at the ecoMOD Fabrication Facility (Photo: ecoMOD4 team)

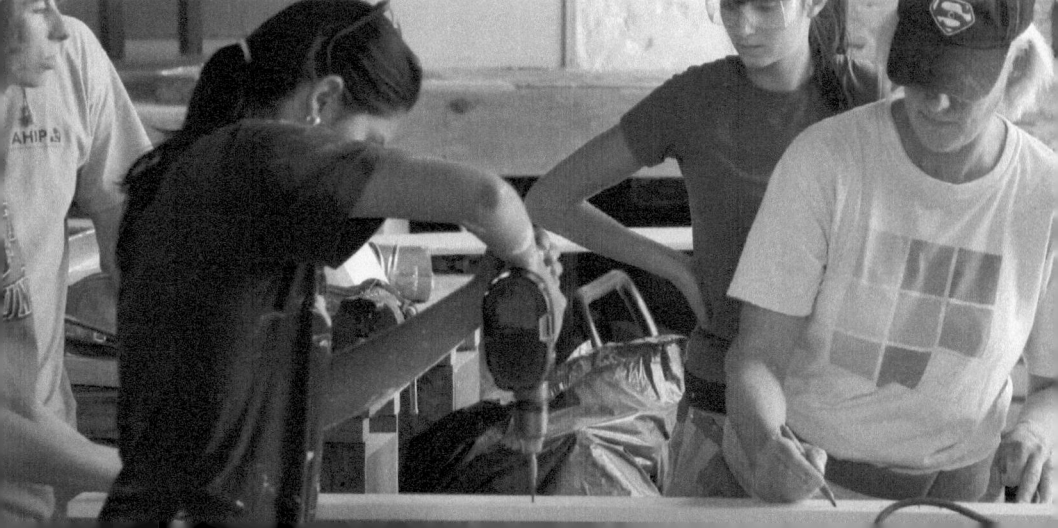

SERVICE-LEARNING INTERNSHIPS
FOR LOCAL ORGANIZATIONS

From 2005 through 2008, SARC conducted the Public Service Fellowship program. The program gave participating students a $5,000 stipend to work as part-time interns for a nonprofit organization during an entire academic year. The students worked for organizations involved in community design, energy and water policy, environmental issues, historic preservation, public health, and affordable housing. The stipends were funded by a local philanthropic organization, but unfortunately after three years the grant was not renewed, due in part to the faltering economy. The nonprofit organizations appreciated the program and provided a lot of positive feedback on it. The program was also hugely popular with students, as evidenced by the large number of applications, which always far exceeded the available positions.

However, the school learned some lessons from the experience. After three years, we felt it needed to be reconsidered academically and financially. The students did not receive any academic credit for participating; therefore, they did not have many opportunities to formally discuss their experiences or place their fellowship in a larger academic context through research and writing. For this reason, individual experiences varied considerably. The school decided it was necessary to refocus the concept to provide a more organized academic context and engage more purposefully with issues related to the environment, energy, and water. In addition, it became clear that to make the program financially viable and less dependent on the status of the economy, we would have to do three things: (1) move the program from the academic year to the summer; (2) expand the nonprofit catchment area to the entire state, rather than just Charlottesville; and (3) offer academic credit with a fully integrated seminar to make the program more financially independent and not linked to annual giving. By offering the program for academic credit, we are making the initiative more like other academic internships offered by UVA and other schools around the country. However, very few of these programs focus exclusively on community engagement, and as far as we know, none of them focus exclusively on sustainability or offer an overlapping seminar.

The new program is called S4, the SARC Sustainability Service-Learning Seminar. By combining service-learning internships with an academically rigorous sustainability seminar, we aim to challenge UVA students to understand and challenge accepted notions of sustainability while gaining valuable real-world experience. The first set of interns will enroll during the summer of 2011. As with the previous program, the students will work for various nonprofits, but we are also targeting local governments around the state that might have a specific sustainability-related project for an intern. S4 will be open to all four disciplines in the school, and the

"We want this approach to lead to a richer experience that more closely mimics the challenges they will face in the professional world."

students will receive three or six credits for their eight-week internship, depending on the time commitment with their sponsor. Some internship sponsors may offer stipends to students to offset their living costs.

The seminar will meet once a week for two hours. Students will be expected to participate in person at the School of Architecture or in a video conference, because we expect that several of the organizations will be outside the Charlottesville area. The seminar will be held in the Insight Lab, the school's new collaborative research and teaching space. The lab space, which was renovated in 2010, contains videoconferencing equipment, smart-screen technologies, and a multitouch Touchscreen Table for group work. The students will discuss their experiences and research the issues they are exploring in their internship. The goal is for the students to enrich their own education at the same time that they expand their internship sponsors' appreciation of sustainability issues.

The possible topics for interns to address vary widely, ranging from research on energy usage in the built environment for a green building organization to stormwater design strategy research for a regional planning district, or the development of sustainability assessment strategies for a regional architectural preservation group. The partners will be expected to provide adequate mentoring and regular feedback to ensure a successful experience for the student. The faculty director will have regular contact with the interns and their sponsors to ensure a positive experience for all.

The S4 program is somewhat similar to clinics found in many law or medical schools, where students serve society during their education. Gaining real-world experience is difficult to do while enrolled in architecture school because of the highly rigorous and time-consuming curriculum. Students need opportunities like these to acquire professional experience while in school, with the added benefit of learning the value of supporting communities through design and research. The sponsors and the students will benefit from an eight-week long "job interview," allowing both sides to

"Beyond exposing students to community needs and providing real-life experience, this program will directly benefit an array of design- and environment-related nonprofit organizations and local governments."

determine whether a long-term job after graduation might be a good fit. The summer 2011 trial run for S4 will be thoroughly evaluated in a variety of ways, to ensure the proper evolution of the program. The students and the internship sponsors will participate in both anonymous and non-anonymous evaluation surveys. This feedback will allow the faculty director to assess the suitability of the 2011 intern sponsors for future internships.

Based on what our students have told us, we believe this is precisely the kind of civic engagement and community outreach that many of them entered the school to pursue. Beyond exposing students to community needs and providing real-life experience, this program will directly benefit an array of design- and environment-related nonprofit organizations and local governments. These groups, which are typically understaffed and overworked, will gain direct access to the energy and intellect of the student interns, and indirect access to the research and intellectual resources of the University of Virginia.

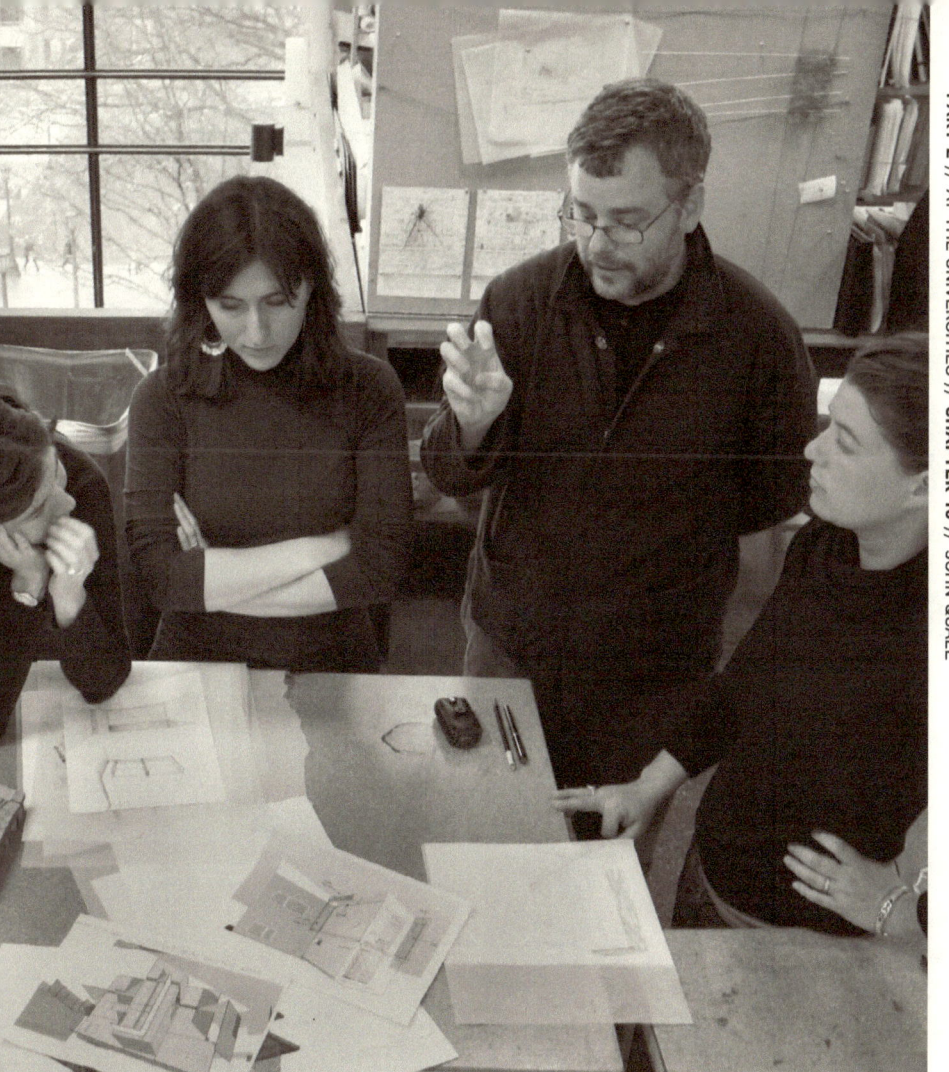

Architecture and landscape architecture students in design studio working on the design for ecoMOD4 (Photo: ecoMOD4 team)

JOHN QUALE is associate professor and ecoMOD Project director at the University of Virginia School of Architecture. He also serves as faculty director for the S4 program.

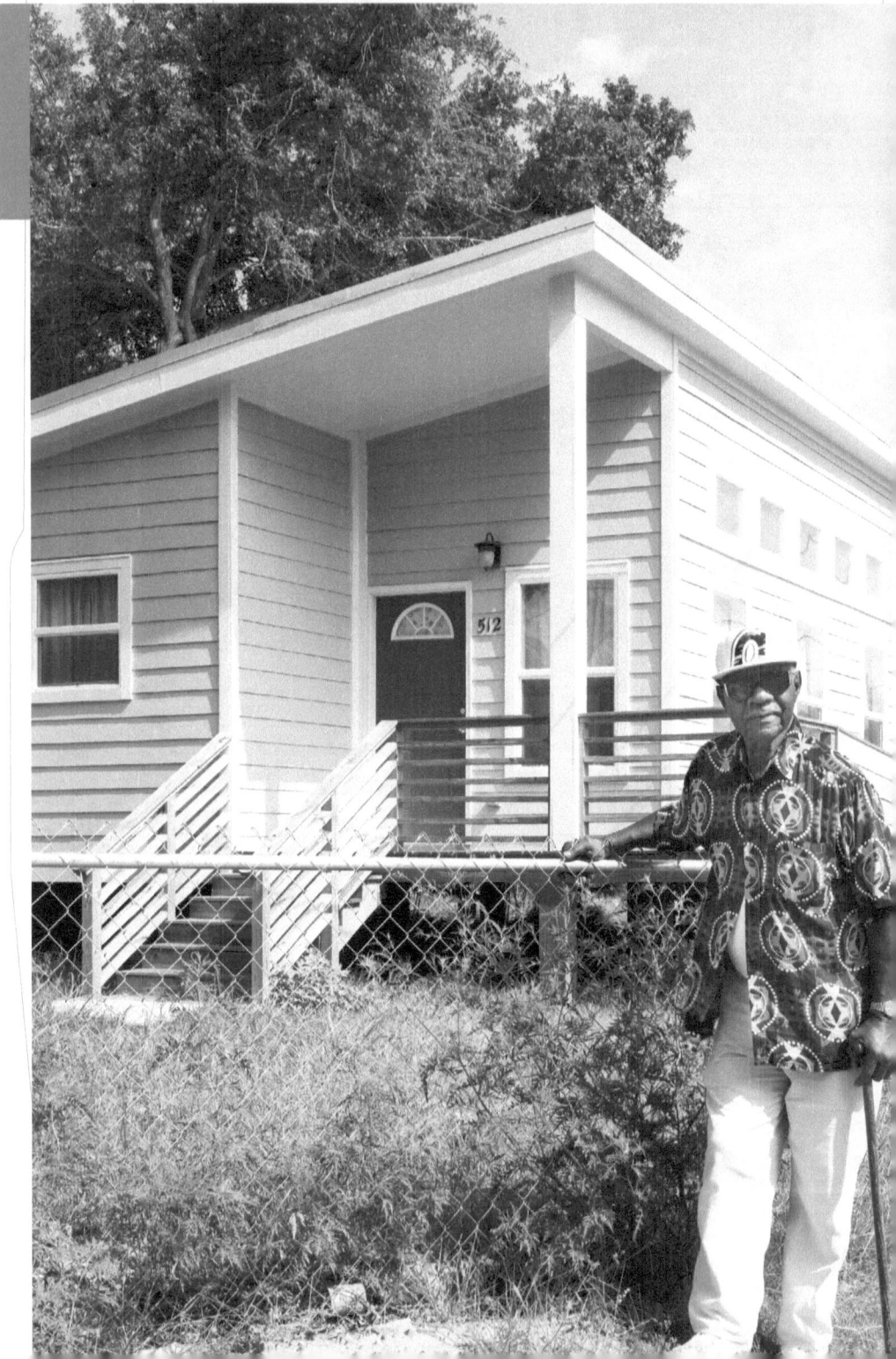

Direct funding enables the Gulf Coast Community Design Studio to provide design services to low-income households without adding costs for the homeowners or our building partners. (Photo: © Alan Karchmer/Sandra Benedum)

DAVID
PERKES

REINVENTING
PRACTICE

You are not a profession that has distinguished
itself by your social and civic contributions
to the cause of civil rights, and I am sure
this does not come to you as any shock. You
are most distinguished by your thunderous
silence and your complete irrelevance.[1]

—Civil rights leader Whitney Young to the 1968 national convention
of the American Institute of Architects

Architecture or Revolution.
Revolution can be avoided.[2]

—Le Corbusier, *Towards a New Architecture*

I expect architectural practice will make progress as long as there are
interns who aspire to social relevance. It seems that in any school
of architecture there are a number of students who do not envision
themselves working in a traditional commercial firm and who are
looking for a practice that addresses social needs. At the same time, a
relatively smaller number of practitioners and educators are creating
intern opportunities as alternatives to a job in a traditional practice. The
demand for such opportunities appears to exceed the supply, indicating
that we are in the early stages of a transformation of architectural
practice that will reach beyond a few experimental projects.

The idea of "public architecture" is gaining momentum and is bringing
the work of diverse organizations onto a common stage.[3] One of
these alternative practices, the Gulf Coast Community Design Studio
(GCCDS), is an experiment in noncommercial design work that offers
lessons in intern training. I believe a new public-interest design
profession is taking shape in this type of nontraditional practice and
will continue to develop and expand by way of a growing number of
interns who are being transformed by working in these environments.
Because practice is the subject of change, we can anticipate that a
reinvented design profession will come as much from new models
of practice as it will come from new educational programs, and we
should expect intern training to be central to this reinvention.

ARCHITECTURE, LIKE MODERNIZATION, REINVENTS ITSELF

Architectural practice is not inclined to revolution, probably because of a built-in hesitancy to bite the hand that feeds it. The architect's fee is a payment for services as well as an obligation to the interests of a client. We should not be surprised to learn that the word "fee" comes from feudal law, referring to land that a lord granted to his vassal on conditions of homage or service. In his 1968 address to the AIA, Whitney Young said that an architect's obligation to a client is an "easy way to cop out … You have a nice, normal escape hatch in your historical ethical code or something that says after all, you are the designers and not the builders; your role is to give people what they want." We should consider the words of a civil rights champion suggesting that "giving people what they want" is not necessarily socially responsible.

Architectural practice is more inclined to invention than it is to revolution. This is because the culture of architecture, following the culture of modernization, is shaped by an urge to solve problems so as to avoid revolution. However, events of the twenty-first century are dramatically challenging the fundamental premise of modernization—that new inventions will solve new problems. The key question we are now confronting is whether the historical symbiosis between capitalism and democracy can be generalized on a global scale without exhausting its physical, cultural, and social foundations. With such a question in mind, "invention" is better thought of as "reinvention," because the problems to be solved are not obstacles to achieving modernization; the

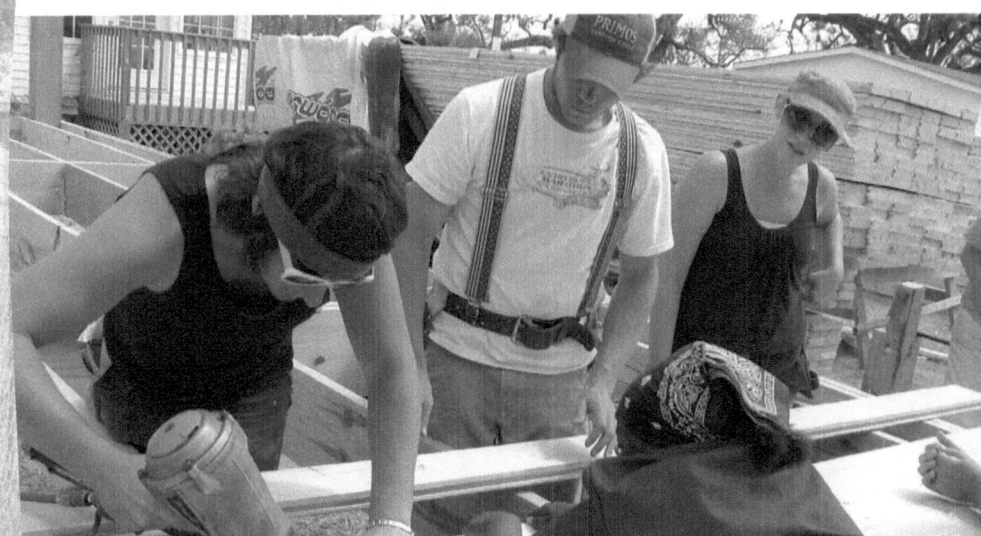

Construction gives interns confidence on job sites and helps them appreciate the craft of building.
(Photo: GCCDS)

problems are products of the victory of modernization. In other words, if simple modernization means the replacement of traditional social forms by industrial social forms, then reinvented modernization means the replacement of industrial social forms by another modernity.[4]

Modernization is not static. As Karl Marx proposed, "The bourgeoisie cannot exist without continually revolutionizing the instruments of production, that is, the relations of production, hence all social relations."[5] Thus, today's modern society is destroying the previously created industrialized social formations of class, occupation, gender roles, and business sectors, and is questioning the status of expertise and specialization. Terms such as "class struggle" and "labor rights" are outdated. Even the language of civil rights does not produce social action to the degree witnessed in an earlier generation. As Le Corbusier expected, revolution has been avoided, not by the work of politics but by the normal regenerative process of modernization.

SOCIAL REINVENTION REQUIRES MORE EFFORT THAN TECHNICAL INVENTION

The reinvention of architectural practice is following the same path as reworked modernization, experimenting with new relationships between the architect and the public. These experiments typically stem more from critiques of the social forms of practice than from its technical aspects. Technical progress in architecture advances effortlessly as building science and product development inform the design and construction of structures. Such progress is built into the building industry because technology is already driven by capitalism and does

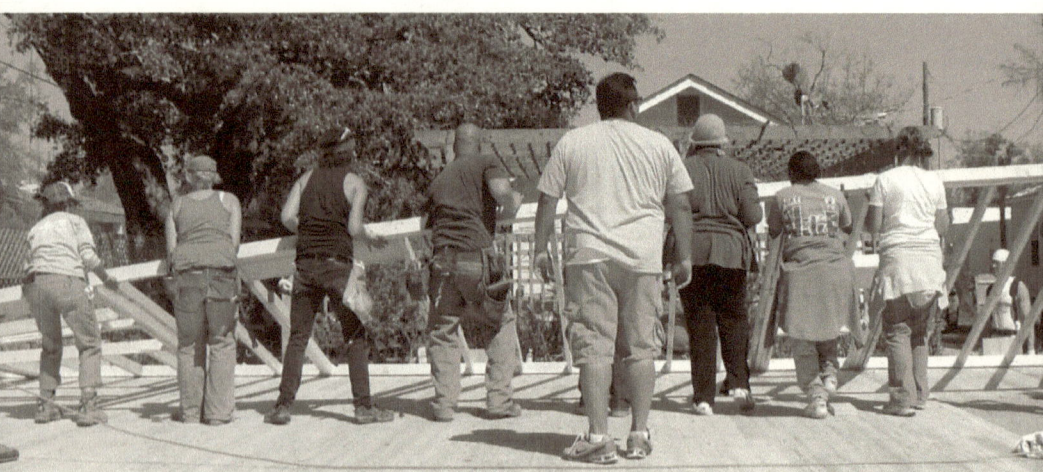

Building is often a group effort that teaches interns teamwork. (Photo: GCCDS)

not require any practical changes to make progress. However, social progress in architecture does not happen without effort. Changes in the social forms of practice are less apparent, in part because defining and measuring social progress is not yet institutionalized to the degree of technical progress, as evidenced by the popularity of LEED and the relatively unknown status of SEED.[6] Nevertheless, if we want to move practice forward we should be able to define social progress and consider the effectiveness of a practice accordingly.

A comparative view of progress in health care offers a way to look at progress in design practice. In health care, technical progress can be seen as advancements in the tools, procedures, and treatments that help people get well more effectively. Social progress can be seen as improvements in access to health care and as an increase in preventive activities among the population to reduce health problems. In short, progress is being made if more people get the care they need and if fewer people need medical treatment to begin with. We might ask: Can the definition of social progress in health care inform a definition of social progress in architectural practice? Can we define progress similarly, as increasing people's access to design and reducing problems of the general population resulting from deficient physical settings? Can defining social progress in a design practice be so simple?

I suggest that even though we don't often define social progress in design, offering a definition is simple; the challenge comes from making changes needed to accomplish that progress. Traditional social formations within architectural practice are often obstacles to accomplishing social progress. Reinventing architectural practice starts with overcoming the limitations of the traditional relationship between an architect and a client, which is built on a fee for professional services; thus, access to design is limited to those who can afford it. It is impossible to increase public access to design if each additional person with access is expected to be a client who can pay for design services. Likewise, preventive public design to address problems of the physical environment would take a rare client, one who was willing to pay for work beyond the self-interests of the project and to take responsibility for problems beyond his or her control.

Increasing access to design requires a reinvention of the way a practice is compensated. To begin with, extending design services to more people in any sustained way requires the architect to be compensated by sources other than the paying client. The two-party relationship between the architect and the client must be replaced by a three-party relationship among the architect, the people receiving the services, and a separate source of funding. Furthermore, once this new relationship has been worked out, the next step would be to expand the scope of the practice so it can use multidisciplinary design skills to address the multiple deficiencies of physical places. Problems with physical places are not limited to architecture; they include environmental problems, land-use issues, and infrastructure limitations that call for landscape architects, urban designers, and planners working alongside architects in the design practice.

INTERNS LEARN BEST FROM EXAMPLE AND EXPERIENCE

To extend progress in architectural practice beyond a few supported programs, it will be necessary to make such practices into places for training interns. In the nearly five years since its establishment, the GCCDS has provided employment and work experience for dozens of interns, students, and volunteer professionals. For the past several years the GCCDS staff has consisted of about fifteen full-time professionals, including architects, architectural interns, planners, and landscape architects. Along with the full-time staff, the GCCDS creates opportunities for students to live and work on the Gulf Coast. The GCCDS is an off-campus program of the Mississippi State University College of Architecture, Art and Design. From the university's point of view, the GCCDS is a university research center, even though the day-to-day work is more practice than research.

The GCCDS was created under unusual conditions in response to the devastation of low-income communities by Hurricane Katrina. The amount and complexity of the work, the level of funding, and the interest in community collaboration have all been unusually high, combining to create a context for a new form of practice to develop. However, even though the GCCDS is a product of disaster recovery, it is a model of practice that would be useful in any metropolitan area. Community-design studios can pursue long-term initiatives in collaboration with multiple partners at the planning, landscape, and building scales. External funding enables a community-design studio to provide the benefits of design to people who cannot afford professional services. In addition, along with providing professional services to low-income residents, a community-design studio such as the GCCDS can be a teaching practice, creating an environment for interns to develop skills in public design.

Design interns, whether from architecture, planning, or landscape architecture, learn best from example and experience. Such learning opportunities are generally not found in school because the primary modes of education used in architecture schools are instruction, experimentation, and testing. The GCCDS is organized to maintain an environment for interns to learn from example and experience. The GCCDS shares an unusual work space with other organizations in a repurposed church sanctuary and rectory. The two buildings make up what the community calls "the coordination center," which comprises a group of organizations that evolved from a relief distribution and volunteer coordination center into a case management, house repair, and building program, and then into a community redevelopment corporation. The GCCDS staff interacts daily with the case managers and construction managers of the coordination center as well as with community members and workers for other nonprofit organizations.

Situating the design studio in the coordination center creates a unique working environment that teaches interns by experience. In a traditional design firm, the interactions between clients and architects are typically limited and formalized by structures such as receptionists, artfully furnished lobbies for waiting visitors, conference rooms for formal presentations, contracts, submittals, and other devices that maintain the firm's image, control outside visitors, manage the delivery of professional services, and reinforce hierarchy within the firm. The work space of the GCCDS is less controlled than that of a typical design firm, and the presentation of the work is less selectively managed. Case managers, homeowners, construction managers, and others are welcome to come into the studio work space freely and unannounced. The effect of this open structure and informality is an increased tolerance of others and an appreciation of the beneficial instability that comes from outside influences.

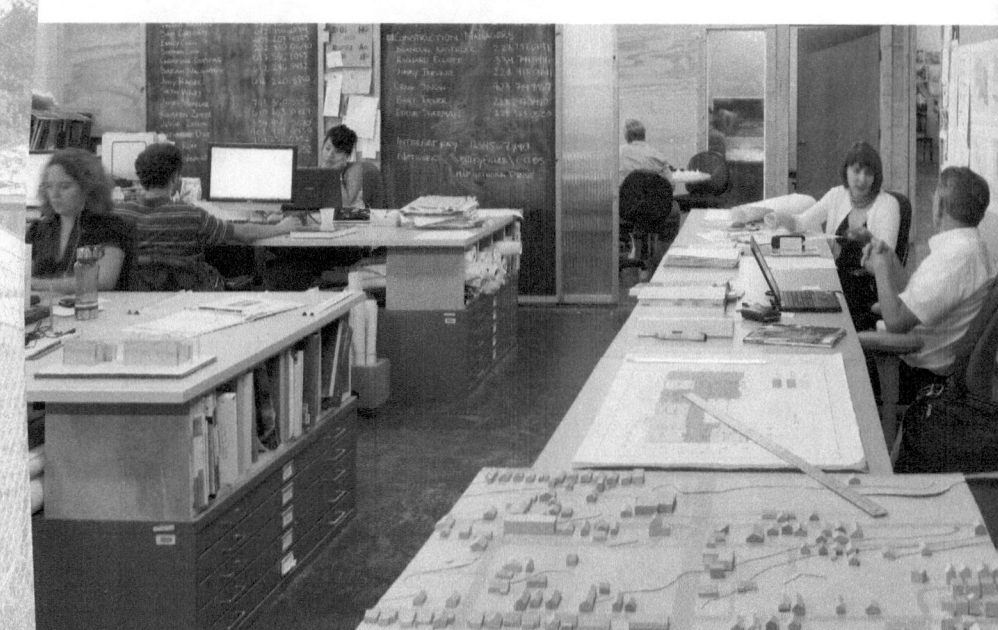

The Gulf Coast Community Design Studio working space is situated within a local nonprofit organization that provides housing-related services to the residents of East Biloxi. (Photo: © Alan Karchmer/Sandra Benedum)

The GCCDS's open work environment keeps every person in the design studio in view of each other. The open work space makes it easy to learn from example, if only by overhearing conversations and phone calls with community partners, which can help interns understand that a public-design practice is built upon sincere appreciation of the people they work with. Interns perform well in such an active work environment because they are learning by experience. When interns are isolated in the back of a traditional office and only get information about clients through the filter of more senior architects, they suffer an all-too-familiar apathy toward their work and make the mistake of thinking that architecture is primarily technical.

The architecture profession would do well to treat developing architects as interns, not as apprentices. Unfortunately, some senior architects like

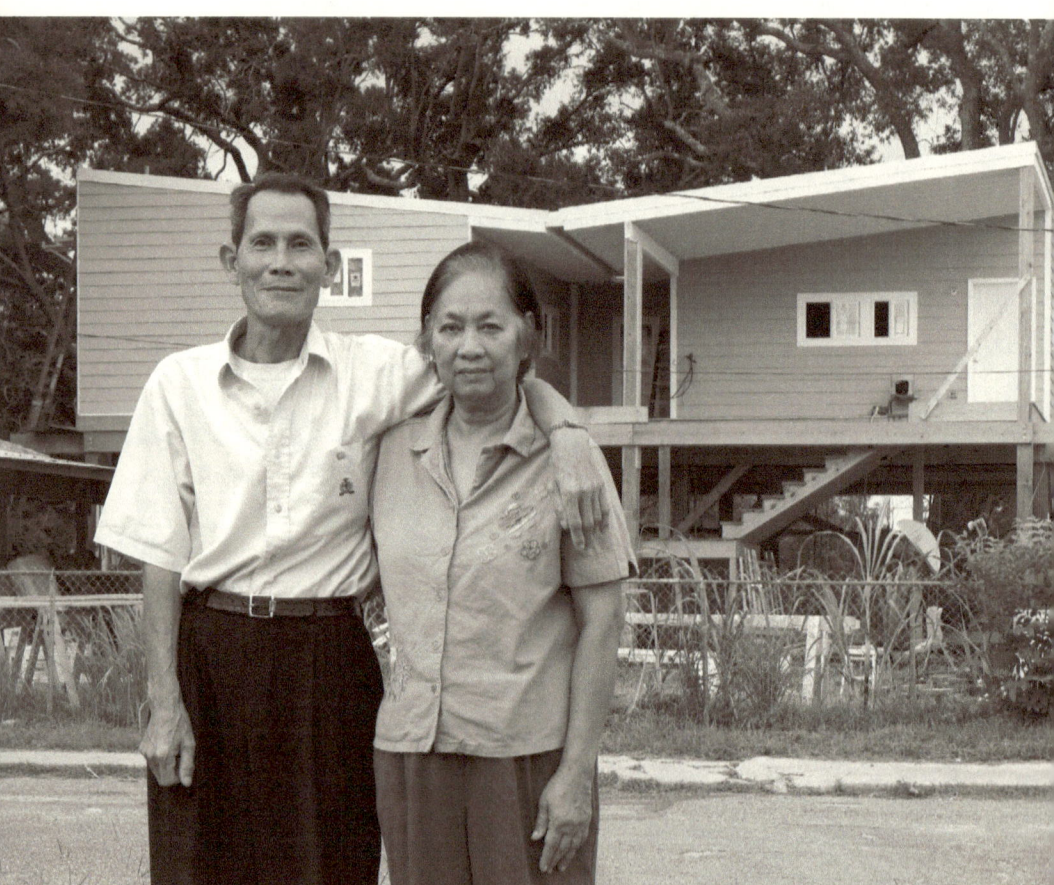

The Gulf Coast Community Design Studio has worked with over 150 families to provide replacement housing following Hurricane Katrina. Many of the houses are elevated to meet new flood requirements. (Photo: © Alan Karchmer/Sandra Benedum)

"I expect architectural practice will make progress as long as there are interns who aspire to social relevance."

the idea of apprentices working for them, learning the trade of architecture from a master. Architecture took the term "intern" from the medical profession, in which a doctor in training works in a hospital and learns how to work with patients. Likewise, an architectural intern should be immersed in a practice and learning how to work with clients. An intern should learn from experience that she is not working for the principals of the firm; she is working for people outside the firm.

SOCIAL PROGRESS IS MADE
BY INCREASING ACCESS TO DESIGN

We have learned many lessons about public design practice in the house design work that we have been doing in the GCCDS over the past several years. To date, more than 150 individual houses have been built with architectural services provided by the GCCDS. Each house was designed for a particular site with involvement from the future homeowner. All of the homeowners are receiving some type of financial assistance and have benefited from our design work without paying for our services. The compensation for the house design work comes from funding provided by the federal Department of Housing and Urban Development and administered through the state's development authority. Such an arrangement is an effective way to increase design access to low-income households without adding cost to the project. The GCCDS manages the accounting of the work internally so that our building partners don't need to include design fees in their project budgets.

Subsidized funding has practical advantages over a traditional fee-for-service approach. Most importantly, it pays for design services for low-income families that have particular needs such as wheelchair use, live-in health care, and multigenerational households. Many of the houses in our area are required to be elevated up to twelve feet above grade, and most of the houses are replacing a larger old house that was destroyed by Katrina. In other words, not only are our professional services too costly for these families that need them; these projects often have complex needs that require careful design work to create well-used, well-loved houses within limited budgets.

Each house project is assigned to one of the architectural interns, who works on the project from initial design meetings with the family to completion of construction. The interns become very familiar with the family, the site, and the construction. The people who are getting design assistance lost their homes and most of their belongings in Katrina, and they have been suffering this unexpected loss and the frustration of bureaucratic delays for much longer than they expected. At the point when they have made it through case management and are ready for a house design, they often still don't know whether the grant funds will work out and whether there will be enough money to build a house. Collectively, the architectural interns in the design studio have worked with more than two hundred such families.

Individually, each of these prospective home owners has a difficult story to tell. It is not unusual for an intern to find herself sitting in a meeting, reassuring a discouraged person who is in tears over the challenges and uncertainty of her life. Such experiences, repeated over and over, shape the working environment of the GCCDS. The interns come to know firsthand that architecture is not a self-serving pursuit and that learning to work helpfully with people who need help is a skill as useful as learning how to work out and dimension a floor plan.

SOCIAL PROGRESS IS MADE BY ADDRESSING DEFICIENCIES IN THE PHYSICAL ENVIRONMENT

In addition to making it possible to sustain a practice that serves people who can't afford professional services, external funding also supports efforts to address issues beyond the interests of a single client. Today's most serious problems, such as climate change, health risks from industrialization, displacement of jobs, decline of cities, and loss of biological species extend well beyond the boundaries of an individual project. Such problems require a broad view of physical places and a practice that is paid to work from within a multidisciplinary, long-term perspective. There is undoubtedly a need to increase design access to people with low incomes; however, if we merely replace a paying client with a nonpaying client, we will be doing little to address today's problems because we will still be limited to working within a single project's boundaries. The general public is becoming increasingly aware of the fact that individual actions—the things we do with and on our own property—can cause injury to others. Similarly, we have come to realize that our lives are affected by events that happen far away. A globalized view reveals that remote actions have local consequences and helps us see that twenty-first-century problems are largely due to the effects of industrialization on people and ecologies beyond a particular building site.

A familiar aspect of reinvented modernization can be seen in mechanisms created to mitigate the self-interests of private ownership. For example, as energy use becomes a more prominent part of building codes, the role of codes evolves beyond addressing public safety to encompass regulations that require property owners to limit the impact of their buildings on the environment. Likewise, many land-use zoning regulations function to control property owners' actions that might affect their neighbors. While these types of regulations function negatively to limit the off-site consequences of private actions, subsidization functions positively to counteract the self-interest inherent in capitalism. Subsidization is a pragmatic tool of capitalism; it is more interested in outcomes than in ideology. It is a both-and type of arrangement, in which we can both have private enterprise and compensate for capitalism's self-interest.

A reinvented practice such as the GCCDS operates with subsidization, recognizing that external funding increases access to design while it broadens the work beyond the interests of a single client. Funding entities, whether governmental agencies or private foundations, provide more than money; they give direction to public design by their sponsorship. The interns in the GCCDS are working on projects that do not have a simple set of client needs; rather, the projects have public-design objectives that are educational and transformative. The work is funded by various sponsors: flood-proof construction research funded by the Department of Homeland Security; energy conservation design tools funded by the Department of Energy; alternative construction systems funded by the Small Business Administration; community arts and education funded by the National Endowment for the Arts; studies of the environmental impact of dispersed development funded by the Department of Housing and Urban Development and a local organization called the Renaissance Corporation; and evaluations of the local

"... along with providing professional services to low-income residents, a community-design studio such as the GCCDS can be a teaching practice, creating an environment for interns to develop skills in public design."

economic development potential of building systems funded by the Hearin Foundation. Such work is well-suited for interns because interns come from school with well-developed skills in research and the presentation of information. Interns learn as they do the work and share information with other design-studio interns in project team meetings and studio presentations. The audience for the research is broad, and there are many opportunities for interns to be part of community-education activities.

The goal of funded design research is implementation. The GCCDS has ongoing partnerships with many building partners so that the knowledge being produced by research can be applied directly to building projects. Knowledge is one of the outputs of a public practice; the implementation of knowledge benefits the local community with improved buildings and neighborhoods, and it benefits the sponsor by advancing its mission. A knowledge-based public practice is a good fit for a design intern. In a traditional practice there is an obvious gap between an intern's limited technical knowledge and that of the firm's more experienced architects, because most of the missing knowledge is internal to the practice. In a practice with research projects, an intern is not at a technical disadvantage and can be productive from the start because the missing knowledge is external to the practice. In fact, the newest intern is likely to bring new-media skills to the practice and will be immediately rewarded for creativity and leadership.

INTERNS LEARN TO BE USEFUL BY BEING USEFUL
The GCCDS is proving to be a model of intern training within a practice. However, intern training was not primary in the practice's formation. The primary goal of the GCCDS was and still is very simple: to be useful to the community. As it happened, the devastation wrought by

"Interns will work with care and commitment when they know that their work is relevant and when they are rewarded with the satisfaction of working with people in the community who need help."

Hurricane Katrina motivated many young people to take action, and the GCCDS became a framework to support their work. The results of our efforts to be useful are a work environment that likewise encourages interns to be useful to the community. One lesson learned from the history of the GCCDS is the importance of creating and maintaining a positive environment in which we are close to the people for whom we work. Interns will work with care and commitment when they know that their work is relevant and when they are rewarded with the satisfaction of working with people in the community who need help.

I often notice that interns who work in the GCCDS don't like being called "interns"; they seem to think that the label "intern" devalues their work. I agree. And I see this resistance to professional tradition as a promising sign. These people who are in the early years of their careers are shaping their aspirations and have a clear sense of the needs and opportunities of their work. I believe the reinvention of practice will be energized by the people who don't accept the inherited class structure of architecture and who look for and create alternative ways to practice.

In closing his speech to the AIA, Whitney Young offers a path for reinventing practice: "An ancient Greek scholar was once asked to predict when the Greeks would achieve victory in Athens. He replied, 'We shall achieve victory in Athens and justice in Athens when those who are not injured are as indignant as those who are.'" And so shall it be with the problems of physical places. The future of design practice will be shaped by those who see how the design profession has traditionally kept its distance from the injured and who are inventing ways to work closer to the need.

DAVID PERKES is the founding director of the Gulf Coast Community Design Studio and an associate professor in the College of Architecture, Art and Design at Mississippi State University. He has a Bachelor of Science in Civil and Environmental Engineering from Utah State University, a Master of Architecture from the University of Utah, and a Master of Environmental Design from Yale University, and he is a Loeb Fellow at the Graduate School of Design at Harvard University.

CHRISTINA
CALABRESE

SYSTÈME D:

SELF-PROPELLED EXPLORATIONS OF DESIGN EDUCATION IN THE PUBLIC INTEREST

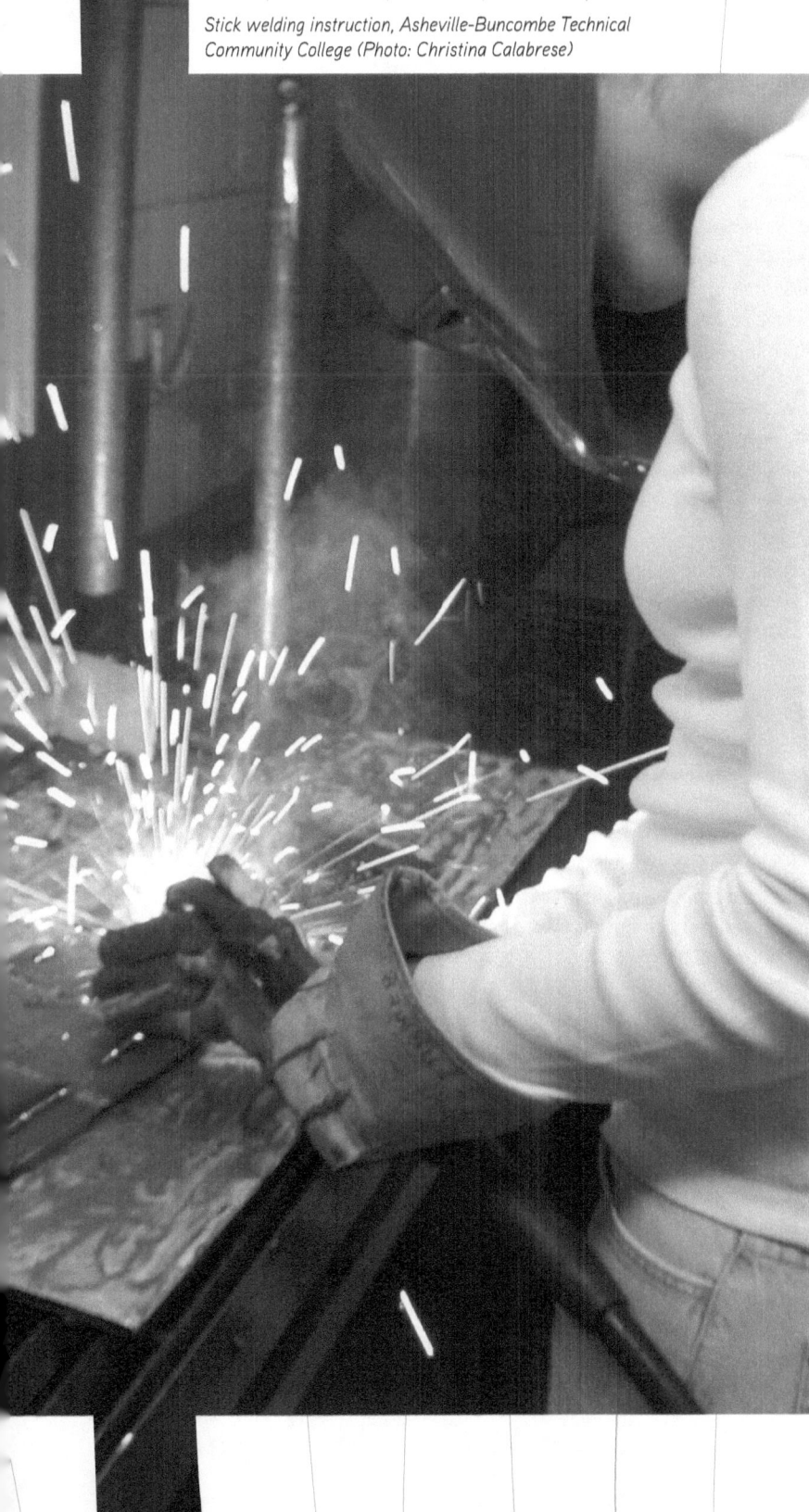

Stick welding instruction, Asheville-Buncombe Technical Community College (Photo: Christina Calabrese)

The trajectory I want to discuss begins with the education I received as a student at the Design Corps Summer Studio; then as a Public Service Fellow for Habitat for Humanity of Greater Charlottesville, Virginia; as a fully funded, independent researcher on public housing in Paris; and finally as a student fellow for ecoMOD, a design-build research project at the University of Virginia (UVA). In French this path is known as *Système D*, named for *débrouillard*, a word that literally means "resourceful" but is culturally defined as the alternative route that individuals carve around established obstacles in various regulatory processes. I would like to demonstrate that although I initially viewed my alternative recourses independently from my academic studios and coursework, by the end of my undergraduate education I was fortunate enough to see my opportunities in these arenas as mutually reinforcing.

I think it is important not only to explain the substantive content of each of the opportunities but also to detail the various costs or forms of compensation given or received, the conditions under which I was eligible to participate in the opportunities, the expectations established by my superiors, and my own expectations. This path was formed outside of the overarching requirements for internships established by the Internship Development Program (IDP) of the National Council of Architecture Registration Boards; it was designed instead to match my specific strengths while identifying areas for improvement so that I could become a well-rounded public servant.

DESIGN CORPS SUMMER STUDIO, 2005
As a rising third-year undergraduate architecture student, I had completed two pre-design studios and two design studios, and I felt comfortable using sketching, hand-drafting, and basic computer modeling to render small-scale design concepts. With an eye toward summer internships, I resisted researching design firms for two reasons: I had little interest in drawing CAD files for projects to which I made few (if any) conceptual contributions, and even if that type of experience proved to be tangentially informative, I would not yet be eligible to count the experience toward IDP credit. Instead, I gave myself a certain degree of latitude to use the summer as a way of identifying what type of design work I found to be truly fulfilling, and I sought to maximize my direct involvement in this work alongside personal development.

I was compelled to take this approach while reading *Rural Studio: Samuel Mockbee and an Architecture of Decency* as a graduating high school student, and again after hearing Bryan Bell speak as a guest lecturer at UVA during my second year there. I wanted to

"In French this path is known as *Système D,* named for *débrouillard,* a word that literally means "resourceful" but is culturally defined as the alternative route that individuals carve around established obstacles in various regulatory processes."

design for "the other 98 percent." I wanted to design for "their" needs and work in "their" communities, which I initially conceived of as being different, more challenging, and thus more rewarding. When Bryan returned to UVA to discuss plans for the first Design Corps Summer Studio—working with a historically marginalized African American community in Asheville, North Carolina, to design and build a bus shelter—I jumped at the chance to participate.

My nascent understanding of architectural pedagogy and practice was shaped by this eight-week design-build experience, which combined coursework in community development and design activism with hands-on training in basic carpentry, welding, and CNC fabrication to produce a bus shelter in collaboration with the Shiloh community and the City of Asheville. While the completion of the bus shelter was immediately gratifying, my engagement with the studio's comprehensive process triggered my motivation to develop an alternative plan for my design education that allowed me to continue to serve the public interest. As our Summer Studio coursework indicated, this path involved piecing together grants and fellowships to finance projects and pursuits relevant to this goal, and it existed parallel to my foundational design curriculum, which—for purposes both practical and otherwise—traditionally trained architects to design *for* people instead of designing *with* people.

Students from various design backgrounds, at all skill levels, were eligible to apply. Eight students—ranging from those at my level to graduates from Master of Architecture programs—were selected based on personal essays, résumés, work samples, transcripts, and recommendation letters. We were not compensated for the experience; I viewed the opportunity as a gateway into nonprofit design and as a supplement to my design education. I was also fully aware of my basic skill set and my capacity to produce design work independently. Thus, the necessary expenses for eight weeks—approximately $800 for tuition, $1,200 for accommodations, $1,500 for board and miscellaneous supplies—paled in comparison to the direct tutelage I received from leading design practitioners, teachers from the local community technical college, and community members. Though I elected not to receive elective course credit for the opportunity, this possibility was offered to students through the University of North Carolina at Charlotte.

The organization of the eight weeks was exhaustive and transparent. We began as a team by establishing, in writing, our goals and expectations for the bus shelter project, for the development and enforcement of design practices, for the team members, and for the studio. This document was drafted with attention to the diverse capacities of the team members, relying on their collective energy and enthusiasm.

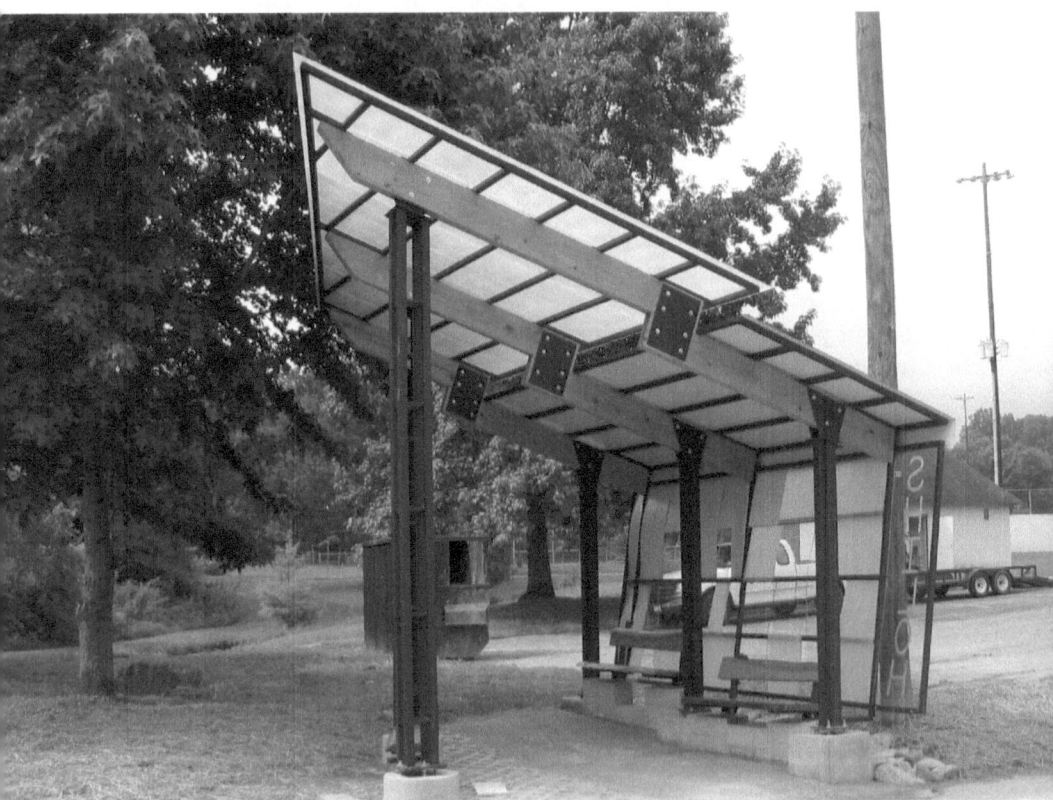

Shiloh Community Bus Shelter, Asheville, North Carolina
(Photo: Christina Calabrese)

The eight weeks were then divided into four weeks of design work and four weeks of one-to-one detailing, prefabrication, and on-site implementation. We worked from roughly 9 a.m. to 6 p.m. Monday through Friday. For the first four weeks, the mornings rotated among coursework in community development, design activism, professional development, and fabrication training. In these courses we collaboratively learned the principles of identifying the assets and challenges of a host community, mobilizing the community toward a common cause, finding and procuring funding for projects and programs from public- and private-sector sources, and maximizing this funding for effective project implementation. Afternoons were typically devoted to design studio meetings, pin-ups, and community meetings, where we established the bus shelter's position as a physical landmark for the neighborhood, debated appropriate sites and iterations to fulfill the project's potential as a landmark, and developed specific sub-projects to engage the community in the shelter's construction. For the remaining four weeks, the team made a full-time commitment to material selection and procurement, physical design mock-ups, and construction, all within a $5,000 budget from the City of Asheville.

While I could list the vast array of skills I acquired through the experience—including site surveying, grading, adaptive reuse of materials, and three types of welding techniques, to name a few—I believe the most valuable skills I gained from the studio are those that paid forward, planting seeds in my design thinking that sprouted after the summer in Asheville. I learned how to be not only a successful public servant, but a public leader. I learned that this position does not exist in a hierarchy of authority or experience but is calibrated by a relentless optimism in the face of unanticipated challenges or dead ends; humility, as defined by the ability to ask sensitive, thoughtful questions; and constructiveness, the capacity to advocate for effective, efficient solutions despite mounting frustrations and time constraints.

PUBLIC SERVICE FELLOWSHIP, HABITAT FOR HUMANITY OF GREATER CHARLOTTESVILLE, 2005–2006

These skills put me in a prime position to apply for and receive one of ten public service fellowships awarded to School of Architecture students at UVA for the 2005–6 academic year. The fellowship paired individual students with local nonprofit organizations based on the students' abilities and the organizations' needs, with the understanding that the students would devote ten hours per week throughout the academic year fulfilling fellowship tasks. Fellows were given $5,000, divided between two semesters, for their commitment.

"With each step I took away from the path of the traditional architecture student, I found support from advisors—both within and outside of academia—who could guide my energy and momentum toward positive change."

I was paired with Habitat for Humanity of Greater Charlottesville, and I worked one-on-one with the affiliate's construction supervisor to first research green building certification programs and then to create a plan for the affiliate to update and align its construction practices according to the certification standards. Though I initially feared that the weekly ten-hour commitment would compromise my design studio and academic coursework, my supervisor and I scheduled regular meeting times, one to two weeks in advance, with a built-in tolerance for school deadlines and holidays.

Together, we focused upon the construction of a series of duplexes scheduled to be completed during the spring and summer of 2006, and we developed an Energy Star and EarthCraft "punch list" whereby the affiliate's existing construction techniques and details were identified alongside potential upgrades to save energy throughout the life span of the home, based on a basic cost-benefit analysis. Part of the fellowship included attending an EarthCraft certification course to become versed in the certification's vocabulary and expectations, and I used the course to convey my findings to the affiliate's building committee, which decided to adopt a pilot certification program for construction of the duplex.

The experience provided a practical way for me to bring my newfound skills "to scale," beyond the design and construction of a single project and into systemic change. As housing prices continued to rise in Charlottesville, Habitat for Humanity was still striving to provide affordable homes to low-income families. The challenge first prompted a shift from single-family residential construction to the construction of duplexes; with the increased demand for homes came a commitment to higher-quality, healthier dwellings that had lower operational and maintenance costs.

I gained tremendous on-the-job education, but I also felt that my position served as a catalyst for innovation within the affiliate's work flow. Skilled, long-time construction volunteers embraced the shift to green building

techniques and respectfully engaged me in their dialogue as they
began to elaborate the process by which they would test the
techniques themselves before training unskilled volunteers in how
to use them. The mutually reinforcing relationship that developed
over the course of the year equally fostered my own progress
within my third year at UVA, where I was pursuing coursework
in building structures, materials, and climatic concepts.

At the end of my fellowship I presented my work to my peers,
design faculty, and the donors who had made the fellowship
possible. The work of each of the fellows was compiled into an
online database that remains active at press time, and the work of
subsequent fellows continues to enlarge the depth and breadth of
the fellowship's impact.

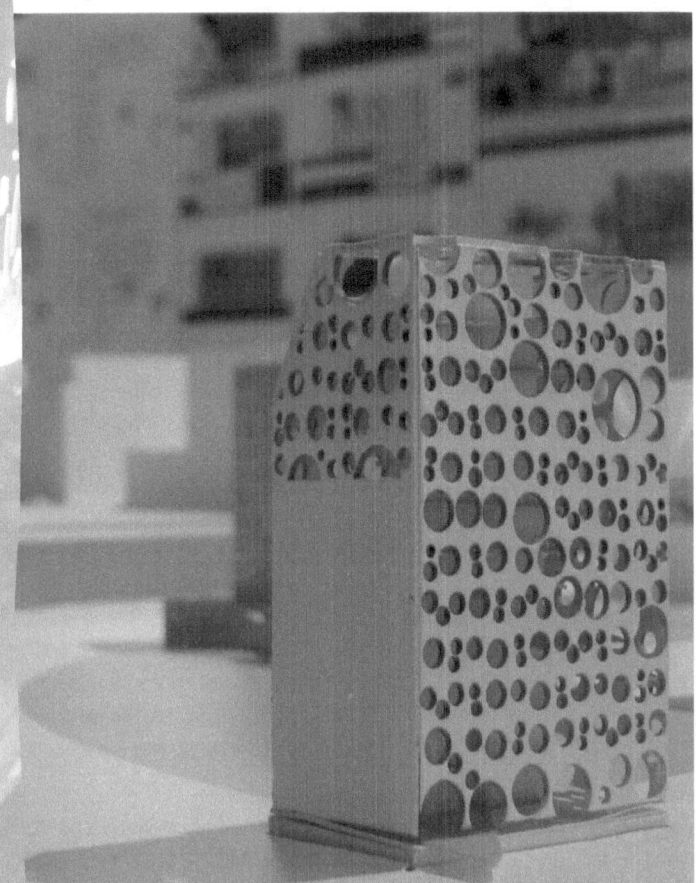

Public housing research, Pavillon de l'Arsenal, Paris, France, 2006
(Photo: Christina Calabrese)

HARRISON UNDERGRADUATE RESEARCH AWARD; SARAH MCARTHUR NIX FELLOWSHIP, 2006–2007

By the end of my third year at Virginia I felt fully empowered to pursue independent projects outside my design curriculum. Through my experiences with Design Corps and Habitat for Humanity I developed a sense of agency that allowed me to actively shape my design education toward public service, which I found incredibly fulfilling. With each step I took away from the path of the traditional architecture student, I found support from advisors—both within and outside of academia—who could guide my energy and momentum toward positive change.

At this point, I was confident that my skill set was accomplished enough to allow me to be compensated for all of the work I devoted toward this effort. It was clear to me that this compensation would not come from the communities in which I worked but from relevant funding sources that advocated for the communities' well-being. When I chose to expand my understanding of affordable housing strategies from the design of multifamily dwellings (as I had experienced firsthand at Habitat) to housing's social and political dimensions, I also shifted my focus from grants and fellowships offered by the School of Architecture to awards given university-wide.

With this mentality I was fortunate enough to bridge a research project between my architectural studies and French, my second major. I crafted my project proposal with the help of my undergraduate advisors in both disciplines and prepared a precise budget for a summer of research in Paris. I wanted to compare two public housing projects—one in the city and one in the suburbs—as a case study for population-integration efforts in France. I believed that through a combination of site observations and analysis, library research, and an evaluation of demographic data, I could demonstrate that the physical isolation of minority and low-income communities compromised France's ability to achieve social stability. This belief first surfaced when working with the Shiloh community in Asheville, where I witnessed the impact one bus shelter could have on the community's sense of collectivity and connectivity with the rest of the city. Although one isolated project could address symptoms of larger social and political disparities, it did not tackle the root causes of public-policy issues affecting marginalized communities.

With my project proposal, budget, faculty recommendations, and transcript, I applied for and received a research grant and a fellowship to pursue the project. The Harrison Undergraduate Research Award gave $3,000 for project travel and accommodation expenses from UVA, and the Sarah McArthur Nix Fellowship awarded $5,000 through the School of Architecture to pursue independent research in France. With the awards I was able to live comfortably and independently as a young, foreign female student for two months in Paris during the summer of 2006 while visiting the housing projects and numerous other institutions. I compiled my research into a thesis-like document—an opportunity I would not have had otherwise as an undergraduate in the School of Architecture—and presented my findings to my two departments and at two undergraduate research conferences.

My trajectory from summer studio participant to public service fellow and on to research fellow showed the cumulative effect of my extracurricular opportunities. As a student I was accustomed to receiving my education through lectures, seminars, field trips, etc. But as an independent designer, builder, and researcher, I learned how to seek experience. I became aware of my inclination toward holistic practices that allowed me to fulfill these three roles, either simultaneously or sequentially.

DESIGN-BUILD FELLOW, ECOMOD3, 2007

My position as a Design-Build Fellow for ecoMOD3 was a perfect capstone to my undergraduate experience, in light of my belief in well-rounded approaches to design challenges. ecoMOD is an ongoing interdisciplinary project between the School of Architecture and the School of Engineering and Applied Science, both at UVA, and Piedmont Housing Alliance, a local nonprofit affordable-housing organization in Charlottesville. The project is responsible for the design, construction, and post-occupancy research of prototypical housing units that incorporate ecological, modular, and affordable housing design principles. The post-occupancy research on ecoMOD1 informed the design and construction of ecoMOD2, the post-occupancy research on ecoMOD2 informed ecoMOD3, and so on, generating a feedback loop between the theory and practice of establishing and maintaining the environmental, economic, and social value of architectural design.

As a part-time fellow for the design and construction of ecoMOD3, I received $1,800 for a summer of work following graduation. Prior to this paid commitment, I was a student designer in the project's spring studio, the second half of the year-long architecture studio run by Assistant Professor and ecoMOD Project Director John Quale. Following the studio's design work, I was specifically tasked with researching and implementing LEED for Homes criteria. My work drew upon

"... for me the long-term takeaways derive from the project's ability to generate design concepts in direct response to the demands of real-life occupants."

my knowledge of EarthCraft and Energy Star rating systems, and it necessitated an awareness of and participation in the project's various design and construction decisions so I could align the project's internal limitations and ambitions with the certification's rating levels. As a team we aimed for LEED's highest rating, Platinum, with the goal of achieving these standards regardless of our project's formal identification as a LEED Platinum home. In other words, knowing the various costs associated with project certification alone, we prioritized design and construction decisions that we believed would most benefit the project's residents.

This priority was made with particular regard to the fact that ecoMOD3 was a unique project that combined the historic preservation of an existing home in Charlottesville with the addition of three new modular units. The modules were fabricated off-site in an airport hangar and were craned into place behind the home, where necessary on-site construction (mostly related to the project's envelope and exterior access) was completed. One of the modules was directly attached to the existing home as a bedroom, while the other two were connected to each other as a separate unit. The project was thus designed as a single-family home with an accessory dwelling unit so that together the modules could accommodate a multigenerational family or two different sets of occupants.

As with my previous opportunities, I could list the many technical skills I acquired throughout the course of the project relative to modular prefabrication, construction sequencing, and construction waste management, and the various skills I improved relative to material selection, construction detailing, and ecological design; but for me the long-term takeaways derive from the project's ability to generate design concepts in direct response to the demands of real-life occupants. In the Design Corps Summer Studio I had the preconceived notion that the needs and desires of "the other 98 percent" were somehow different from those of the 2 percent for whom architects normally designed, and that because of their financial limitations, design programming for the other 98 percent should pay greater attention to creating opportunities for social cohesion.

However, my experiences with Design Corps, with Habitat for Humanity, in Paris, and with ecoMOD proved that essential design priorities apply to all members of society, regardless of economic status. The use values of passive design principles of lighting, shade, and ventilation greatly transcend the use value of surface material treatment and innovative detailing, though their exchange values are inversely proportional. Whether creating inviting public spaces or unique private dwellings, the binary between populations traditionally served by architects and populations living in communities historically overlooked by architects is perpetuated solely by the degree to which architects are self-propelled to engage these respective communities. These lessons may be simply stated, but they are not widely reinforced by the practice of pursuing traditional internships with design firms.

In the *Système D* approach, design education in the public interest can be acquired through a variety of outlets; funding for design programs and projects in this vein is available to those willing to find it; and the benefits of sustainable, holistic communities can thus be made accessible to all. This path may not begin on the first day of a design-school curriculum, and it may not formally follow the design studio sequence, but academic and extracurricular opportunities to develop today's public leaders in design can be made mutually reinforcing for those designers who are ready to serve. I have been fortunate to directly experience the great challenges and rewards of this path, and I can only hope to have the opportunity to facilitate similar experiences for other students and professionals in the future.

CHRISTINA CALABRESE received her Bachelor of Science in Architecture from the University of Virginia and her Master in Urban Planning from the Harvard University Graduate School of Design. She received the Thesis Prize in Urban Planning and Design for her master's thesis, "Reading and Constructing Spatial Narratives."

PART 3:
BEYOND THE
IVORY TOWER

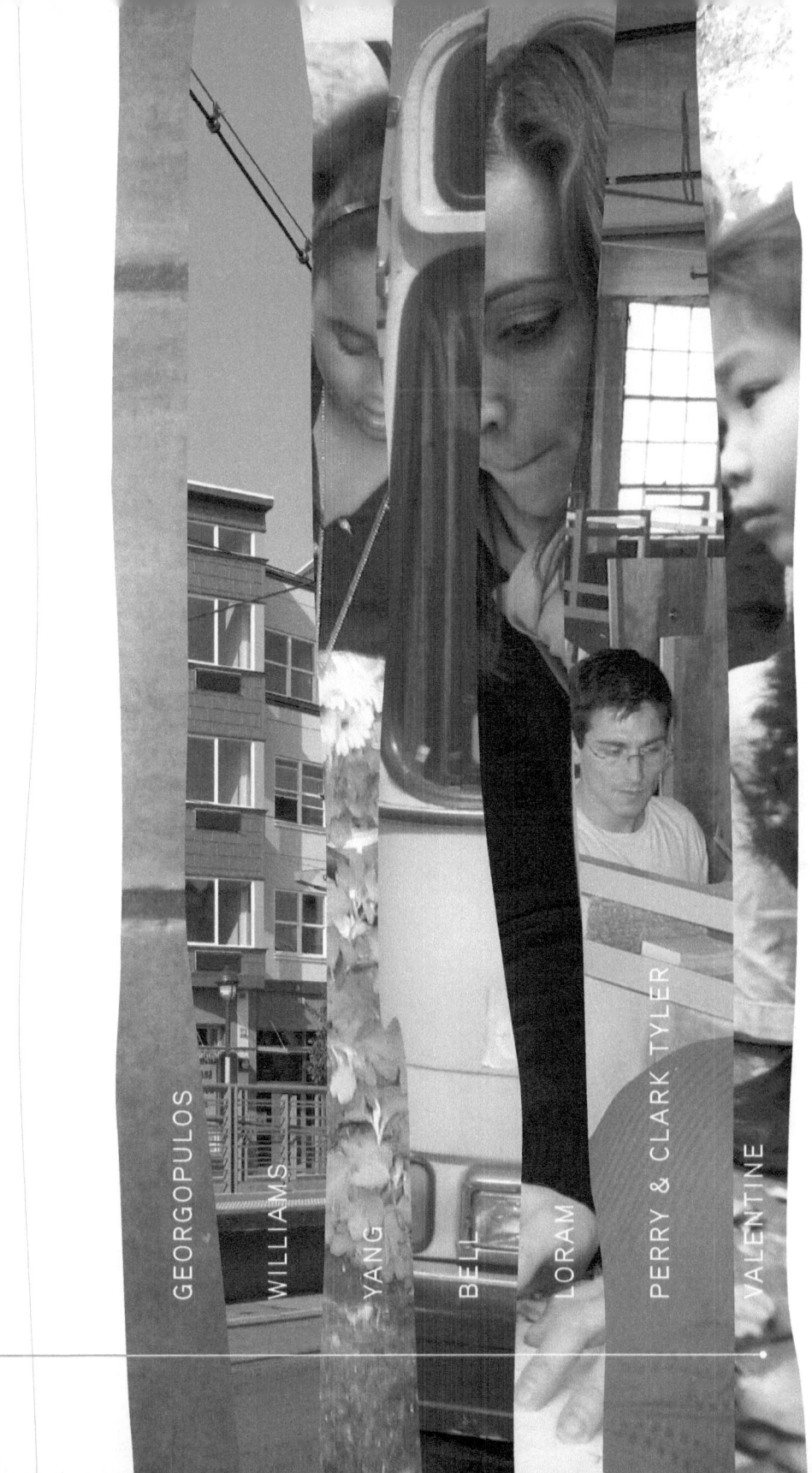

GEORGOPULOS

WILLIAMS

YANG

BELL

LORAM

PERRY & CLARK TYLER

VALENTINE

DIANE
GEORGOPULOS

NOTES FROM THE
BUREAUCRACY

For the past twenty-five years, I have been an architect employed by a quasi-public agency that provides affordable housing to those in need. I consider myself one of the luckiest people in the profession, although, like anyone who has worked in any office for twenty-five years, I see the warts of this bureaucracy alongside the wonders it can achieve. In this essay I discuss what I understand about bureaucracies, and I offer some advice about how interns could be best deployed by them.

When I graduated from MIT's architecture program in 1982, I was attracted to public service because it was apparent that the path to economic self-sufficiency would be more arduous for a woman in private practice. At that time, 1.5 percent of the registered professionals in our field were women. While there were some extraordinary women who were principals of firms in the Boston area, I imagined that this was probably a consequence of the fact that both Harvard and MIT were located there. Boston's architecture community spawned an incredibly rich diversity of practices that opened their doors to talented graduates, male and female alike. Because I did not have any experience in construction, I felt hampered in applying for those jobs, and I actually volunteered in an architect's office to gain experience doing working drawings. But the nation was in a recession and the architecture profession was still primarily a male domain. Although there had been some growth in the numbers of registered professionals and principals who were women, the numbers did not even come close to reflecting the ratio of women to men in the classroom or in society at large. I eventually landed a job in a small practice, where I got direct experience in every phase of design and construction. I passed my exam and decided to move into public service, where I thought my prospects of advancement would be better.

In retrospect, I now see the contribution that diversity makes by encouraging new ways of thinking and approaches to understanding. At the time I entered public service these thoughts were not on my mind. Yet now, I am restored in my sense of the possibility of the future. Yes, it may initially be uncomfortable for older practitioners, be they male or female. The capacity to conceive of alternatives to conventional ways of collaborating and imaging space can create new opportunities for practice. These nascent models urgently need to be explored and refined as with any design process if our intention is to grapple directly with increasing environmental, social, and financial complexity.

AUTHORITY FLOWS FROM AN ELECTED OFFICIAL

What is important to understand about a bureaucracy is that, like a private practice, it is structured as a hierarchy. In government, that hierarchy is usually headed by an elected official. Key executives lead cabinet agencies, but the executives are typically accountable to an elected official. All policy flows from the elected official through the key executives to appointees and staff; at least, that is what a flow chart of the hierarchy would reflect. However, each functionary in a new administration probably has a critical view of the ancien régime, which generally fuels the development of new policy directives, along with campaign promises. At the same time, there are legions of people who work in the bureaucracy for many years. Some would call this the permanent bureaucracy. I myself have made my professional career as a bureaucrat working in the state service to provide affordable-housing opportunities to people of low income, which makes me one of them.

WHEN I WAS MYSELF AN INTERN

I was an intern at the New York City Department of Housing Preservation and Development while studying for my Master of Architecture degree at MIT. As a New York City Urban Fellow (a program that is still in existence; see http://www.nyc.gov/html/dcas/html/employment/urbanfellows. shtml), I received a stipend that was enough to pay for a share of an apartment in Brooklyn and other necessities. It was very exciting to return to the city of my birth and actually contribute something at a time of extreme duress in the city's history. The south Bronx was afire with arson, the Brooklyn apartment house where my grandparents used to live was a bombed out shell, and the hospital I was born in was boarded up.

Within a few days of being assigned to my department, I helped my supervisor negotiate with the New York State Department of State to receive support for the city's weatherization program. This program financed the installation of new roofs, double-paned windows, building-entry doors, and dual-fuel boilers in very distressed buildings that the city had seized due to tax foreclosures. The work I was performing was critical to restoring habitable conditions for residents whose landlords had walked away from their buildings. It felt good to be able to go to my office on Maiden Lane in lower Manhattan, take a look at the morning newspaper, and not see any stories about somebody dying due to the lack of heat in any of the addresses in my portfolio. My supervisor, who had no other employees to develop the weatherization program, was thrilled with my work—so much so that when my fellowship year ended, he found the salary to hire me. I worked for another year at Housing Preservation and Development and then returned to school to finish my degree. By the time I graduated, however, the economy had continued its decline into a full recession, and job openings in New York were nonexistent. I stayed in Boston, where I have remained.

THE CONCRETE DOUGHNUT VS. THE HOTHOUSE GARDEN

For the sake of illustration, let us say that there are two kinds of bureaucracies: concrete doughnuts and hothouse gardens. I am describing essential tendencies or types, and I do not know of any bureaucracies that correspond exactly to these depictions; but hopefully the metaphors will prove informative.

A public agency that is like a concrete doughnut can withstand virtually anything—droughts, hurricanes, monsoons, pollution, or vandalism— because it is so resistant to external change. There is no entrance or exit door in a concrete doughnut; there is no on or off ramp. It is the sort of place that one needs to know the secret handshake to penetrate. There may be sprinkles on top or fillings inside to give it a particular identity, but concrete doughnuts are impervious to invasive species. Agencies like this can be big or small. When a member of the public has to interact with a concrete doughnut, exasperation, frustration, and irritation are the words most commonly used to characterize the experience. They operate only to deliver services and they seem immune to leadership changes. They exist almost as forgotten places on organizational charts. Communication between leadership and staff in agencies like this is typically infrequent and one-way. They survive by sheer dint of invulnerability to exogenous forces.

At the other extreme are the hothouse bureaucracies that need copious amounts of light and water to survive, and special rules like the freedom to spend public funds without depending on the normal budgetary processes. A hothouse bureaucracy is not self-sustaining as it depends upon sustenance from external resources. It is a parasite that usually is hosted by some other office with a budget big enough to nurture its creation without too much administrative oversight. When these hothouse gardens are attacked, they die. When they succeed, they bring forth hybrids and rare species that are cultivated for specific reasons. These offspring are sometimes transplanted into the larger environment, spawning the development of practices and products that support the health of the larger system. Communication in this type of agency is characterized by leadership being networked with staff. Agility,

> "These nascent models urgently need to be explored and refined as with any design process if our intention is to grapple directly with increasing environmental, social, and financial complexity."

pragmatism, and urgency are often evident. These bureaucracies generally do not last longer than the administration under which they were initiated. As a matter of fact, if a hothouse bureaucracy is successful enough to survive a change in administration, its name is often changed to prevent acknowledgment that the previous leader has anything to do with its success.

WHICH TYPE OF BUREAUCRACY IS BEST FOR AN INTERN?
All interns are not created equal; and bureaucracies, as I have tried to characterize them, have personalities too. An intern navigating these questions would be best served by seeking the advice of a counselor who can help match the right intern with the right agency. Counselors play a significant role in creating positive outcomes for both the intern and the bureaucracy.

An objective of the bureaucracy is to provide a program or service that is responsive to the needs of a constituency or target population. There are a number of metrics for assessing a program's benefit. One measure is financial. Success may be measured by a budget decrease due to more efficient delivery of service. Another measure may be higher satisfaction with services provided; or growth in the general fund as a result of increases in tax revenue caused by expanding economic activity. However, a public official will generally expect her reward for good performance at the polls, when voters express their satisfaction with her work when she is up for re-election.

Not unlike delivery of a drug from a pharmaceutical company, delivery of a new service or program in the public sector is normally preceded by high outlays for program development. Unlike new drugs from a drug company, however, new programs in bureaucracies are rarely in place long enough to actually repay the investment. And unlike pharmaceutical companies, the public sector is generally loath to impose or increase charges for services. Patience for return on investment is no more a virtue in the public sector than it is in the private sector. We love quick results and are very disappointed when we don't get them. The appetite for innovation in an agency has to be tempered with knowledge of the time it takes to build a constituency for a program, design it, implement it, and have it in place long enough to measure its benefit to the target population, the general fund, and the administration. For this reason, the concrete doughnut is perhaps the place for people who have skills that can streamline work processes. Their contributions will be appreciated in a situation where current employees lack the skills, or the time to develop the skills, to make the agency more efficient.

For example, at my current agency, we currently have an intern from the Boston Architectural College helping us calculate square footage on a large number of projects. He knows how to use a particular software package that transfers scanned images of properties we have financed into our database, to be used for reference when we establish comparables for construction and operating costs. This is highly routine work, but our intern seems to be accomplishing the tasks with good humor and skill. The benefits of our intern's work are manifold.

In a hothouse garden, the tasks assigned may be much more difficult to anticipate. The nature of work in this kind of setting usually requires flexibility and the ability to live with high degrees of ambiguity. Self-directed personalities function more effectively in circumstances like this. Supervisors of hothouse departments are typically deeply involved in managing the expectations of superiors or putting out fires. Thus, they have less time to direct staff, and an intern who needs direction will likely not be an ideal fit.

But let us not be so naive as to imagine that everyone will view interns positively in an environment of high unemployment and cost cutting. There must be a clear signal from the top that internships are a valuable part of the culture of an organization. This signal must be evident from the outset, because efforts to bring interns into the workplace can run headlong into the public's demand for fiscal accountability. The recent increase in negative sentiment directed toward bureaucracies has unleashed a torrent of criticism of the work of bureaucracies. Key executives may be forced into making budget cuts to appease the desire for greater efficiency.

Firing or furloughing employees, restructuring departments and divisions, and eliminating what seem to be "luxuries" are common ways that executives demonstrate responsive, transparent leadership. Ironically, the overriding focus on performance usually coincides with low employee morale. The need for training to update and streamline methods is greatest when there is no budget for training. Introducing an intern into this situation can exacerbate workplace tensions. Workers will likely view interns as job threats in an atmosphere of uncertainty about layoffs and reduced pay.

OPPORTUNITIES FOR TRANSFER OF KNOWLEDGE

Every bureaucracy has employees who are affectionately called "white hairs" or "lifers," those who have withstood the ebbs and flows of early retirement buyouts and layoffs or enticements into the private sector to become long-term employees. These people hold the institutional memory of a bureaucracy. Economies are cyclical, and in recurring situations for which no written documentation exists, these are the people who can recall which programs and methods were used to advance a public policy at earlier times where comparable limitations or restrictions existed.

They are also likely to be the holders of rare copies of dog-eared, coffee-stained handbooks or documents that may have at one time been issued to assist in the administration of a new program. For instance, I am currently hoarding an old copy of the federal Department of Housing and Urban Development's 1979 *Minimum Property Standards*; the fifth edition of Sleeper and Ramsey's *Architectural Graphic Standards*, where the graphics look like the materials they are supposed to represent; and the second edition of *Site Planning* by Kevin Lynch. I find the usefulness of these antiques to more than justify

"...I do not know of any [university] program that deliberately trains architects for public practice, which is astonishing considering the amount of work that is constructed with public funds."

their place on my bookshelf. I have seen interns light up when they look at these books and see something they have not seen before.

I recently used a young colleague's PDA to see if there are any iPhone or Android apps that impart the same information. My failure to locate a source may have been caused by my lack of dexterity at navigating through options. Getting familiar with the process was beneficial to me, as much as the knowledge transfer. It is crucial to understand the maturing age of the workforce in these bureaucracies and be alert to the population of those who are ready to take the lifers' places when so many are slated to retire over the next 10 years.

In 1996 the American Institute of Architects issued the *Boyer Report* (officially titled *Building Community: A New Future for Architecture Education and Practice*), which examined the relationship between academia and practice. The report was groundbreaking in that it called the professional degree-granting institutions to account for their programmatic design. Schools have implemented some of the report's findings, and some innovations have been introduced into the educational process for a professional degree. But these changes were years in the making. Now the workplace is changing because of technology's vast influence on the design process. The schools are facing enormous challenges to provide an education in the overwhelming number of skills and knowledge bases that a practicing architect must master before being able to build well and beautifully. Yet, I do not know of any program that deliberately trains architects for public practice, which is astonishing considering the amount of work that is constructed with public funds.

Historically, positive outcomes were achieved when the profession articulated clear expectations about the skills and abilities that architects needed to master in order to practice responsibly, and the schools largely (although not completely) designed programs to mirror those skill sets. Now, however, it cannot be denied that we as a profession seem to be running at a very high number of revolutions per minute without making much progress in effecting the change to environmental quality that is necessary to ensure our future on Spaceship Earth.

ASKING UNCOMFORTABLE QUESTIONS

Transportation agencies are using cell phones with GPS tracking capability. Housing authorities have Facebook pages. Police departments have Twitter accounts where citizens can report crimes in progress. There are blogs and RSS feeds for community-design projects that use public funds. Collective intelligence models are transforming the

"Many young practitioners could be persuasive advocates for federally sponsored internships in federal and state bureaucracies."

way we think about participation in the design process. An emerging professional spoke recently about the geospatial world that we live in and how extraordinary it would be to capture its power to create living maps and histories of city streets. Bureaucracies are not yet geared to use those methods, but the next generation is already thinking about space in an entirely new way. Isn't collaboration necessary for our mutual survival? Haven't job definitions that sprang from old models of information transfer been transformed by new technology? Isn't that precisely what is going to happen to bureaucracies in the near future?

We should remind candidates who run for elected office that students vote. Many young practitioners could be persuasive advocates for federally sponsored internships in federal and state bureaucracies. The federal government used to have a very active internship program. Young architects, lawyers, planners, and other liberal-arts graduates were invited to try the public service for a year. At the end of that time, the supervisor of the department and the intern would discuss whether or not there was a good fit. A job offer to stay on generally accompanied the understanding that the experience was not only worthwhile but had opened a career opportunity that had not been previously considered. A dramatically scaled-down version of the program, with no job offer at the end of the year, continues today (see http://www.usajobs.opm.gov/). Clearly, capturing the imagination of leaders and cultivating their enthusiasm for engaging the next generation of practitioners is a key to success.

The contributions that interns can make to the workplace are perhaps best epitomized by their enthusiasm for the future and their commitment to making the world a better place. I, for one, am happy that they feel that way. I have felt that way in the past. But I think it is inaccurate to imagine that they will simply be taking over the controls of the current machine. If we were seeing the picture clearly, we would understand that they are driving an entirely new technology that will revolutionize the way bureaucracies work. And it would be wise to try to learn as much from them as we can.

"The contributions that interns can make to the workplace are perhaps best epitomized by their enthusiasm for the future and their commitment to making the world a better place."

DIANE GEORGOPULOS, FAIA, has worked for twenty-five years as an architect for MassHousing, the country's leading affordable-housing finance agency. Her professional work was recognized in 2005 when the American Institute of Architects gave her the Thomas Jefferson Award for Architecture in the Public Service.

KATHERINE
WILLIAMS

STEPPING OFF
THE MERRY-GO-ROUND:

A ROSE FELLOW
CHOOSES
COMMUNITY
DESIGN

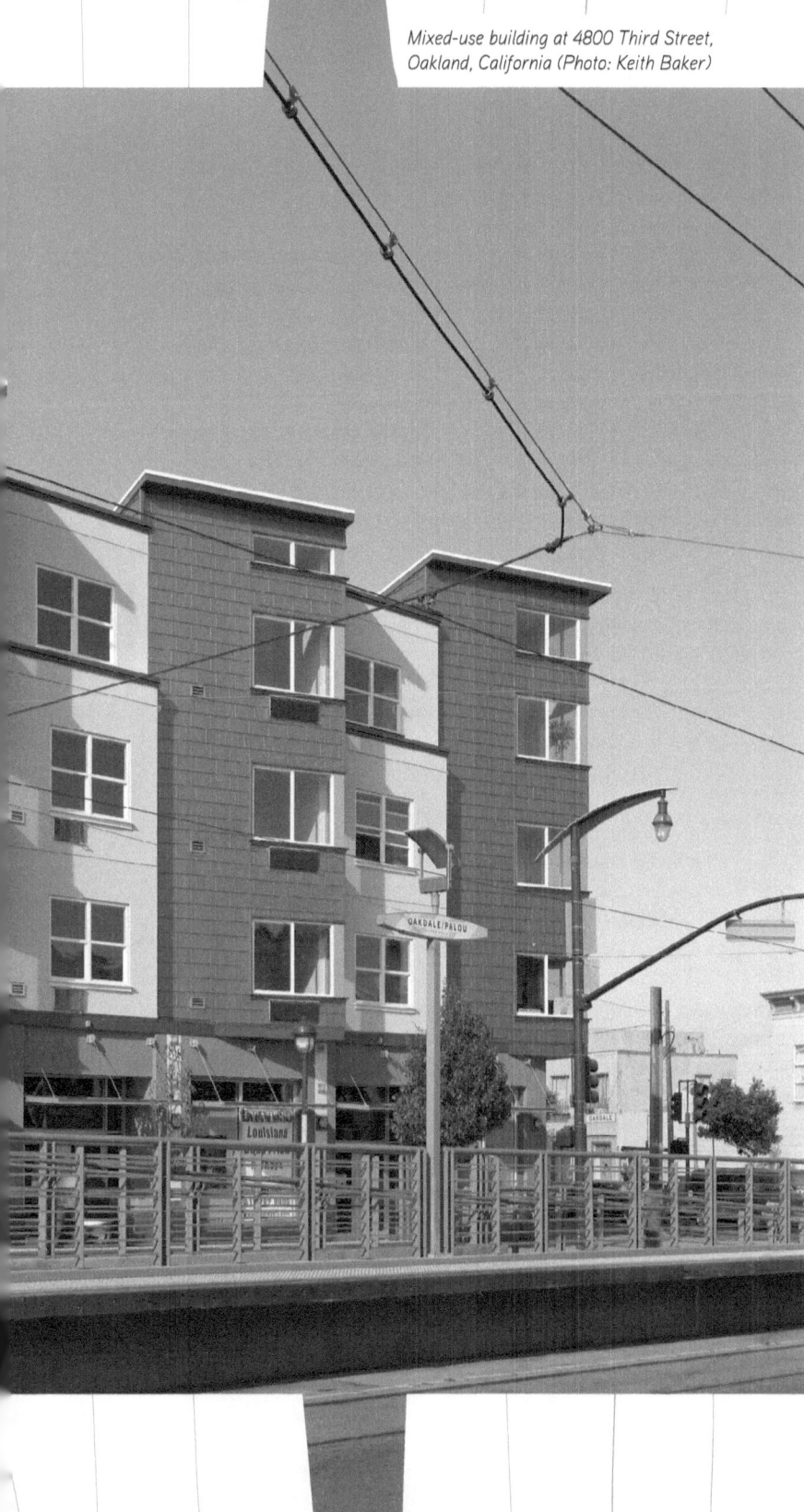

Mixed-use building at 4800 Third Street, Oakland, California (Photo: Keith Baker)

Is it possible for an architect to have a career in community-based design? (For the purposes of this essay, my definition of community-based design follows the core principles of the Enterprise Rose Fellowship and the Association of Community Design, including the use of participatory planning to create design solutions for a community.) In my opinion, most architects come to the conclusion that the answer is no. Most would acknowledge that community-based projects, usually for nonprofits or other community entities, can have a role in practice; but in many instances, community-based work becomes something that a practice will get to "when we have time." In some offices, that time rarely comes unless the architect is intimately involved with a community-based group or has close associates, friends, or colleagues who are involved with such a group. If interns want to use their architecture skills to make a difference in a community, how are they ever to get a chance?

For most interns, getting experience in work that truly helps communities boils down to fitting it in on their own time; they volunteer with groups like Habitat for Humanity or take on a side project for a community group. Thus, architects have created a never-ending merry-go-round where community groups are begging for services they need and wind up settling for design work that is less than ideal.

For young architects to step off the merry-go-round during the crucial period of internship takes courage.

When I attended architecture school in our nation's capital, I had dreams of designing grand projects like art museums; I. M. Pei's East Wing of the National Gallery in Washington, DC, especially inspired me. Yet I was disheartened by the condition of the city, and I felt that the built environment demonstrated a blatant disregard for the poor. In Washington, as in many cities in the United States, disadvantaged neighborhoods were plagued by neglect. Governmental efforts to remedy the situation often involved razing entire poor (usually majority black) neighborhoods to make way for "revitalization," highways, or other projects, relocating whole neighborhoods of unwanted people. For me, a suburbanite, the city held great possibility. I did not understand how all the wonderful old buildings I saw could be sitting unused when I saw so many homeless people. Living in the city and learning about urban policies and development made me rethink my career goals. Architecture could be more than just designing buildings; it could help communities recover and thrive.

Once I graduated, I worked in traditional architecture firms. I was spoiled by my first position out of school because I worked for Terry Ammons,

"For young architects to step off the merry-go-round during the crucial period of internship takes courage."

an architect who was embedded in his community of Petersburg, Virginia. He was one of few architects in a small city, which meant that lots of community members sought his advice and help. His specialty was historic preservation, and many of the old buildings in Petersburg seemed ripe for opportunity. While much of the work I did with Terry was fulfilling, I still felt as though some of the community's most important revitalization needs remained unfulfilled. Like many old cities that had been vacated by a flight to the suburbs, Petersburg saw a resurgence in the early 2000s, but hurdles including funding, politics, and community mobilization left many needs unmet and many projects languishing at the idea stage.

Small projects were happening, but these seemed piecemeal; I longed for work that would have an impact on the community at large. I also wanted to learn how to initiate projects that tapped directly into the needs of the community, so I began thinking about a new step in my career. I looked at local housing groups and community development corporations, but a lack of available positions forced me to move to another traditional firm. This gave me the chance to be in a larger firm, but I experienced an even wider disconnect from the community-based work I wanted to do.

During my transition between firms, I learned about the Enterprise Rose Fellowship, which places an architect into a community-development corporation (CDC) for three years. The architect gains experience in real-estate development and the professional nonprofit world, and the CDC gets to have an architect on staff, a rarity for such organizations. It seemed an ideal position for me; I could work for a nonprofit, using my design skills while learning about the development of projects from start to completion.

After five years of working in traditional practice, I applied for and became a Rose Fellow in San Francisco. I started my fellowship at the Visitacion Valley Community Development Corporation, a small CDC started by residents who did not want to be displaced when their low-income housing site was being rebuilt. I started with the organization during their tenth year of working to improve Visitacion Valley. Initially my fellowship focused on the design of a multiuse classroom and activity space in the building where I worked. I was able to translate the needs of my colleagues, who had no architecture background, into sketches and drawings for our project architects. The project involved transforming an underutilized garage into a functional classroom.

On the architecture side, I was able to refine the design with the project architect. I guided this project from design development through construction document completion. On the ownership side, I had to help my organization lobby for additional funding to fill budget gaps related to the scope of work we wanted to achieve. I also had to be mindful of requirements that were attached to changing the use of the space, such as giving written notice to neighbors within a certain vicinity. After additional funding was obtained, the project was constructed and is now complete.

My work also included thinking about regional development across jurisdictions in the Visitacion–Guadalupe Valley Watershed. This culminated in a collaboration with a nonprofit design firm to create a publication used to provide a snapshot of the neighborhood and upcoming developments that would influence future growth. The goal was to give residents and developers a picture of current conditions that would then inform regional development.

I spent the last half of my fellowship term at the San Francisco Housing Development Corporation, a twenty-year-old organization founded by community members to assist low- and moderate-income families. Similar to the Visitacion Valley group, the founders of the San Francisco Housing Development Corporation wanted to stop displacement of families from San Francisco. In addition to building housing, the organization counsels people who need financial training, foreclosure intervention, or home-buying assistance.

My time as a fellow culminated with the construction of an affordable-housing development. The project was small enough for me to be able to touch on every aspect, from the closing of the financing through construction and on to the sale of the condos and the build-out of the commercial space. I was able to contribute to the design of some of the spaces, like any intern architect. Traditional architects often do not get to do the kinds of work involved with this project, such as navigation among community and city stakeholders who are invested in the project's success, the thought process that goes into selling homes, and negotiation with a commercial tenant.

The Rose Fellowship gave me the opportunity to connect my community work to my skills as an architect. I had many experiences during my fellowship that I would not have had any other way. One of my greatest fellowship experiences was sitting in a community meeting and thinking that this was now part of my job, not just something I did in my free time.

"One of my greatest fellowship experiences was sitting in a community meeting and thinking that this was now part of my job, not just something I did in my free time."

The fellowship experience also taught me that I was not the only architecture graduate looking for these opportunities. I have presented my work to design students and graduates who want to know how to engage in this type of work. During the fellowship, the Fellows communicated regularly to discuss our work, support each other, and provide advice. We were also part of a larger network of people who wanted to improve communities. I became exposed to a new world of organizations and events that were at the forefront of community-based design. One, the Association for Community Design, is a network of community-design centers from across the United States that supports CDCs and is a place to learn about best practices. Another group, Design Corps, convenes an annual event called Structures for Inclusion. This two-day event showcases architects and designers practicing in alternative settings. The work they do usually has a socially conscious purpose and shows people that architecture can have a greater role in society.

The success of my fellowship can be measured in many ways. I truly became embedded in two communities, and the starts and stops of all the projects I worked on taught me many aspects of the development process—including the fact that no two projects are exactly alike. My work in the housing arena has given me insight into many issues related to affordable housing and the need to keep people of all incomes in the community where they want to live. I am now involved in all levels of development in the communities where I live and work.

I found a way to step away from the merry-go-round.

This year I earned my architecture license. I was able to accomplish this by staying focused and relying on the resources I had at hand. I completed all of my internship requirements during my years in traditional practice, so I only had my exams to complete during my fellowship. I used my local library, on-line study groups, and fellow interns to support my efforts to pass my exam.

My time at a traditional architecture practice was important and necessary. Without it, I would not feel comfortable giving critiques to architects for whom I am now the client. I know what goes on in an office, so I can articulate the needs of a project and know what limits to push. I would have had a more difficult time completing my internship if I had not worked in an office. For instance, although I use CAD occasionally now, I do not spend months putting together construction documents as I did in an office.

A year after my fellowship, I am still working for the organization that was my host. This was possible because I was still actively engaged in an ongoing project. Part of my role now will be to secure funding for future projects, which will allow my position to be retained. In the nonprofit sector, unrestricted funding is hard to find, so a development organization has to have a pipeline of ongoing projects or other constant streams of income, like rental property, to support staff.

The Enterprise Rose Fellowship provided me with the opportunity to use my architecture skills to help underserved communities. Even as the program celebrates its tenth year, I cannot say that it has gotten easier for architecture interns to find a path into community-based work. Over the last year I have seen people create their own opportunities. Like a developer, architects may have to use more of this creativity and gather the components—funding, community support, and entitlements—to implement projects that improve communities.

During my fellowship, I became part of a larger network of community designers who are not talked about much in traditional architecture circles. Now my challenge is to continue doing this work over the long term. Initiating projects and completing them within a nonprofit setting has advantages, but options like consulting are also available. In the nonprofit world, securing funding to continue to build projects, staying aware of the political and economic climate, and being mindful of changes in the neighborhood where I work are critically important. I have my architecture skills, but the past four years have helped me expand on those skills so I can make meaningful contributions to an underserved community.

At the intern level, architects only tend to talk about their career with other architects. We need to interact with other groups because these are future clients and stakeholders, and these intersections also bring new perspective. Once I sat on the client side, I became aware of a whole new set of issues that I had not even known about while sitting in an office drawing details.

My hope is that the work I do will have long-term impact and help achieve better integration between community design and traditional practice. Ultimately I hope to achieve the goal I set for myself long ago: to help revive communities in need.

"My hope is that the work I do will have long-term impact and help achieve better integration between community design and traditional practice."

KATHERINE WILLIAMS is an architect, mom, project manager, community do-gooder, native of Virginia, and current resident of San Francisco who loves books, sharing time with friends and family, and listening to others' stories. She writes online at katherinerw.com.

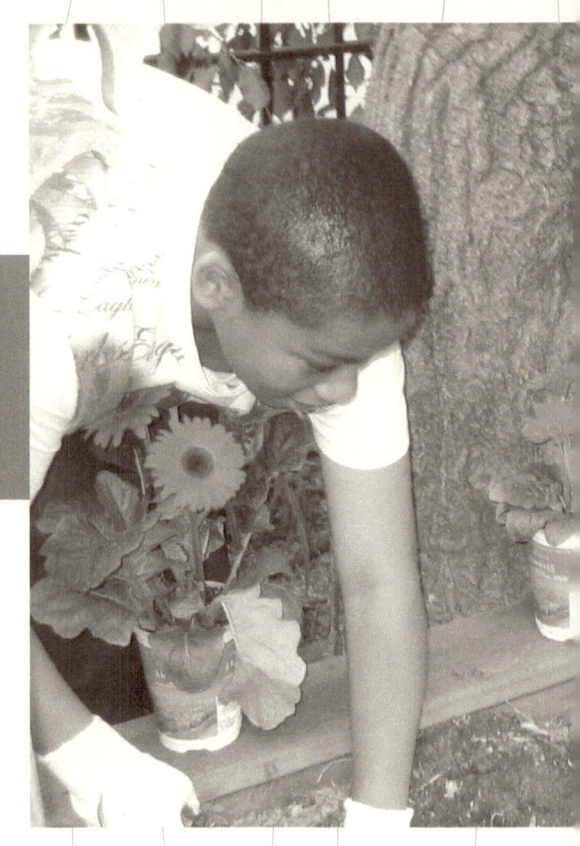

ESTHER
YANG

DISSEMINATING DESIGN THROUGH THE ENTERPRISE ROSE ARCHITECTURAL FELLOWSHIP

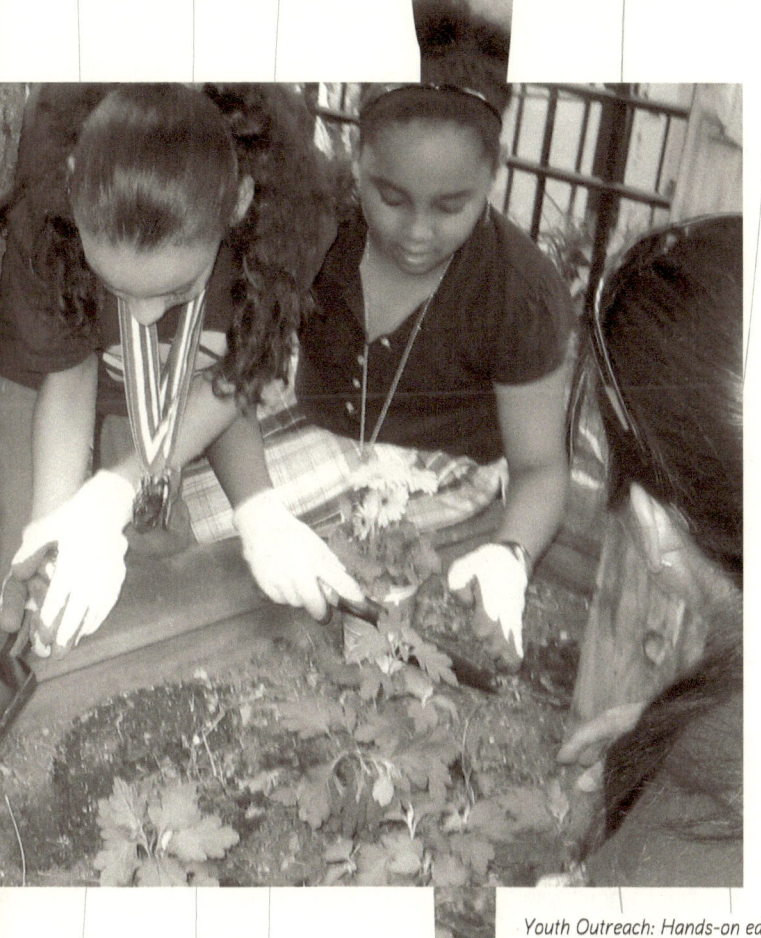

Youth Outreach: Hands-on education programs raise awareness about environmental concerns. (Photo: Esther Yang)

The Enterprise Rose Fellowship provides a unique opportunity for an architect to take unconventional career paths by working in a collaborative partnership with a nonprofit housing developer—a sphere in which the influences of design are often overlooked. The fellowship gives selected individuals the opportunity to inject fresh insights into established development practices and to expand, refine, and influence industry improvements.

THE OPPORTUNITY: BRONX, NY

In the fall of 2007, I started my Rose Fellowship with Fordham Bedford Housing Corporation (FBHC), a group that works for the preservation and provision of affordable housing in the Bronx. FBHC was founded in 1980 when the Bronx was rapidly deteriorating; it began its work with the acquisition and rehabilitation of abandoned and endangered buildings. Three decades later, FBHC combines these efforts with a new focus on preservation that fine tunes its portfolio and practices to increase building performance, reduce demands on environmental resources, and protect the health and livelihoods of their residents.

My admittance into the fellowship program extracted me from professional stagnancy and injected me into a fast-paced, unfamiliar environment. Like a koi fish, which will grow in proportion to its environment, I embraced the collection of projects before me and let my professional curiosities unravel. Despite our unique points of reference, FBHC and I aligned with a shared mission and methodology to enhance the quality of life and housing for neighborhood residents by recognizing areas in need of improvement, investigating and implementing solutions, evaluating our collective successes, and identifying challenges for future improvements. As a result, the fellowship was an ingenious mechanism for broadening my professional horizons and perspectives through a sharpened sense of purpose.

FBHC applied for an Enterprise Rose Architectural Fellow to fill roles within project management and construction oversight. However, beyond the scope of these tasks was a platform of projects that provided me with mentorship within established practices that helped me better understand how the influences of design can be used as a framework for the efficient delivery of high-quality housing. My participation in development meetings, construction supervision, design collaborations with the project architect, funding application processes, and peripheral property management not only enlightened me about development dimensions but also introduced me to the myriad of nested, conflicting forces that projects had to contend with. As an Enterprise Rose Fellow representing the field of design, my growing familiarization with various projects, policies, and development politics motivated me to filter new information so I could specifically understand how the industry of architecture could better alleviate persistent development concerns.

The host of projects within my fellowship work plan strengthened my conviction to redefine the way design is usually conceptualized, i.e., isolated within the boundaries of aesthetic design and construction. Design insights and actions influence ongoing concerns regarding long-term building performance as well as property and tenant management. My involvement in a cross-section of activities offered me glimpses of how the architectural sector could knit a variety of development interests together to deliver high-performance housing. My insights revealed the following facts:

- Architects have the expertise and skill to address restricted construction budgets by stitching developer interests, contractor/construction practices, and green-certification requirements together through a more a deliberate and calculated design process.

- Architects have specification resources and insights on post-occupancy performance that can be itemized and evaluated to anticipate, track, and monitor building performance and maintenance needs for the building owner and property manager.

- Architects hold specialized knowledge about building practices, and communicating that information to building owners, property managers, and tenants can foster accountability efforts to prolong the life of the project.

These three points became the bases for my fellowship investigations. My fellowship provided an environment in which I could reveal that design does more than just deliver objects; it is an influential component of a process that engineers the vitality and longevity of those objects within a community.

To moderate the volume and scale of FBHC's entire project pipeline, my fellowship work plan gave me ownership over a number of smaller-scaled projects. These endeavors permitted me to closely evaluate design and development decisions by testing specific tactics intended to refine performance and reduce the environmental impact of FBHC's portfolio. These project experiences also revealed to me the influential relevance of design within local, national, and international spheres.

Over the course of the fellowship's three years, I worked on the design, construction, or maintenance of 14 sustainable initiatives and supervised two green-building certifications. These projects included four green roofs (two extensive, two intensive), five rainwater systems (four simple landscape irrigation systems and one system to service residential toilets), two solar electric systems, one solar thermal system for heat and domestic hot water, and two lighting retrofits. My active participation in these projects gave rise to a forum in which FBHC and I could test and validate new tactics within standard practices. Through a macro lens, I was able to relay information about implementation practices and anticipated performance, suggest resources for further technical assistance, share advice with colleagues to prevent pitfalls, introduce in-house tracking measures, and project a system's collective impact on urban infrastructure. Through a micro lens, I was able to calculate specific reductions in water or fuel usage, project cost savings and performance payback, and assess a system's feasibility for future projects.

My fellowship work functioned in synergy with rising levels of interest in sustainable construction and conservation, mobilizing a diverse network of local, national, and international conversations in which I could position my work. Locally, my colleagues and I were able to compare systems and practices to learn about alternate construction, design, and financing solutions. Nationally, colleagues reviewed and revised resources to help developers better navigate certification programs, as a way to achieve environmental objectives with the support of a critical mass. On an international level, environmental advocacy groups provided feedback about the impact of U.S. development decisions on global communities. These discussions were the pinnacle of my fellowship. It was exciting to see ideas finally explode out of industry compartments and spill over to alter perspectives and policies amongst domestic and international colleagues.

FELLOWSHIP ACHIEVEMENTS
Development practices are tethered to and governed by established policies, so I was eager to transform the rich insights collected from my fellowship experiences and network of colleagues into tangible resources that demonstrated how design can guide various development sectors through shared challenges and mobilize reforms within the architecture industry. Fortunately, the Enterprise Rose Fellowship exposed me to the conduits and contacts through which ideas could be widely circulated.

Challenge: Establishing Development Priorities
Achievement: Schematic Decision-Making Resources

In the midst of performance objectives, sustainable practices, and restricted construction budgets, it was important to use weighted priorities to guide development and design decisions. Based on conversations with colleagues and lessons learned from my fellowship projects, I created two schematic graphic resources that illustrated development and design priorities in proportion to performance, cost savings, and relative impact on property maintenance. As a result, FBHC was able to convey to their community colleagues the benefits of thoughtful, holistic evaluations before implementing newly marketed sustainable strategies that may only offer limited benefits. These two development schematics were used for many presentations throughout New York City and are now in the hands of many local city and community development agencies.

Challenge: Restricted Construction Budgets
Achievement: Design/Cost Estimation Tool

The imperatives of design are notoriously in conflict with the realities of project budgets. I drew upon my design background, my fellowship construction experiences, and my relationships with contractors to initiate the design of a new 8,000-square-foot green-roof garden terrace, using a homemade low-tech cost-estimation spreadsheet. This tool granted me design freedoms and informational leverage with various contractors and vendors while concurrently monitoring the design's cost effects. This process protected me from unfortunate design adaptations during our industry's beloved "value-engineering" process when projects exceed budget limits.

There are advanced software counterparts to this tool, but using it at FBHC allowed me to level the playing field with my contractors by empowering me to budget a total development cost, rather than depending on a contractor to quote one. This cost-estimating tool has not been widely shared beyond a group of colleagues, but such tools allow developers and architects to proactively engage design within budgetary constraints.

"My involvement in a cross-section of activities offered me glimpses of how the architectural sector could knit a variety of development interests together to deliver high-performance housing."

Challenge: Evaluating Speculative Environmental Initiatives
Achievement: Performance Evaluation and Tracking Tools

The difficulty with implementing speculative sustainable practices is that they hold no value until they demonstrate worth through performance. With an ensemble of 14 sustainable projects, I was able to use costs from utility invoices, consumption readings from system meters, and performance updates from Web-based tracking systems to extrapolate raw information into productive evaluation resources.

My design background and exposure to development work and property management prepared me to assemble this information into assessment tools and to effectively communicate my observations to a variety of teams. Development team members will want to compare annual operating costs to upfront costs to determine the feasibility of an investment. On the flip side, development teams may elect to move forward with projects that have predicted losses if doing so would address local concerns regarding burdened city infrastructure. For example, a solar-thermal project that we worked on boasted drastic reductions in fuel consumption and utility bills, but a rainwater system did not. However, the rainwater system was able to retain and detain stormwater to alleviate the volume of water challenging New York's sewer systems. Also, these evaluation resources helped me communicate certain concerns to the property management team. Collected data could highlight maintenance needs or possible concerns about tenant behavior, or it could alert contractors to defects in construction or components.

Consistent monitoring and exchange of information facilitates feedback toward system and operation refinements. Several organizations are currently reviewing and refining these tools for property and asset management purposes.

Challenge: Green-Building Certification Compliance
Achievement: Project Management and Assessment Tools

Development and design teams face two challenges when seeking green-building compliance: a lack of resources to properly guide developers through compliance decisions, and the conflict between criterion mandates and performance realities. Two peer Rose Fellows (Ophelia Wilkins and Jessy Olson) and I drew upon our design and fellowship experiences within the construction field to revise a compliance workbook for Green Communities, an affordable-housing green-building certification program administered through Enterprise Community Partners. Our objective was to transform a document conventionally isolated within specific moments of development into a working document/resource that would serve multiple development and property management interests during many stages of a project.

The revised workbook gives developers and architects a snapshot of compliance tactics and associated costs, it allows project managers to track explicit and implicit compliance requirements, and it itemizes and documents implemented practices. This tool holds an invaluable amount of information and observations that can encourage policy reform, communicate to manufacturers about specific system component defects, and streamline efforts within the maintenance department. For example, if an item breaks or malfunctions, the property management team can reference the workbook for appropriate replacements or consultant contacts. The contractor may tell the building owner that certain materials or products are not performing well; the workbook can be used to document those comments and influence future project specifications. Furthermore, product feedback given to manufacturers may lead to manufacturer improvements or replacements. With regard to policy reform, the tracking of building performance could encourage green-certification administrators to consider revisions to their rules, if compliance mandates show significant performance compromises. Amid a sea of "green" development checklists, this resource aims to activate observations and design insights and to support further conversations and conclusions.

The workbook was adopted by Enterprise Community Partners and was distributed to a network of developers across the nation in January 2010.

Challenge: Long-Term Building Maintenance
Achievement: Leasing Protocol Modifications

Tenants are significant figures who influence the longevity of a building. As a result, FBHC supported three outreach efforts to educate tenants about the environmentally conscious practices within their buildings to foster tenant/owner commitments to the quality, performance, and maintenance of rental units and property.

Pre-lease orientation sessions were held to educate tenants about sustainable building features and to introduce them to the community of neighbors they would be living with. Modified leasing documents endorsed partnerships and accountability between tenants and owners. The distribution of welcome packages containing household implements and instructions served to introduce and encourage tenants about specific cleaning strategies appropriate to the building's new materials. These methods threaded the products and practices of design and construction into tenant protocols that worked to prolong the life of the building and to promote the health and well-being of the tenants.

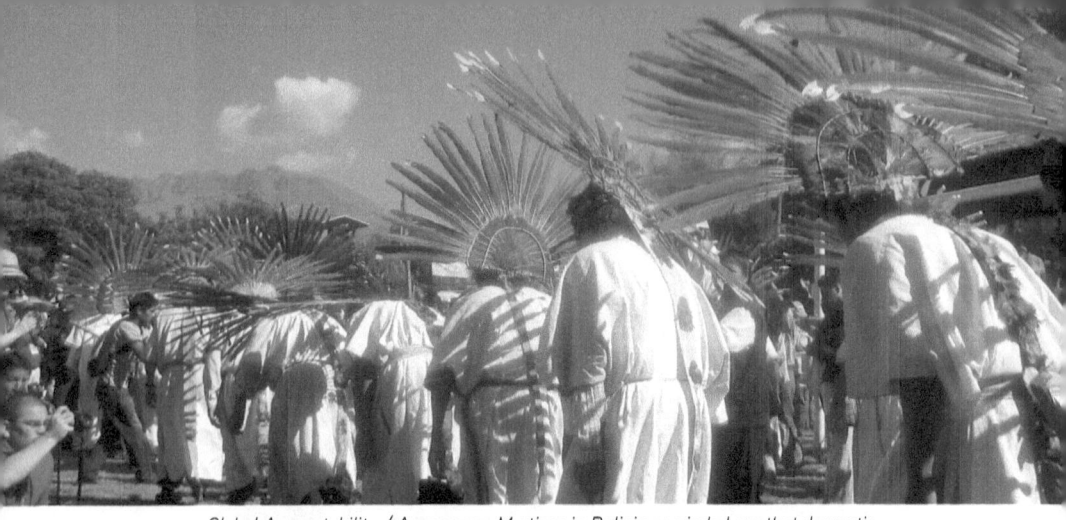

Global Accountability / Awareness: My time in Bolivia reminded me that domestic architectural practices and specifications are not always accountable to global/cultural concerns. (Photo: Esther Yang)

These practices have been shared with a wide array of property owners and managers and have been standardized into FBHC practices.

Challenge: Ignorance of and Indifference to International Realities
Achievement: Education and Advocacy

Despite sustainable initiatives in the United States, our overall development practices and consumption patterns do not often prioritize environmental stewardship or the preservation of communities beyond our borders. During my fellowship, my work on sustainable initiatives enabled me to receive an invitation to serve as a delegate representing the Bolivian Mission to the United Nations at a climate justice conference in Cochabamba, Bolivia, hosted by President Evo Morales. My time in Bolivia immersed me in a myriad of cultures, contentious conversations, and strategy sessions, and it exposed me to populations who were burdened by extravagant exploitation, the privatization of natural resources, and consequentially forced migration. These grievances significantly affected my outlook on my industry.

For example, upon returning from the conference I was presented with a Forest Stewardship Council–certified Brazilian wood product for a rooftop project. Despite this product's appealing aesthetic, performance, and validating certificates, I was unable to approve the product because I understood that regardless of these factors, the delivery and use of this product might harm the livelihood of particular communities from which it was extracted. This dilemma provoked discussions with my wood distributors about decision impacts, international compensation, and potential reforms intended to eliminate endangered resources from our domestic construction palette. While this experience did not lead to the creation of a particular policy, I did what I could at the moment to heighten awareness within specific groups and to encourage more conscientious and compassionate decisions.

NEW THRESHOLDS

Today, in the immediate wake of my fellowship's expiration, I feel that the vast collection of my fellowship experiences and achievements have impressed a significant set of new professional perspectives upon me. On the technical side, the fellowship offered me a spectrum of work to fulfill licensure requirements and patched holes of information that previous jobs did not fill. I now have access to a range of potential professional outlets that include hybrids of design, development, construction, policy, education, and community outreach. However, my main fellowship achievement is proof that design insights, properly disseminated, can radiate beyond the field's conventional boundaries, influencing mechanisms that can lead to more efficient and effective delivery of housing. In coming years, I hope to have opportunities to continue refining and articulating the work started during my fellowship.

I am deeply grateful to the fellowship that rescued me in a moment when I was extremely displeased with the direction of my career path; offered me a professional lifeline in an economic moment when desirable employment opportunities were scarce; empowered me to cultivate experiences, partnerships, and career options that would align with my professional convictions and personality; and now grants me a greater sense of confidence to seek out diverse professional directions that will continue to advance our mission of public service and community empowerment. It is with this strength and support that I move forward.

ESTHER YANG is a designer with an array of professional experiences within multiple architecture firms, academic teaching, and social justice initiatives. Esther recently completed the Enterprise Rose Architectural Fellowship with a refined set of skills, resources, and a network of domestic and international colleagues to promote more conscientious and compassionate development practices. Consistently involving herself between practice and policy, Esther maintains her hunt for fresh and productive perspectives to inject into the housing industry.

BRYAN
BELL

INTEGRATING FORM AND CONTENT: TRAINING PUBLIC-INTEREST INTERNS

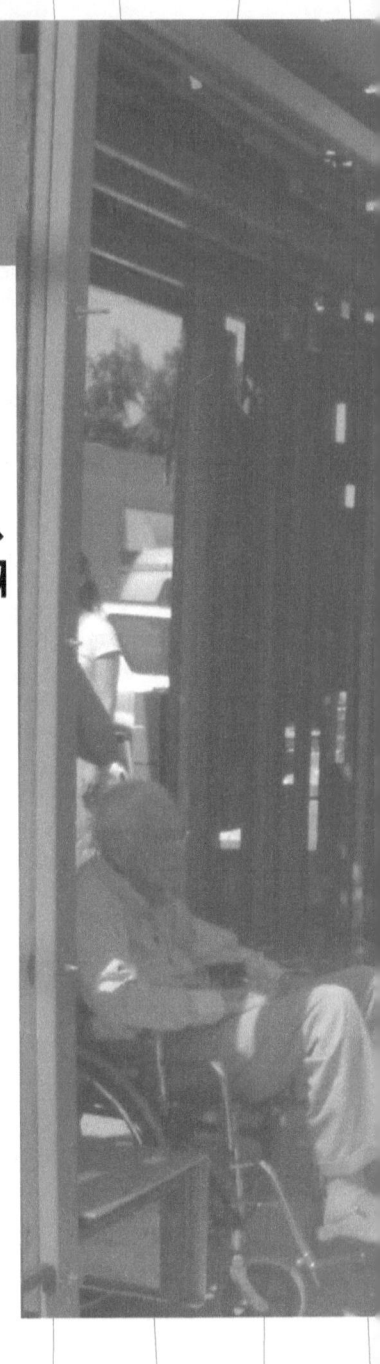

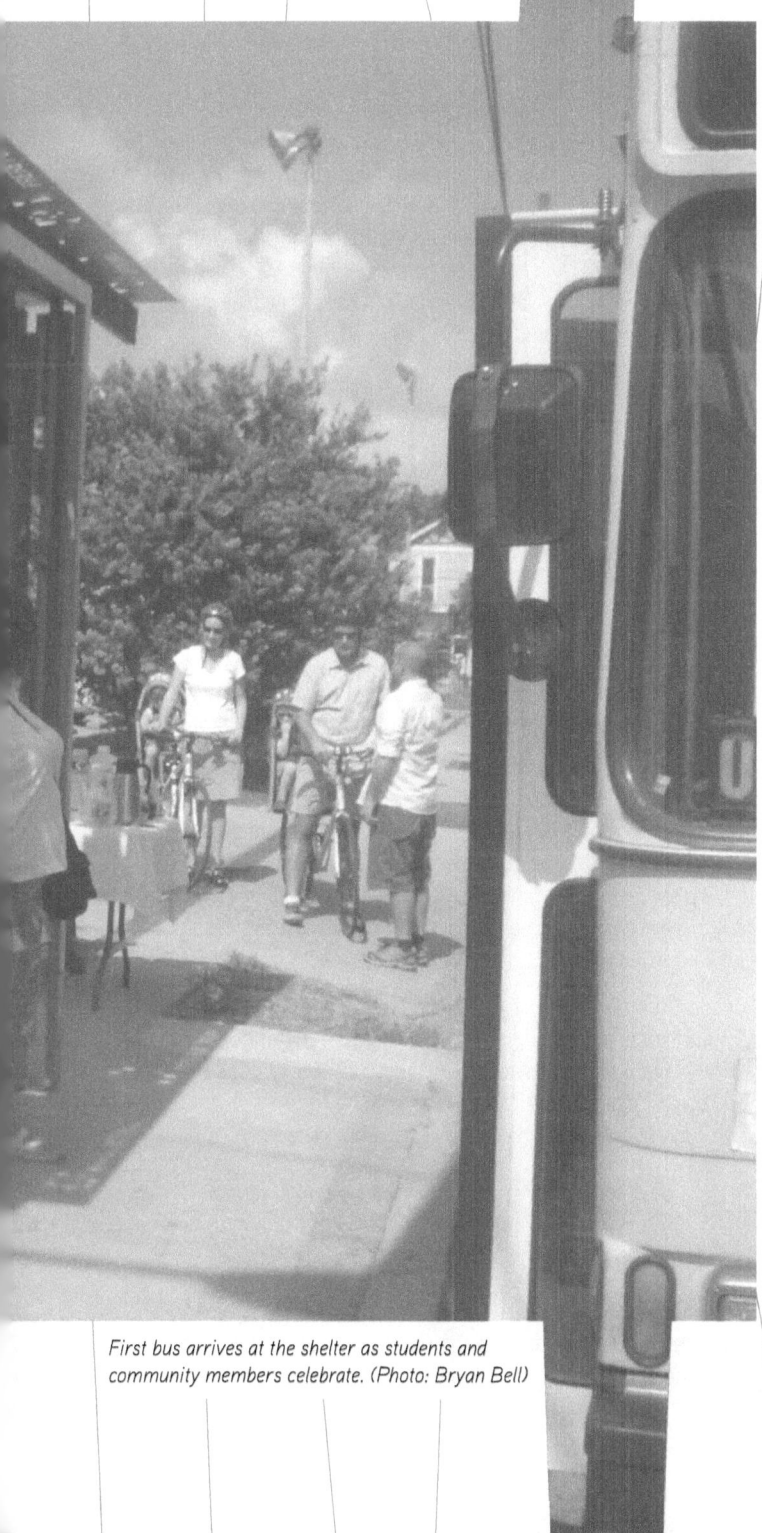

First bus arrives at the shelter as students and community members celebrate. (Photo: Bryan Bell)

New roles are emerging for architecture graduates to address the critical issues that challenge societies, both in America and around the world. How can recent graduates be prepared to take on these new roles? What skills do these graduates need to pursue this new professional path? While design remains the most critical skill, schools are not providing the training and knowledge needed in many other areas. Why? Faced with a full curriculum required by the National Architectural Accreditation Board, can schools teach architecture and add the additional skills?

From the first design-build students at Yale to the seminal work of Sambo Mockbee and the Rural Studio, learning through real projects has been the model for public-service education. Those who have worked in design education bring their knowledge to the field. However, even completing real projects through the academic studio model doesn't allow the extra time for students to develop needed skills. As proof, note that almost no Rural Studio graduates have pursued a career in public-interest architecture. The only solution is to provide full-time fieldwork as part of architectural training. This can currently only happen through summer studios or postgraduation internships.

DESIGN CORPS OPPORTUNITIES

Design Corps, a nonprofit organization in Raleigh, North Carolina, has two types of opportunities for students to pursue the learning objectives we believe are necessary for a career in public-interest architecture. One program is offered during the summer, and the other is offered as an internship that we call a fellowship. Both are full-time. Design Corps' goal is to address local needs with a model that emphasizes process so that transferable knowledge can inform similar efforts across the nation.

The Design Corps Summer Studio functions as an independent training center for community service, designing and building to meet local needs. The purpose of the studio is to provide the benefits of quality design to communities through inspired built form while training future architecture professionals in community visioning, organizing, and leadership.

In the fellowship program, the goal is to provide each fellow (or intern) with a broad range of skills to enable career advancement and personal goals. These positions are funded through AmeriCorps, the domestic Peace Corps program. Fellowships provide a living stipend that is set by the national office of VISTA (a unit of AmeriCorps), as well as health insurance and a $5,000 education award for completing the full year of service. (For details, see http://www.americorps.gov/about/programs/vista.asp.) The fellows are responsible for coordinating community-based projects. They learn specific

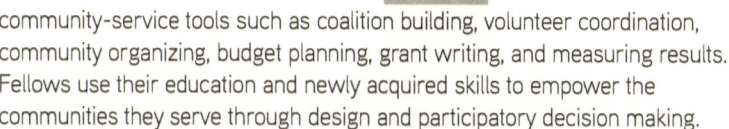

"Fellows use their education and newly acquired skills to empower the communities they serve through design and participatory decision making."

community-service tools such as coalition building, volunteer coordination, community organizing, budget planning, grant writing, and measuring results. Fellows use their education and newly acquired skills to empower the communities they serve through design and participatory decision making.

FORM PLUS CONTENT: THE DESIGN CORPS APPROACH

Both intensive full-time immersion programs, the summer studios and the year-long fellowships, share a common philosophy and are built upon the Design Corps methodology of integrating form and content.

Form = the arrangement of material and space.
Content = the relation of design to people, time, and place.

We believe design can make social contributions when it responds to both form and content. The Design Corps process involves discovering the relationship between these two critical components through a series of interwoven explorations that generate a built project for those who are not traditionally served by architects.

We cross-pollinate content and form. This is similar to moving from drawing to 3D modeling. Each method gives different information about the same thing. The dialogue between the two enriches a design process and ignites fresh ideas.

"Community projects are not like the neat assignments that are typical in architecture school; they are messy and require creative problem-solving in many areas."

Designers are givers of form. This is our skill. We can give three-dimensional reality to the needs and dreams of individuals and communities. But every form is packed with cultural values and social implications, i.e., the content. We must understand the social implications of what we create. We will not create random forms. Beautiful: Yes. Functional: Yes. Meaningful: YES.

To create meaningful form, Design Corps takes an approach called asset-based design. Traditional community assistance focuses on a community's deficiencies and problems; this method remains the primary approach in providing services to communities in need. The asset-based approach, on the other hand, insists upon identifying a community's assets and capacities as integral to community building. We untangle needs-based models of community building from asset-based models by exploring case studies in which architects have worked with those who are not traditionally served by design. We explore an asset-based approach because we believe communities must be deliberately and intricately involved in the design and redesign of their own spaces. In the process of identifying the assets of the community, students and fellows also define the assets they each bring to the work.

We seek beautiful form, both invented and found. We study properties of materials and how to apply them creatively. We research architectural solutions to social needs. We learn how to make a solution into a project so we can contribute our skills and show others what design can do for them. We seek inspiration from the local and the regional. We seek to identify and express the poetry of both people and the environment.

LEARNING TOGETHER IN THE FIELD
In both Design Corps programs for students, the community-engagement experience requires a proactive approach. Community projects are not like the neat assignments that are typical in architecture school; they are messy and require creative problem solving in many areas. Community projects are not assured of success. They are not "done

deals" that will be accomplished with a token effort. They ask a lot of the students and fellows, but most critically they require hard work and initiative. Completion and success are entirely up to the students.

Architects are good at saying, "Here's my great idea. Now it's your headache." On our projects we make sure to say instead, "Here's my great idea. Now it's my headache." Another of our guiding principles is: "Underpromise and overdeliver." It is very easy to make promises to communities and partners, but much harder to keep them.

Students are asked to be fully responsible for becoming independent, creative problem solvers in any area required to get the project done. One does not learn to drive a car by being a passenger. Students are expected to define their design intent, explore materials required to implement the design, and figure out how to build the project. The mantra is "build first, talk later," because ideas have a way of reconfiguring, and answers of emerging, when material hits material. Creativity is necessary not just in design but in approach and method as well. Participants gain knowledge through learning by doing. The students also get the opportunity to define a future project and write a grant to get it started. These skills will be invaluable to their later careers.

We emphasize that teachers don't know the perfect solution for a project, but the best answers emerge through an intense collaborative process. The aim of the studios and fellowships is to teach young designers how to create the method that the projects and communities require for successful resolution. While there are some organized class sessions, most of the students' work is done outside the traditional classroom, working on the projects and figuring out what needs to be done on their own, not at the direction of the teachers.

Our students tend to discover a number of common themes:

- The people doing the work make the decisions.
- Resolved ideas that are well-represented through drawings, models, and details will move ahead.
- If you don't, nobody will.
- Do not expect anyone else to finish your work.
- Design only what you can complete.

Our two programs for students teach six areas of skills, each with its own set of educational goals. The successful achievement of these goals gives each student and intern knowledge of a transferable process, empowering

them to pursue this work and preparing them to work as designers.
The skills we teach and their associated educational goals are as follows:

Asset-Based Community Context

- Distinguish between needs-based (top-down) and asset-based (grassroots) community building.

- Discuss practical case studies of successful asset-based strategies.

- Explore the challenges and advantages of an asset-based approach to community work.

Student Assets

- Identify individual assets students bring to the work of the summer studio.

- Collaborate and apply individual assets toward common goals.

Communication

- Listen to real clients and understand their needs.

- Present design solutions to clients' problems.

- Refine presentation skills in oral presentation of research and design ideas.

Community Understanding

- Understand the diverse needs, values, and backgrounds in our culture.

- Observe the social needs existing in the world.

- Understand the role designers can play in addressing identified community needs.

Collaboration

- Define big-picture objectives and shared goals with others.

- Understand the benefits of pooled abilities and energy.

Form Making

- Define and create a design proposal for a community.

- Research the relationship between materials and design objectives.

- Identify and apply the qualities of materials to a full-scale detail considering the design intentions.

- Construct the project, understanding the choices of materials and their connections.

Summer studio student Andrew Bryan, otherwise a graduate student at Harvard, sets the newly painted frame on the Rock Bottom Towing Company truck. (Photo: Bryan Bell)

A DESIGN CORPS CASE STUDY[1]

Freret Street, once the main street of a vibrant, diverse neighborhood in New Orleans, has not recovered from years of abandonment beginning before Hurricane Katrina and continuing afterward. As part of the city's recovery plan, the New Orleans Recovery and Development Administration has contracted for streetscape improvements for Freret Street. Included in these improvements are bus shelters, which are severely needed at the street's eight bus-stop locations.

In an effort to have the local community participate in the changes in their neighborhood, Neighborhood Housing Services contracted with Design Corps Summer Studio to coordinate a participatory-design process with local residents and organizations. The "program" for the built work was to create a public project that would visibly jump-start improvements along the street and inspire further economic development.

Summer architecture students organized meetings with a community group called Neighbors United and members of the Freret Street Business Association. An advisory group of twelve stakeholders was formed. The resulting design for a multiuse shelter responds not just to sun, rain, and seating, but also to the diverse needs of bus riders such as young children and wheelchair users. Like a Swiss army knife, the shelter has many other features, including bulletin boards, a bike rack, a planter, and a child's toy.

The primary material is durable heart pine salvaged from homes destroyed by Katrina. The wood slips into a steel frame that was fabricated off site. Other built shelters using this design could use the same steel frame and insert other local material as the infill. It is our hope that this bus shelter will be a visible symbol of renewed vigor and health in the neighborhood and that future neighborhood-specific models will be built. It is not envisioned as a generic off-the-shelf design but rather a symbol of improvements to be made by the New Orleans Recovery and Development Administration, which can be localized for each unique New Orleans neighborhood.

EVALUATING SUCCESS

The advantage of being a part of a community-based project is that it teaches skills that cannot be learned as effectively in the classroom. One disadvantage is that success is not easily measured. Without concrete evaluations of success, project results can be ambiguous, with the possible unfortunate result that weaker projects are replicated while better projects are not.

One of the reasons why green design has registered so strongly in the public consciousness is that LEED began to measure success. Prior to this development, there were many misleading claims of green design, and the public had no tools to compare or measure results. Communities would look to designers for assistance with social and economic challenges if there was a similarly accepted tool to measure positive impact in these realms.

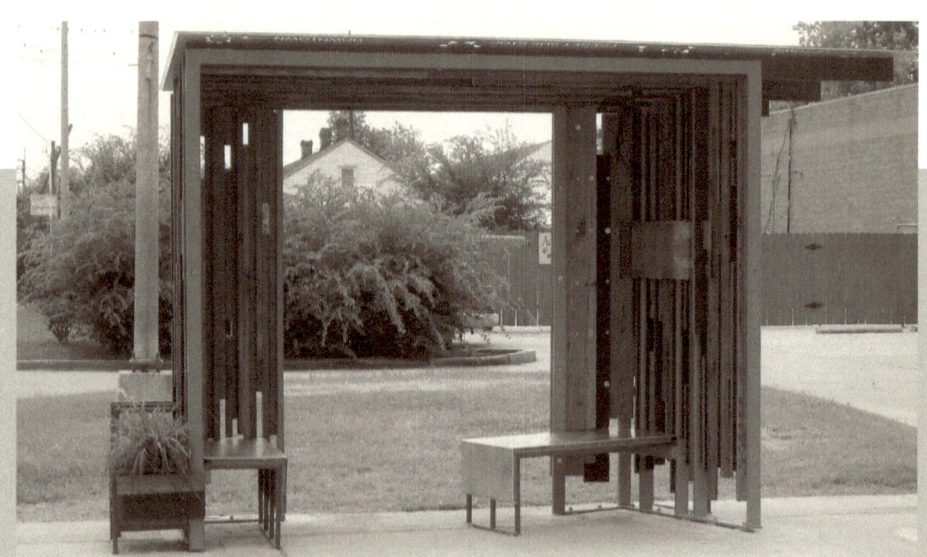

The completed "swiss army" shelter (Photo: Bryan Bell)

Design Corps and its fellows are now part of a multiyear collaborative effort to establish a new standard for design projects. The standard is called SEED: Social Economic Environmental Design®. An actionable version is available as a new online tool, the SEED Evaluator, at http://www.SEEDnewtork.org The online tool guides design professionals in working with locals to achieve buy-in and cooperation for projects, increasing their sense of inclusion and empowerment. The SEED standard addresses the triple bottom line of critical issues—social, economic, and environmental. SEED is a tool for developing design projects, evaluating them as they progress, and assessing them when completed. It can be of critical value to communities, designers, and architects who want to ensure that they are developing responsible projects that are transparent and accountable to the public. In addition to being a guide through the design process, SEED also can provide a stamp of approval, a third-party certification that the community's goals are being met. Resulting projects will maximize the positive impact of a community's limited resources.

For organizations like Design Corps that work with communities and train young architectural professionals, this type of tool will help us more effectively leverage our work. It will establish a standard for measuring results and sharing best practices. We will learn from each other as we demonstrate effective, meaningful, relevant, and often new approaches to design. This is a significant step in teaching the skills needed for the best community-based design. Projects designed and constructed using SEED as a tool will demonstrate the accountability and transparency needed in design education and the entire practice. The public deserves this, especially for projects that claim to benefit them.

BRYAN BELL is a design activist advocating for proactive design in the public interest. He is the executive director of Design Corps, a nonprofit organization he founded in 1991 "to provide the benefits of architecture to those traditionally unserved by the profession." Bryan is a 2010–11 Loeb Fellow. He is working to grow the Social, Economic, and Environmental Design (SEED) Network, researching and documenting design projects that address the critical issues faced in the world today.

Drew Lavine, Jill Lavine, and Andrea Marzolf sketch up ideas during a community-based design charrette. (Photo: Mark Garvin)

HALEY
LORAM

THE COMMUNITY DESIGN
COLLABORATIVE:
AN ALTERNATIVE
MODEL FOR
PUBLIC-SERVICE
ARCHITECTURE
INTERNSHIPS

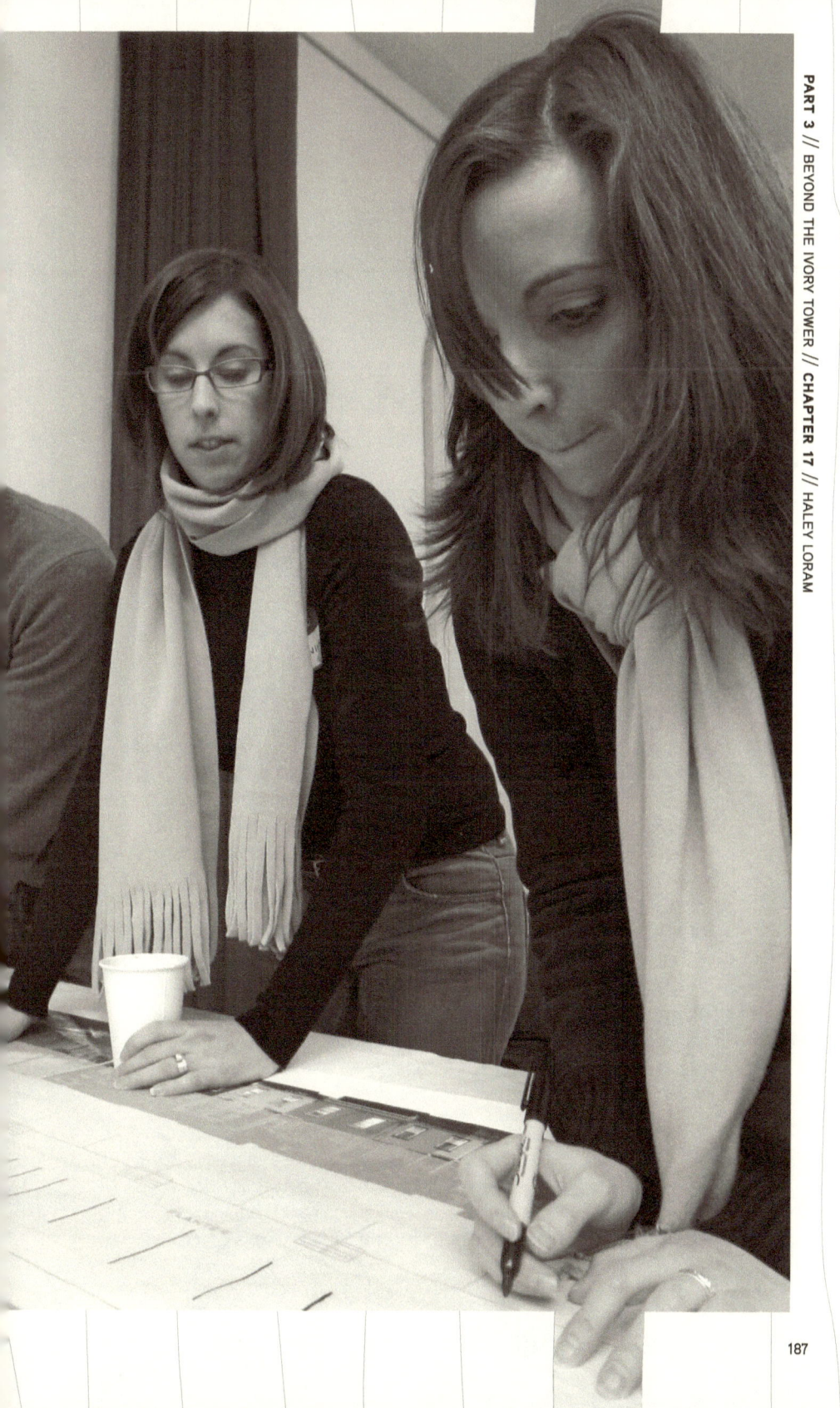

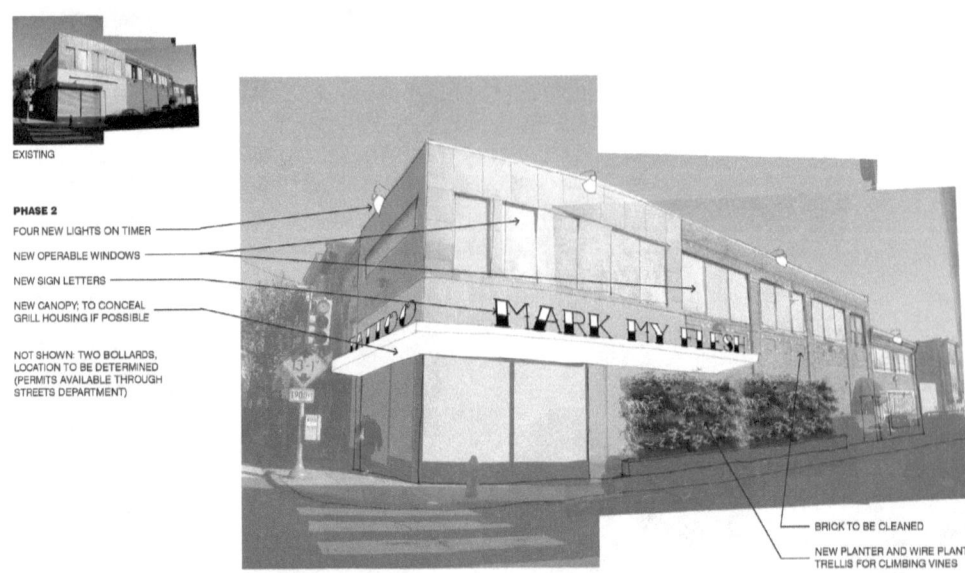

EXISTING

PHASE 2

FOUR NEW LIGHTS ON TIMER

NEW OPERABLE WINDOWS

NEW SIGN LETTERS

NEW CANOPY; TO CONCEAL
GRILL HOUSING IF POSSIBLE

NOT SHOWN: TWO BOLLARDS,
LOCATION TO BE DETERMINED
(PERMITS AVAILABLE THROUGH
STREETS DEPARTMENT)

BRICK TO BE CLEANED

NEW PLANTER AND WIRE PLANT
TRELLIS FOR CLIMBING VINES

Volunteer intern architect Michelle Shuman recommended increased lighting and a
bright canopy for a business on Philadelphia's Frankford Avenue Commercial Corridor.
(Graphic: Collaborative)

The conversation between intern architect Michelle Shuman and Fernando
Torres, the owner of Mark My Flesh Tattoo, was focused on barriers—
specifically, those that could help prevent cars from hitting Torres's building
in the Frankford neighborhood of Philadelphia. The young designer,
who worked with the Community Design Collaborative, was conducting
a design consultation with the seasoned business owner to discuss
options for improving the safety and visibility of the corner tattoo parlor.
The Collaborative had teamed with Frankford Community Development
Corporation to coordinate working sessions between volunteer designers
and a group of business owners to develop designs that would guide
storefront renovation and improve foot traffic. Shuman suggested that
Torres use a combination of increased lighting and a brightly colored
metal canopy to make the building stand out, along with bollards and
planters as a security buffer between the street and the sidewalk.

This working session was one of more than thirty partnerships between
community groups and designers that the Collaborative arranged in 2009.
The majority of these gave intern architects direct responsibility for
providing design concepts on projects such as the relocation and expansion
of a beloved neighborhood food co-op in West Philadelphia, a conceptual

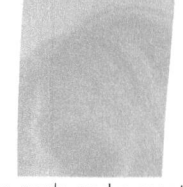

design for the renovation of a steeply sloped urban park, and a master plan to guide the reorganization of the headquarters of a social services agency in Philadelphia's Kensington neighborhood.

The Community Design Collaborative is a nonprofit community-design center that connects Philadelphia designers with local nonprofits that need help planning for physical improvements in their neighborhoods. A group of young architects created the organization in 1991 to serve as a transparent hub for providing their design skills to grassroots organizations that could not afford predevelopment assistance. Through the Collaborative, they could contribute their skills pro bono to feasibility studies and conceptual design work that demonstrated a project's potential.

The Collaborative was founded during an economic downturn as a special project of the associates committee of AIA Philadelphia. Job opportunities for recent architecture school graduates were scarce. Meanwhile, intern architects employed at large firms were often treated like "drafting fodder," as one Collaborative founder put it. Volunteering on projects with the Collaborative gave these young designers opportunities to actually do conceptual design, interact with clients, lead cross-disciplinary teams, and work with designers from a variety of firms.

However, the Collaborative has never compensated any of its volunteer designers for the work they do. All the work done through the Collaborative is strictly pro bono, and while it provides a valuable source of learning, networking, and exposure, it does not provide designers with a livelihood.

Nevertheless, the Collaborative is popular with young designers in the greater Philadelphia area. Currently, intern architects make up slightly more than 25 percent of the Collaborative's volunteers (391 of 1,457). Since 2000, intern architects have contributed more than twelve thousand hours of time worth more than $830,000 to hundreds of Collaborative projects in the Philadelphia area. A large portion of these interns have become repeat volunteers who make public service through the Collaborative an integral part of their careers.

Natalie Malawey-Ednie, AIA, found the Collaborative while pursuing a Bachelor of Architecture at Drexel University. She has volunteered more than two hundred hours on Collaborative projects, including a design for a community information kiosk and a master plan for the renovation of a West Philadelphia commercial corridor. Since graduating in 2003, she has worked primarily for larger architecture firms with fairly delineated paths

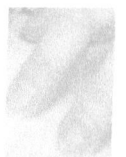

for young associates. She notes that Collaborative projects allow recent graduates of architecture school to continue to develop their own designs while real-world parameters and money constraints push them to be more creative. In her words, "The Collaborative is a conduit: you can come in and do what you're good at."

HISTORY OF THE COLLABORATIVE
The decision to provide design assistance strictly on a pro bono basis was influenced by the collapse of another Philadelphia community design center, the Architect's Workshop, which was funded by the City of Philadelphia. The Architect's Workshop paid both individual architects and firms to work with community groups that could not otherwise afford design services. Donald Matzkin, AIA, did projects with the Architect's Workshop that helped him launch his firm, Friday Architects/ Planners. Although the Architect's Workshop provided community-design opportunities, it folded, due in part to concerns about the role that politics played in selecting projects and volunteers. Years later, Matzkin guided the formation of the Collaborative and focused on making it as "open as possible to professionals with the skills to aid community groups in bolstering their communities." Alice Berman, AIA, another founder of the Collaborative, also worked for the Architect's Workshop before pursuing her Master of Architecture. She shared Matzkin's goal of creating a transparent organization; not paying designers for their public-service work helped to dispel concerns about politics and about the Collaborative taking work away from the private sector.

Several of the Collaborative's founders worked at small firms or went on to start their own firms, and they were sensitive to the concern that the Collaborative would siphon work from the private sector. This led to a core tenet of the Collaborative's scope of work: to focus only on early design assistance that gets projects off the ground and helps nonprofits obtain funding to hire design consultants to further develop and implement the design. The narrow scope of services that the Collaborative offers its clients is an important reason behind the success of its projects and its retention of volunteers. Collaborative volunteers focus on early design and development challenges, offering tailored feasibility studies. They evaluate sites; survey buildings; assess structural, mechanical, and electrical systems; analyze space and accessibility needs; help write requests for proposals; design conceptual plans; and offer opinions of probable costs.

Over two years of meetings in 1991–92, the founders of the Collaborative developed an organizational structure that would be responsive to

"Since 2000, intern architects have contributed more than twelve thousand hours of time worth more than $830,000 to hundreds of Collaborative projects in the Philadelphia area."

community-articulated needs and would help get capital projects off the ground. Berman noted that in the 1990s, when the Collaborative was founded, money for community development was "being eviscerated at every level of government," and the Collaborative became an access point for community-design services that might previously have been provided by the public sector. The organization steadily matured, guided by architects with experience in the community-design centers of the '60s and '70s. They hired their first staff member in 1992 and became a 501(c)3 nonprofit in 1996.[1]

HOW THE COLLABORATIVE WORKS

Today, the Collaborative's mission and processes have become more targeted. The organization has a staff of seven, including two from AmeriCorps VISTA and a full-time project manager. Its primary focus is on "building neighborhood visions through communities and volunteer design professionals working together." Its work includes site-specific service grants and theme-based initiatives that highlight citywide challenges such as food access. The service grant model leverages the community's resources, attention, and action, while ensuring that Collaborative projects are responsive to community needs and supportive of community revitalization efforts.

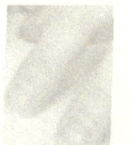

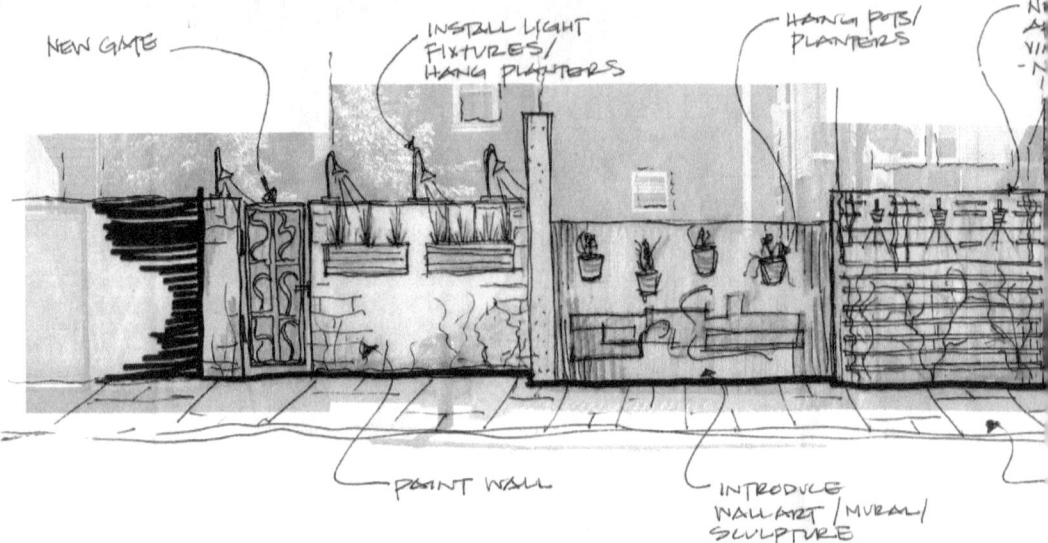

NEW GATE

INSTALL LIGHT FIXTURES/ HANG PLANTERS

HANG POTS/ PLANTERS

N
A
V/
- N

POINT WALL

INTRODUCE WALL ART / MURAL/ SCULPTURE

All of the Collaborative's projects are site-specific and are identified through a systematic application and selection process. As a first step, community groups approach the Collaborative with ideas for capital development, which are evaluated and defined before going through the selection process. The Collaborative's project manager, a registered architect with twenty years of experience, screens these initial applications and conducts a site visit, offering an early consultation and clarifying the types and extent of services that Collaborative volunteers could offer. Following the site visit, the Collaborative gauges volunteer interest in the potential project to assess possible matches.

The Collaborative manages a pool of more than one thousand volunteer designers in the greater Philadelphia area. Volunteers usually work in compact teams of two to six people over a six-month period. Generally the teams comprise individual contributors drawn from various firms and disciplines within the architecture, construction, and engineering industries. Teams may include landscape architects, historic preservationists, lighting designers, graphic designers, planners, and cost estimators. Volunteers are only placed on projects that they express an interest in, and they can sit out as many rounds as they want.

The project selection committee—which includes architects, landscape architects, construction managers, economic development experts, real-estate developers, an attorney, and representatives of the public sector— awards service grants on a quarterly basis. This process for vetting clients and projects ensures that the Collaborative's volunteers work on projects that will truly allow neighborhoods to benefit from predesign assistance.

After an orientation meeting with Collaborative staff, the teams work directly with the client to solicit input and develop a design. Each team has

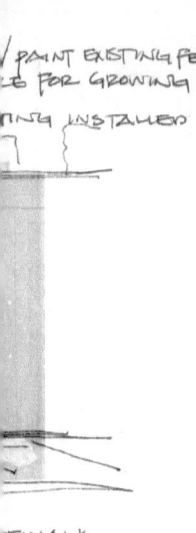

PAINT EXISTING FENCE
...E FOR GROWING
...TING INSTALLED

...EWALK

Sketch illustrating suggestions by residents for sprucing up rundown fences and garages in Fairmount (Rendering: Collaborative)

a leader. To ensure high-quality work, the team presents its design at two peer reviews during the course of the project, one at the midpoint and one just before the conclusion. The project review meetings are usually attended by ten to thirty local design professionals. Richard Winston, AIA, chair of the project review committee, noted that the reviews give experienced design professionals like himself an opportunity to contribute to projects that they may not have time to volunteer for, "in terms of design, of suggesting important questions to ask clients, and sometimes by making simple suggestions such as, 'add another exit on that side of the building.'"

Throughout the process, the Collaborative's project manager provides advice and troubleshooting. Clients and volunteers consistently cite the clearly defined process and expert project management as major contributors to successful projects. For each project, a final report that includes the team's drawings, photographs, a narrative, and a cost estimate is produced. The report gives the nonprofit's governing board solid information to guide a decision about a proposed project's feasibility. Upon completion of the Collaborative project, the team reviews the final report with the client to ensure that they can present it independently to third parties in a way that helps them get the most value out of the conceptual design. If the nonprofit decides to pursue the project, the report will be a powerful tool in community organizing and fundraising efforts.

In 2002, the Collaborative recruited its first project team fully staffed with volunteers from a single firm. The firm of Francis Cauffman Foley Hauffman Architects worked with the Allegheny West Foundation to develop fresh ideas for contextual residences to be built on lots left vacant by selective row home demolition. Participation in the project enabled the firm to offer its associates a professional development opportunity, allowing them to earn credits toward the Intern Development Program (IDP) of the National Council of Architectural Registration Boards. Since then, the Collaborative has expanded its work with firm-organized teams, and the number of "firm volunteers" has grown steadily. In 2008, forty-three firms and 132 design professionals volunteered through the Collaborative, delivering more than $425,000 in predevelopment services to more than thirty local nonprofits. In 2009, seventy-four design firms and 187 design professionals volunteered their skills through the Collaborative on twenty-seven projects whose combined total value of services was nearly $610,000.

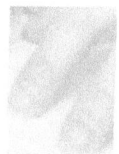

VOLUNTEER PERSPECTIVES ON THE COLLABORATIVE

In interviews with the author, a number of Collaborative volunteers explained why they feel that the Collaborative's work matters. Collaborative board member Mami Hara, AICP, ASLA, explains that although the firm where she is a principal, Wallace Roberts & Todd (WRT), does not have an official volunteer policy, it actively encourages individuals at all levels in the firm to volunteer their time to broaden their exposure to issues that may be relevant to their work at the firm. Hara notes the important professional development benefits of volunteering with the Collaborative, especially for young designers:

"At a midsized firm, the level of involvement that you have with projects has to increase incrementally as you gain the experience to perform at the level needed to take on a leadership role. However, having the opportunity to stand on your own two feet and see a project through early on in your career is very healthy. Young designers need to have new experiences to grow, which include opportunities to engage directly with clients, lead a project, and present to respected design professionals. Volunteering with the Collaborative also allows you to get the perspective of people from outside the firm. It's really important to understand how others can perceive your aesthetic."

Megan McGinley, AIA, a project architect at WRT, has volunteered with the Collaborative since the start of her career. She says that volunteer projects allow young professionals like herself to "take on new assignments with the benefit of an experienced mentor, so that when you use those skills at your firm, it is not the first time." Experienced team leadership, staff troubleshooting, and the two design reviews together ensure the quality of the design work. Doing pro bono projects with the Collaborative allows intern architects to learn skills that are difficult to teach in the classroom and initially difficult to practice in their firms.

Although several Philadelphia-area colleges and universities offer design programs, the Collaborative provides the only local opportunity for designers coming out of those programs and intern architects who may be further along in their careers to volunteer their design skills. The Collaborative's projects offer opportunities to earn Intern Development Program (IDP) credits from the National Council of Architectural Registration Boards.

Volunteer projects with the Collaborative can be counted toward the IDP community service requirement and might qualify for a number of other areas. Heidi Segall Levy, AIA, the Collaborative's project manager, can sign off on IDP credits, although only ten or fifteen intern architects have ever asked her to do so. However, intern architects more often obtain

"Doing pro bono projects with the Collaborative allows intern architects to learn skills that are difficult to teach in the classroom and initially difficult to practice in their firms."

community-service credit for time spent on Collaborative projects by showing the products and their time sheets to supervisors at their firms.

In addition to fulfilling IDP requirements, Collaborative projects give intern architects the opportunity to practice other skills. Unlike work done at firms, where a senior designer develops a design concept that is then executed by less-experienced associates, young designers can and frequently do assume leadership roles for Collaborative projects. As an intern architect, Natalie Malawey-Ednie served as a lead volunteer on two projects, one of which involved a presentation of the final design to more than seventy community members.

Intern architect volunteers also learn how to work directly with clients who may not have worked with designers and aren't necessarily familiar with what design can contribute to a project. Volunteers must respect the client's expertise related to their community while suggesting innovative, useful design features that the client may not know to ask for but that could improve the outcome. Intern architects can work with clients who may not fully understand how design could support their mission, but who in turn can push designers to produce truly creative work under serious constraints. That mutual process of education is at the core of the Collaborative's work: volunteers learn how to collaborate effectively with community groups, and clients learn how design can make a difference in their neighborhoods. That philosophy anchors the work of volunteers like Alexander Chan, who believes that architects "have a responsibility to use our design skills to support communities that use the spaces that we design."

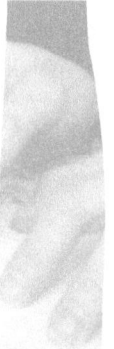

"When these designers are at a point in their career where their jobs may be dominated by mundane tasks, community-based work can provide a creative outlet, prevent burnout, and bring home the relevance of design to the neighborhoods where these volunteers live, work, and play."

The Collaborative's niche of connecting nonprofits with pro bono design assistance for site-specific projects is unique in the greater Philadelphia area. The Collaborative is the only steady opportunity for young and intern-level designers to volunteer their design skills in this region. When these designers are at a point in their career where their jobs may be dominated by mundane tasks, community-based work can provide a creative outlet, prevents burnout, and brings home the relevance of design to the neighborhoods where these volunteers live, work, and play. The local connection between the city's nonprofit sector and area designers builds a rich web of connections between nonprofit professionals who know the needs of their communities and designers who can help ensure that they have the tools to make good decisions about capital projects.

Alice Berman notes that community-based work helps to "guard against building simply as sculpture." It encourages designers to see how the built environment affects the social fabric of the city, and it promotes designers' connection to that social fabric.

Intern architects have contributed more than one-fourth of all the volunteer hours for the Collaborative's projects since 2000. Although Collaborative projects may not be built for years, if at all, the work contributes to outcomes that are not necessarily physical. Volunteer Nissa Eisenberg, an intern architect, helped the Collaborative coordinate a design charrette in her neighborhood of Fairmount. The day-long project brought together a mix of new and long-term residents from adjoining blocks to work with designers on developing strategies to address run-down back

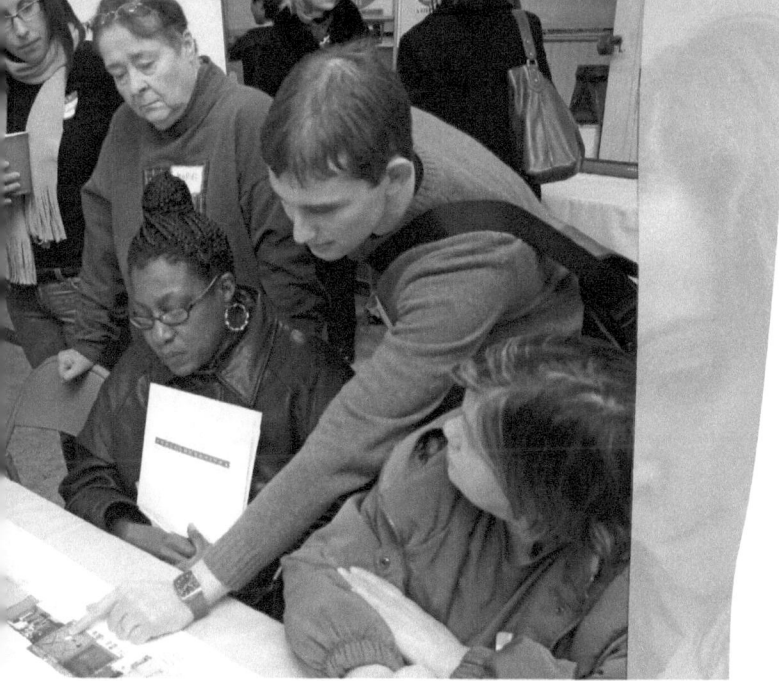

Young designers engage residents of Philadelphia's Fairmount neighborhood in a discussion about block improvements. (Photo: Mark Garvin)

yards, fences, and garages. The charrette got them talking, in some cases for the first time, and brainstorming a solution collectively.

One of the important challenges the Collaborative now faces is how to provide enough volunteer opportunities. With a pool of almost one thousand volunteers and an average of thirty to forty projects a year—few with teams larger than ten people—there is a gap between the demand for volunteer opportunities and the number of projects available. In some rounds, more than twice as many intern architects express interest in volunteering as the Collaborative can place on teams. This imbalance has increased since the start of the recession in 2008, and feeding the pipeline has become an increasingly important part of the Collaborative's work.

HALEY LORAM graduated from Swarthmore College in 2008 with a major in political science and a minor in Latin American studies. She was part of the Community Design Collaborative staff for two years, first as a Philly Fellow and then as an AmeriCorps VISTA Leader.

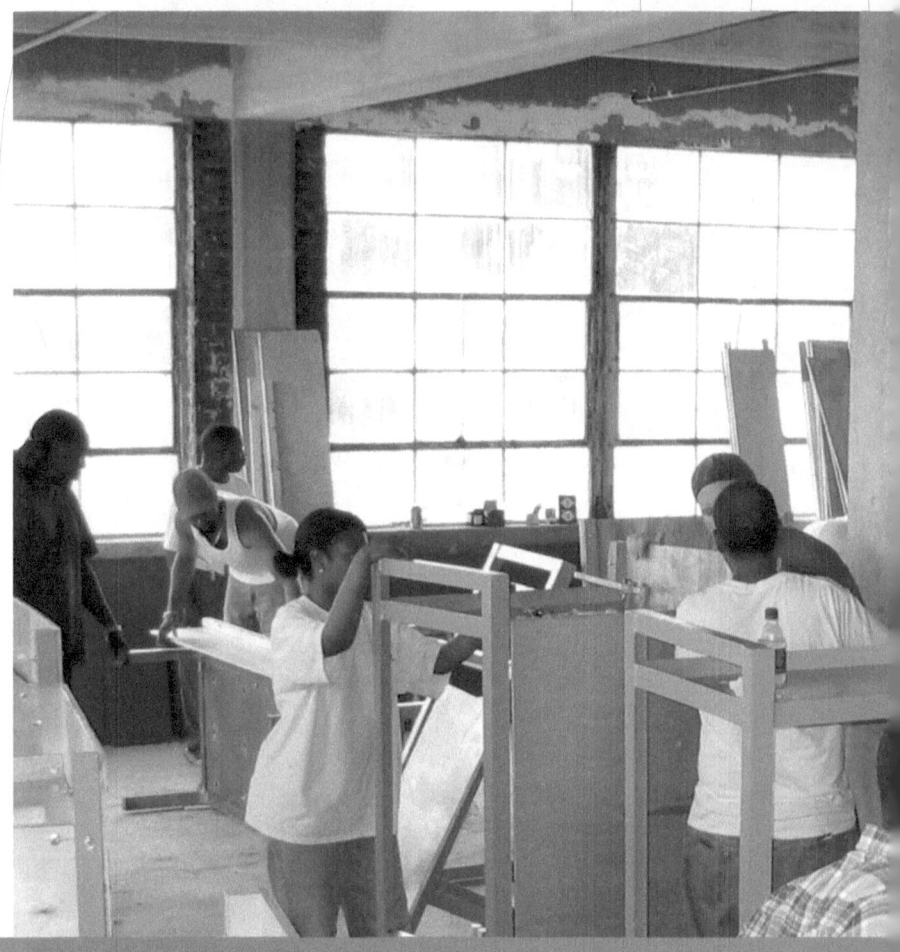

With the help of a local architecture firm, many of the Peachtree-Pine beds were upgraded with a storage unit. (Photo: Luke W. Perry)

LUKE WELDON
PERRY &
LUKE
CLARK TYLER

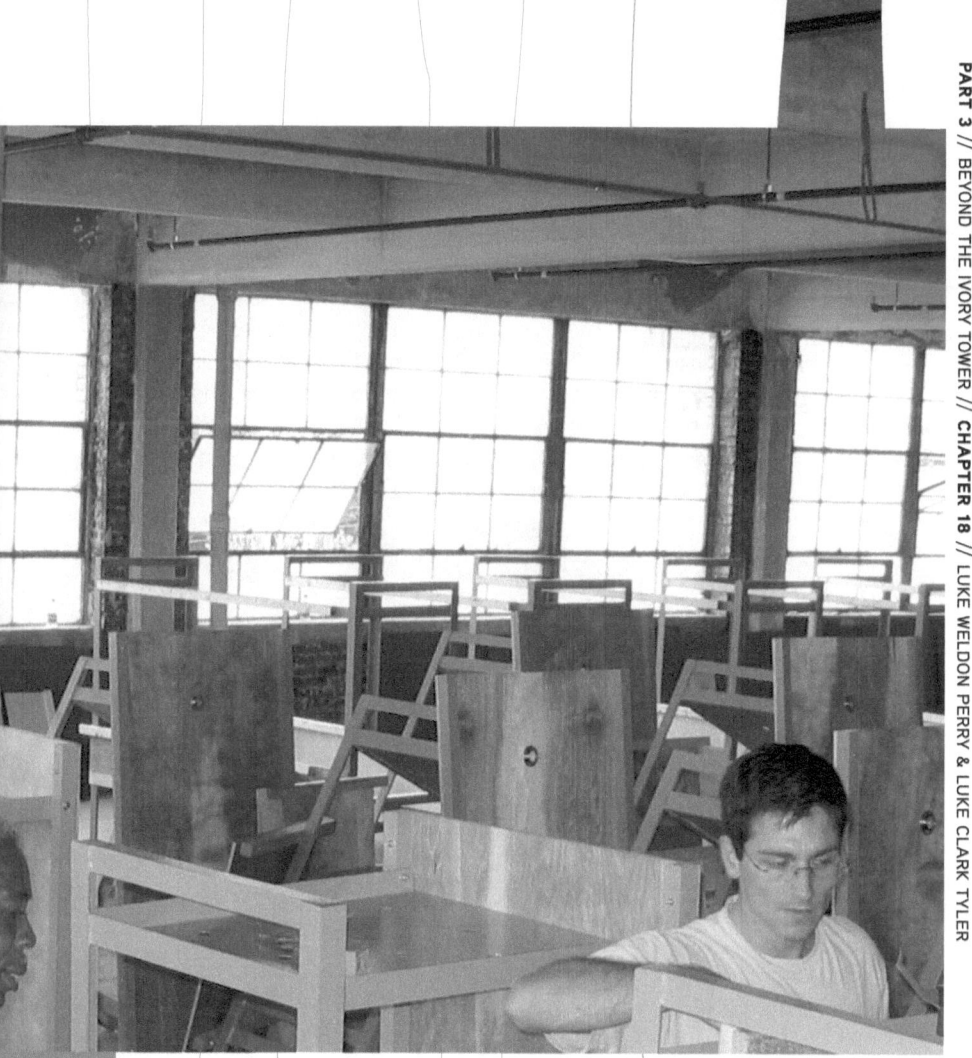

ARCHITECTURAL IMMERSION: THE PEACHTREE-PINE EXPERIENCE

On the northeast corner of the intersection between Peachtree Street and Pine Street in Atlanta, there sits a remarkable building. Known as Peachtree-Pine, it has occupied a prime spot on one of the Southeast's most famous streets for eighty years. Even though it is located at the nexus of midtown and downtown, it was largely abandoned and empty for many years until the Metro Atlanta Task Force for the Homeless acquired the building in 1999. Since then, Peachtree-Pine has provided emergency shelter, comprehensive services, transitional housing, and advocacy support to upwards of eight hundred people daily. However, this facility has sparked fierce debate about the people it serves, the manner in which these services are provided, and most importantly, the location in which such activities should take place, especially in light of the recent economic resurgence of both downtown and midtown.

In 2004, the Task Force embarked on a participatory master planning process to envision a redeveloped Peachtree-Pine. In a unique approach, the Task Force brought Luke W. Perry (LWP) on board as a design coordinator for the redevelopment project. He worked for the Task Force from 2004 to 2006, and then Luke Clark Tyler (LCT) continued the project from 2006 to 2007. Both young intern architects worked and lived at Peachtree-Pine. In the following dialogue, they describe their experiences with this unique project.

THE MASTER PLAN

LWP: In June 2006, during my last week at the Task Force (and Luke Clark Tyler's first week), we held a meeting to introduce the new master plan for Peachtree-Pine to the residents of the building and the surrounding community. It was quite an extraordinary mix of people, representing a broad range of interests. Two years earlier, when I first arrived, it would have been impossible to get some of the constituents to even set foot inside our building, much less to sit at the same table with everyone else involved. But on this night, community members were at the table, political leaders were present, funders were engaged, and Peachtree-Pine residents were already deeply involved in transforming the building. Much of this progress and momentum had been generated through the design process, which facilitated the development of a vision for one of Atlanta's most challenging, but also one of its most exciting, social-service projects.

LCT: And it was a truly compelling plan: one hundred thousand square feet devoted to helping homeless people develop stable lives through emergency services, job training, arts, housing, and leadership

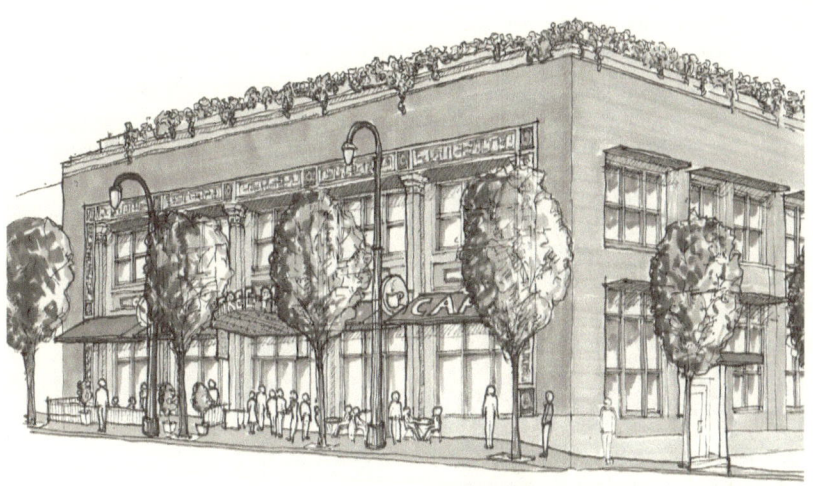

The master plan envisioned new commercial spaces on Peachtree St. to provide jobs and income for the rest of the Task Force's services. (Rendering: Luke W. Perry)

development. There would be a coffee shop and other commercial spaces on Peachtree Street to generate income and provide jobs and training for the residents of Peachtree-Pine. A twenty-thousand-square-foot public space on the roof would offer unparalleled views of downtown while hosting a community garden growing organic vegetables for the agency's future commercial kitchen. Passive heating and cooling strategies were going to make the building more energy-efficient.

LWP: Most importantly, Peachtree-Pine provided a unique opportunity to transform what was quickly becoming an exclusive part of the city into a much more inclusive one. We wanted the building to be a vibrant address on Atlanta's signature street, Peachtree Street, and we believed that some of Atlanta's most vulnerable residents should remain part of the community life of downtown, especially because of the work opportunities, transportation options, and social-service providers already in the area.

LCT: In theory, the opportunities were endless. We were not only planning to fully rehab a nearly dilapidated building; we were also going to create an innovative facility to host a new model of homeless services. With the momentum we had gained, Peachtree-Pine was on its way to being a groundbreaking project.

LWP: But it didn't start (or end) that way. The Task Force was a strong and outspoken critic of the city's destruction of affordable housing and its treatment of homeless people during and since the 1996 Olympics. This resulted in many spirited public battles against the city and its political and business leaders. After the Task Force acquired Peachtree-Pine, the political battles were transferred to the building itself, with many powerful interests determined to see that homeless services were no longer provided there. During this time, many of Atlanta's poor were losing their housing, and the need had become overwhelming. A broken social-services system, a lack of shelter beds, deep ideological battles, and strong opposition to shelters in any neighborhood (especially in central locations) had made the quality of life very poor for a large portion of Atlanta's most vulnerable citizens.

STOP BEING AN ARCHITECT

LWP: In such a fragile, complex social environment, it didn't take me long to question how effective my formal training as an architect would be. I had to think a bit more broadly about what it meant to be an architect and how I would be able to use my skills in such a context.

LCT: As architects, we often see ourselves as problem solvers, ready to cast designs, execute, and get things built. That is what our education prepares us to do. We create design concepts in response to formal, aesthetic, or theoretical "problems." This approach can create incredibly interesting designs, but it doesn't prepare one to take on such significant, real-world issues as those we found at Peachtree-Pine.

Generating new ideas for the building wasn't the problem. Our charge was unique in that we had to get people to consider a plan that included the Task Force as part of its future. While anyone could make Peachtree-Pine into a beautiful piece of real estate, it was our job to integrate the agendas of the Task Force, the residents of Peachtree-Pine, and the surrounding community to make the building a more welcome and integral part of the neighborhood and the city.

LWP: Although Peachtree-Pine had a unique, diverse, and rich internal community of staff, volunteers, and hundreds of people who called it home, a majority of city residents, political leaders, and neighbors had a strong negative opinion about the Task Force. As a result, many would intentionally avoid going near Peachtree-Pine. So no matter how informative, provocative, or appealing our designs were, the negative perception of the shelter prevented most from even looking at a plan that included the Task Force as part of the building's future.

"I had to think a bit more broadly about what it meant to be an architect and how I would be able to use my skills in such a context."

Many parties on all sides of the homelessness issue had given up trying to communicate or were not doing so effectively, so I saw designing the master plan as a process of re-engagement. This re-engagement took place with politicians, business leaders, and other nonprofits and early on it was more of a passive approach. I had to put to the side my formal training and skills so I could instead just listen and observe. Rather than immediately identifying the problems that my experience and background would predispose me to recognize, I had to allow others to tell me what the problems were.

Part of the process included being present at all levels of community meetings, from the neighborhood to the city level, even though we faced constant, vociferous, often uninformed opposition to the work going on at Peachtree-Pine. But we made it a goal to always be present, along with a few of the residents (or "clients") of Peachtree-Pine, to ensure that there was a voice of truth and reason representing the Task Force. We used these meetings as starting points, and many additional conversations took place on sidewalks, over lunch or coffee at neighborhood businesses, and eventually inside Peachtree-Pine.

COMMUNITY ENGAGEMENT
LCT: It was clear the only way we could be effective as designers in this context was by first establishing ourselves as involved and committed community members. We had to engage the social dynamics of Peachtree-Pine to develop a strong voice, rooted both in the realities of the shelter and in a vision for the future. Simultaneously, we actively engaged the neighborhood, becoming involved in a variety of activities. This integration proved to be as essential to the design process as sketching. By working to bridge the divide between the Task Force and the neighborhood, we were able to facilitate productive dialogues that not only helped the surrounding community better understand the Task Force, but also helped generate the most beneficial solutions for the challenges of the redevelopment.

LWP: One reason we were able to effectively represent and speak on behalf of Peachtree-Pine in the neighborhood is that we both lived in the shelter during our time at the Task Force. We had our own private space, and we lived rent-free, which was somewhat of a necessity so we could survive on the small stipend. But we had great views of downtown, easy access to parks and restaurants, and some of the most interesting "roommates" imaginable. Of course we would also witness late-night fights, sleep through constant sirens, unknowingly camp with large rodents, and face persistent pleas for help. But work was the real reason we stayed there.

LCT: Being so exposed to the truth of what happens at Peachtree-Pine around the clock gave us a unique understanding of the place. Not only did we witness the energy; we were a part of it. We more or less lived the challenges and opportunities of the place, which made it so much more viable for us to engage in discussions with both "insiders" and "outsiders" about what the Task Force is and isn't, does and doesn't do. Most importantly, we gave voice to and let others hear about solutions from the perspective of people who were living there.

LWP: As for the "insiders," one of the biggest surprises was the sense of community that the clients built, no matter how transient some of them were. It wasn't the case for everyone, but several found Peachtree-Pine to be a place where they could grow and develop

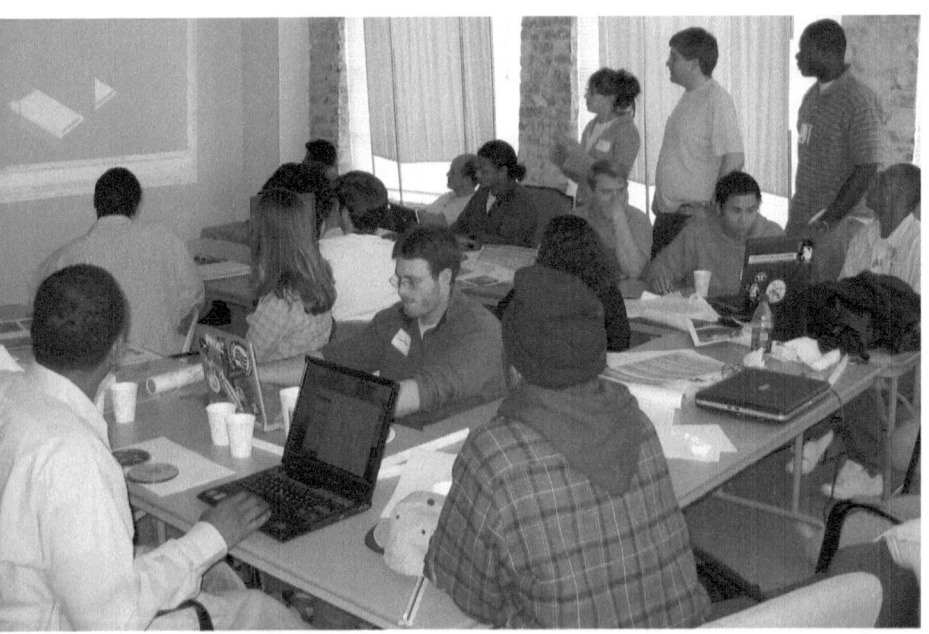

Small design-build projects often began with charrettes involving local architecture students and professionals, the community, and Peachtree-Pine residents.
(Photo: Luke W. Perry)

personally and creatively. The relationships we developed inside the building were essential, as they helped foster critical dialogues and discussions about the master plan we were charged to develop.

We then focused on strategies that would dispel the uninformed public perceptions that had been previously established. Our goal was to demonstrate that Peachtree-Pine was a vital member of the neighborhood instead of the cause of every problem in it. We worked hard to educate others about homelessness in general as well as the range of programs Peachtree-Pine offered. We initiated cleanups that brought clients, staff, and community residents together to beautify the neighborhood.

Finally, we set up an advisory committee of Peachtree-Pine residents, staff, community residents, business leaders, sustainability experts, builders, and architects to help guide the development of the master plan. This group was essential for providing us with mentorship, but also for ensuring a range of voices during critical parts of the process.

START BEING AN ARCHITECT

LWP: Our open, strengthening relationship with the clients and the neighborhood allowed us to begin an active design process. We initiated a number of public design charrettes that gave rise to small projects within the building. Renovating the bunks in the emergency shelter, building a roof garden exhibit, and improving the office space brought together Peachtree-Pine residents and outside community members (many from the architectural community) on projects that had immediate impacts and direct outcomes. We even restored the historic façade of the building, which gave us a new face to show the neighborhood. Most importantly, it provided a welcoming space to bring together different groups of people who would never normally cross paths on equal terms, which was the spirit of Peachtree-Pine.

LCT: The process eventually generated ideas for larger design concepts. Through our community engagement, we could begin to tackle design solutions that addressed the needs of the agency and those it served, as well as the larger needs of the surrounding neighborhood. It was only at this point that we were able to begin to exercise our more formal architectural skills, such as visual communication.

LWP: Graphic representation became an incredibly important tool for expressing the overall vision to our clients, our neighbors, and the larger community. It essentially allowed us to present a socially conscious, just, economically viable, and environmentally friendly community as something tangible and beneficial to all groups. This was something most people hadn't thought possible before.

LCT: In our design, we planned to continue to offer the emergency services offered by the Task Force, but in a new way. It was the emergency services that generated the most criticism, with many (including some Peachtree-Pine residents) insisting that we were just warehousing people without actually helping them. In reality, Peachtree-Pine's emergency services offered a safe and welcoming place for them to be, very different from the streets of downtown Atlanta, where physical abuse was common and extensive laws unjustly criminalized those on the streets. Consequently, we planned a large, open, light-filled atrium space to serve as an entry point for people to access whatever services were needed. Those who needed short-term assistance such as birth certificates, housing advice, or legal assistance would be served through the existing day service center. Short- and long-term housing options were to be expanded in the new master plan, with a diversity of types to serve a range of needs. Emergency shelter and resident volunteer programs would remain, because the Task Force depended on participants to assist with building operations. Transitional housing would be expanded to include a single-room occupancy program and double rooms that would offer more independence and responsibility.

LWP: Beyond housing, existing programs for painting and photography would be enhanced to support people's creativity during times of transition. The idea was that works of art could then be displayed in the public coffee shop or art gallery, both of which would be located at the front of the building on Peachtree Street. These programs were designed to create a space where the neighbors could begin interacting with the activities and occupants of Peachtree-Pine. Additionally, they would offer commercial services to the neighboring community and job opportunities to our clients.

LCT: We also planned to include a community kitchen on the lower level of Peachtree-Pine that would support many programs. It would provide additional job training and income opportunities, as baked goods from the kitchen would be sold in the coffee shop. Additionally, it would feed the hundreds of people who would otherwise go hungry every day.

LWP: One of my favorite parts about the community kitchen was the connection with the building's rooftop. We planned to grow as much of our own food as possible on the twenty-thousand-square-foot roof. There would be gardening plots, recreation space, and walking paths. In addition, we planned to open up the rooftop to the larger community by offering a sculpture garden and a rooftop terrace/performance space for the coffee shop so anyone could enjoy the panoramic views of downtown in a unique setting. It was the crown jewel of the project.

LCT: Overall, the master plan was quite extensive in its scope. It took the very issues and challenges that had provoked deep divisions in the past, and it reworked and repackaged them in ways that people could understand, discuss, and even get excited about. This ability to improve the external appearance of the building, create affordable housing, and develop programs that could both generate revenue and put people to work enabled the conversation to move beyond the political and ideological battles that had been simmering for almost a decade. Architecture and the design process helped give life to all of this.

LIMITS AS OPPORTUNITIES

LWP: Within the context of Atlanta, the master plan's ability to significantly affect thousands of homeless people was evident from the beginning. Yet I believed that the process of developing it could play a significant role in the resolution of the bitter battles that had plagued the politics of Peachtree-Pine and homelessness in general. I also believed that it could facilitate and kick-start all of the other factors that were needed to fulfill the master plan. This included generating the necessary funds, receiving community support, empowering the residents of Peachtree-Pine, and ultimately achieving the political will—from all sides—to move the project forward.

LCT: I think we succeeded in all of those except the last. We brought significant funds and momentum to the project. We engaged previously opposed sections of our community in a process that brought them all to the same table. And I believe we kept the needs, skills, and potential contributions of thousands of homeless people as the primary driving force.

LWP: Unfortunately, the project lost most of its momentum after three years because the organization was unable to move beyond the political battles that had seemed to define the building and its work. The Task Force is still finding a way to keep the doors of Peachtree-Pine open, even though it has lost almost all of its funding, and the building was recently foreclosed on. Still, despite the fact that the compelling master plan was not realized, we did succeed in generating a carefully considered, socially contextual, appropriate design.

Architecture's limits as a tool for social change constantly stared us in the face. At times I even doubted the relevancy of having an architect on staff. With people lined up out the door needing basic and comprehensive services every hour of every day and night, there was always plenty of other work to do. Beyond immediate needs, the many personal, financial, and political forces that shaped and influenced the form of our work were far more powerful than any rendering, charrette, or document we could produce. While many lives were affected and transformed for the better, it is disappointing that this project ultimately was unable to fundamentally challenge and change the way we approach and deal with homelessness and our most vulnerable citizens.

The act of designing was incredibly relevant and necessary throughout the process, but there were still moments when I needed to actually step back and turn off the constant proposal of solutions. Rather than making sure my own ideas were heard, I found much greater value in helping give a voice to people and ideas that might not be heard otherwise.

LCT: In my opinion, the social-service sensitivity brought to the project was both a strength and a weakness. On the one hand, we really expanded our role as architects to make our designs more responsive to the complex needs of everyone involved. But on the other hand, we found ourselves with very little control over the project, especially in our ability to move it forward at critical points. If the schedules, budgets, and efficiency of the professional world could be combined with the sensitivity and contextual attention of the nonprofit/social-service world, such designs could be both contextually appropriate and realizable.

Beyond the disappointments, though, the experience has forced us to really evaluate what it means to be an architect and how we can be most effective.

INTERN DEVELOPMENT

LWP: It is precisely this tension between the professional world and the social-service world that places young architects in a difficult position as they try to develop professionally while doing work they believe in. All too often, these two goals do not coexist. It is clear that there aren't enough opportunities out there for architects who want to be involved in the social sector. Whether due to a lack of funding or a lack of attention from architectural pedagogy and practice, public-service work is not readily available for all those interested in it.

LCT: Even I didn't know about the field of community design until I was just about to leave architecture altogether; a friend introduced me to the field through a similar internship of her own. Even though the field has grown tremendously over the last decade, the needs still overwhelm the available opportunities. Projects like Peachtree-Pine often don't fit within the very structured formal training of an architect. The development of the technical skill set, the requirements of the Intern Development Program (IDP) of the National Council of Architectural Registration Boards, and licensure all require a standardized approach.

"Rather than immediately identifying the problems that my experience and background would predispose me to recognize, I had to allow others to tell me what the problems were."

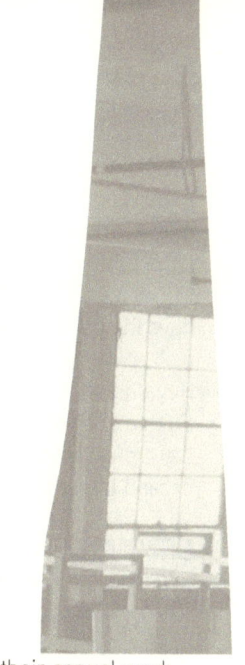

LWP: Many architectural firms now commit 1 percent of their annual work to pro bono efforts, but I think the profession needs to go beyond that measure and really support young architects who are getting hands-on experience, working on the streets, in the gardens, and at the community meetings instead of only in cubicles, conference rooms, and luncheons. The Atlanta architectural community was very supportive, providing resources, technical assistance, and critical guidance. But I operated and worked in a completely different world from theirs. In general, the profession is not set up to support young architects doing years of deep service.

I can't say that much of the work I did there would actually have met any of the IDP guidelines. Because IDP is so professionally focused and limited to the way our field traditionally works, there was not a lot of room to quantify, much less document, the intangible work and experiences offered by organizations like the Task Force. Trying to focus on IDP requirements might also have limited the impact I was able to achieve through the nonarchitectural side of the work, which ultimately made my designs much more appropriate and applicable.

LCT: In my opinion, the most important way to support a shift in our profession is by making it happen in the schools of design and architecture. When people are in school, they are tuning their design sensibilities and learning what is out there for them to participate in after they graduate. By integrating community design into the curricula the same way history, theory, and design are, we could reach many more students who have the interest but are not aware of the possibilities. We might also produce a larger body of architects who are more socially conscious in general and will work harder to provide their services to communities in need.

LWP: We have to acknowledge that this work isn't a good fit for everyone. Expanding the reach of such opportunities might formalize something that may not need to be formalized. Because of the limited number of such opportunities, the process is somewhat self-selecting. Blindly diving in to change the world can actually do more harm than good. If you don't have the capacity or interest to deeply understand both people's lives as well as the forces that shape them, your efforts may very well be in vain. Regardless, we really do need more designers doing this kind of work. Such a change could help decentralize and shift the power balance within the profession away from the traditional office structure, and it might expand the reach of designers in a sensitive, necessary way.

BEYOND PEACHTREE-PINE

LWP: While I have a deep commitment to working with communities who may not otherwise access design services, it has been a struggle to make a living while doing it. I left Peachtree-Pine in 2006 to attend graduate school, where I focused on the design of affordable, self-built, incrementally developed low-cost housing solutions, both in the United States and abroad. I do hope to pursue such work in the future as a way to actually prevent homelessness, but I have also recently decided to try to complete the IDP and pursue my license. While licensure is not necessary, I think it will enable me to be more effective as a designer and have more control over the work I want to do. Unfortunately, the economy in 2010 has made it difficult for anyone to find work. For the last year I have been doing construction work and small design-build projects just to get by. I now teach design in the Department of Technology at Appalachian State University in Boone, North Carolina, and I am running a small community-based design-build practice in Asheville, North Carolina.

LCT: I too have struggled to find similar opportunities after leaving Peachtree-Pine. I ended up freelancing for more traditional design firms. The freedom of self-employment allowed me to engage in community-service opportunities when they arose. One of those was a unique project that was also deeply tied to its broader social, historical, environmental, and economic context. It was a community project in the Nairobi slum of Kibera that focused on reclaiming unusable space for public use. Shortly after joining the project team, I moved to East Africa to once again live in the community where I was working. And while the experience may not have met the financial or professional development needs of a traditional young architect, it was exactly the kind of project I want to be engaged in. We were turning a trash-filled swamp into an active and accessible public space for recreation and income generation for the

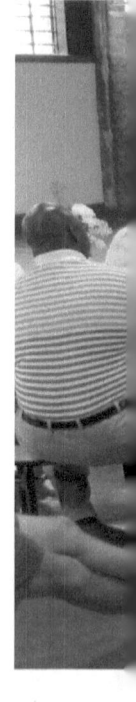

surrounding community. I can't think of more appropriate experience for all of us designers who want to use our skills to meet the social needs of our global population.

LWP: After all the professional challenges I have faced over the past year, I am realizing how fortunate I was at Peachtree-Pine to be agitating for social change and still using my architectural training. The whole experience was messy, painful, and incredibly frustrating at times, yet I have never felt more alive. It exposed me to some of the most challenging people and situations that exist in all levels of our society. Yet, it also put me face to face with the daily struggle of people to rise above such challenges. Far beyond the pen, paper, or computer, it was there in the personal space of compassion, struggle, empowerment, and justice where the greatest triumphs occurred. As such, this "internship" went far beyond typical professional training, setting a very high standard for what I believe architecture

The master plan was introduced to a broad range of stakeholders in 2006. (Photo: Luke W. Perry)

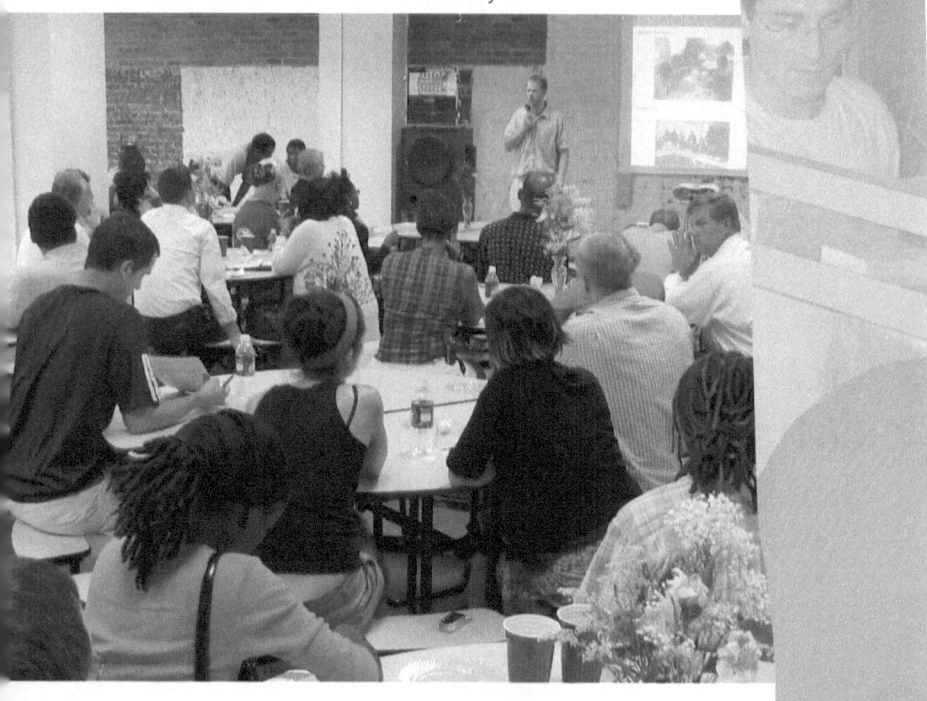

could and should do. While this standard has felt somewhat like a burden during the last couple of years, it has demanded that I expect more from the design field and from the work that I commit to doing. I couldn't imagine learning a more fundamental lesson so early in my career.

"Far beyond the pen, paper, or computer, it was there in the personal space of compassion, struggle, empowerment, and justice where the greatest triumphs occurred. As such, this 'internship' went far beyond typical professional training, setting a very high standard for what I believe architecture could and should do."

LUKE WELDON PERRY earned his bachelor's degree from North Carolina State University in 2000. He then spent several years working for nonprofits focused on affordable housing and homelessness in Washington, DC, and Atlanta. Since graduating with a Master of Architecture from the University of California, Berkeley, in 2009, he has worked in western North Carolina, running a small design-build practice in Asheville and teaching at Appalachian State University in Boone.

LUKE CLARK TYLER received his Bachelor of Architecture from Cornell University in 2006. From 2006 to 2007 he worked with the Metro Atlanta Task Force for the Homeless. Since then he has worked as a freelance designer in New York City. Most recently he has been splitting his time between New York and Nairobi, helping run a nongovernmental organization that works with local Kenyan slum communities to help transform their wastelands into productive public spaces.

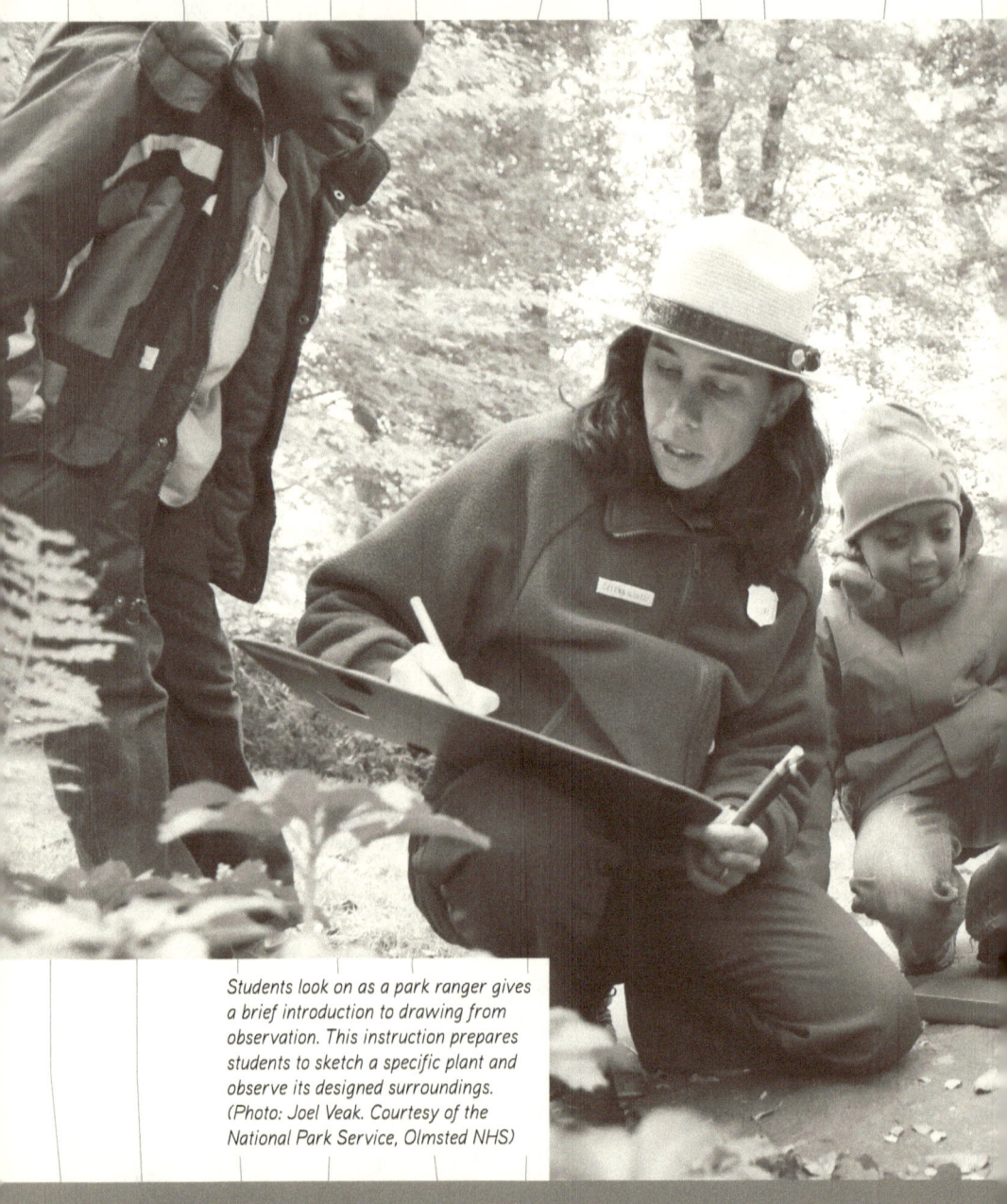

Students look on as a park ranger gives a brief introduction to drawing from observation. This instruction prepares students to sketch a specific plant and observe its designed surroundings. (Photo: Joel Veak. Courtesy of the National Park Service, Olmsted NHS)

SAM
VALENTINE

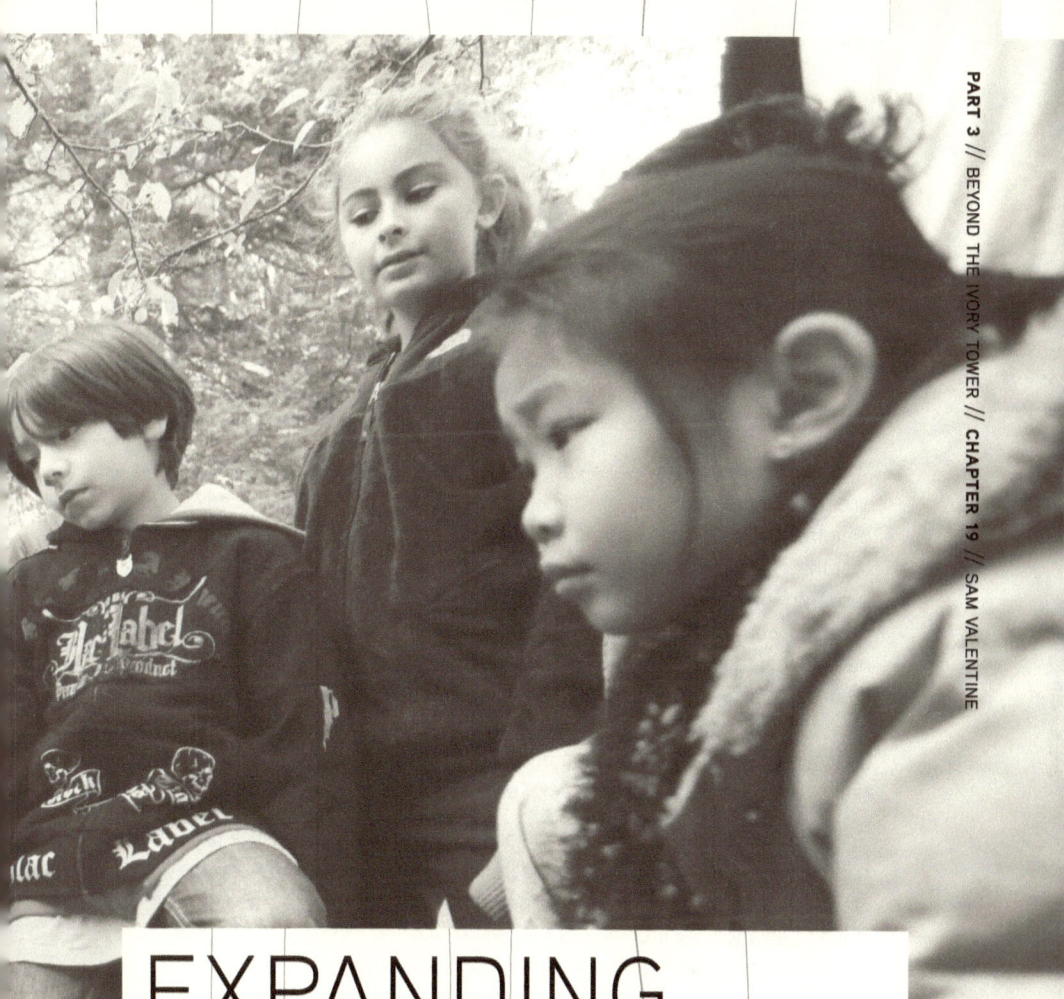

EXPANDING CAREER BOUNDARIES THROUGH PUBLIC SERVICE

There is a well-marked expressway that connects design
schools to private practices across the country. The signage
is clear. The surface is smooth. The lanes are wide.

By contrast, the route from a studio classroom to public-service work
is a winding dirt path. Though scarcely marked and rarely traveled, this
path is much less treacherous than it may seem. Following this trail
may take a designer to a place he or she had never imagined, and there
is something thrilling about not knowing exactly where it may lead.

We environmental designers—architects, landscape architects, and
urban planners—consider ourselves to be among the highest skilled,
best trained, and most influential professionals; and I do not think
that this is an unfair assessment. We are the individuals who employ
research, observation, analysis, and creative thought to create plans that
drastically affect the quality of human lives. Unfortunately, however, I
have detected in my profession the belief that working in public service
means not achieving one's full potential as a designer. (At times I have
even foolishly held this belief myself.) In the past year since graduation
I have learned that when we do not consider internships in the public
realm, we do a great disservice not only to society but also to ourselves.

For many years, my school's Bachelor of Landscape Architecture program
had demonstrated its ability to educate its students so well that most
graduates had multiple job offers lined up by the day they finished school.
But as I finished my fifth year of this well-regarded program in May 2009, I
was frustrated by what appeared to be a total lack of relevant employment
options. With the economy tanking and national unemployment at its
highest rate in my lifetime, much of my grief was clearly caused by
external forces beyond my control. My frustration, however, was also
compounded by my false perception that if there were no private-practice
jobs available, then there was simply no fulfilling, relevant work to be done.

In design school we were taught a great respect for the value of using our
skills to help communities; we were taught that environmental designers
are uniquely poised to have a positive impact on society. From offering
a community-building summer studio in Ghana to teaching a smart-
growth planning studio in an Atlanta suburb, my BLA program strongly
encouraged service-learning opportunities. My coursework guided me
to my first internship, where I was able to document and help conserve
regional tracts of wildlife habitat through a local nonprofit land trust.
(Editors' note: Landscape architects are not certified by the National
Council of Architectural Registration Boards, and the internships described
in this essay are not required for licensure as a landscape architect.) The

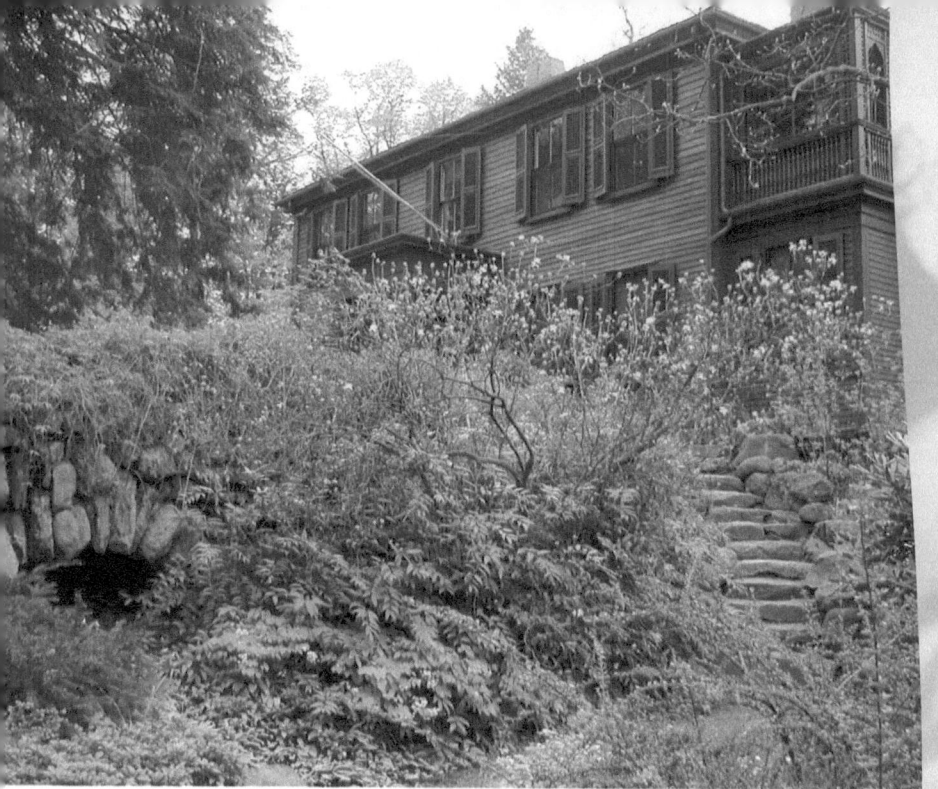

The historic home and office of Frederick Law Olmsted, now a National Historic Site, is embedded in the restored landscape of his original design. Students are challenged to explore and document the many layers of this landscape while describing what makes it unique. (Photo: Courtesy of the National Park Service, Olmsted NHS)

problem, though, is that this pursuit of meaningful public-service work is rarely seen as a viable, logical step beyond school, and most BLA graduates lay down these interests when they pick up their degrees.

When my classmates and I were holding these newly earned diplomas and looking into the void where entry-level employment opportunities had once thrived, we nervously joked that we were doomed to have short, unsuccessful careers in design. For a short time, I took the advice of my elders: I took some time to travel and study the country, and I tried to enjoy my "funemployment." It was not long, though, before I realized that I had to find some way to employ my honed set of skills before I lost them completely. So, gingerly, I broadened my job search, first by including landscape architect positions in government agencies. I knew that some federal, state, and local agencies, such as the United States Forest Service and the Boston Redevelopment Authority, employed architects and landscape architects, but even this widened search yielded no openings. Eventually I reached out to agencies that I had never imagined would have relevant opportunities.

For the position that I eventually did find, I would later learn that even in those hard economic times, when graduate schools and unpaid internship positions were receiving an unprecedented flood of applications, I was the only applicant who came from an environmental design background. To be honest, if not for one seven-letter word—a name—in the job posting, I wonder if I would have even thought to take a closer look. That name was "Olmsted." The posting I had stumbled upon was an advertisement for an internship opening at the Frederick Law Olmsted National Historic Site (NHS) near Boston. It is understandable why the name of this historic site should immediately appeal to a landscape architecture graduate. Widely recognized as the first "landscape architect," Olmsted guided the development of a new profession that borrowed from the traditions of architecture, city planning, art, engineering, and landscape gardening. In the process, he and his immediate successors were largely responsible for the design of America's most celebrated public spaces, including New York City's Central Park, Boston's "Emerald Necklace" system of parks, the layout of the World's Columbian Exposition, and the redesigning of the United States Capitol grounds in Washington, DC.

Despite the intrinsic relevance that Olmsted had to my profession, it was a little jarring to notice that the job description would not engage me in designing any landscapes. Just above "Frederick Law Olmsted National Historic Site" on the listing were two other words that seemed less relevant to the career I had chosen: the advertisement was for an "Education Intern." I am not putting down education; my father is an educator, and in my family education is held in the highest degree of respect. My initial career path, before I entered the wonderful world of design, was headed toward education. Even in my career as a designer I hope to one day share my knowledge through teaching, thereby cultivating a new generation of environmental designers; but it did seem like an education position would surely be a detour from a designer's logical career path.

According to the job announcement, Olmsted NHS was seeking the most qualified candidate to "work within the Division of Education" at the park and to "collaborate with staff within the Divisions of Interpretation, Archives, Maintenance, and Management." The selected applicant would also "work with an array of teachers and school administrators to launch a brand new program for third graders called *Good Neighbors: Landscape Design and Community Building*." Before reading that posting, I had been wholly unaware of the many divisions that can operate within just one National Park. I knew what an Interpretive National Park Service Ranger was, but it was certainly news to me that there was also a Division of Education within the Park Service. Though I could not immediately imagine

"There is a well-marked expressway that connects design schools to private practices across the country. The signage is clear. The surface is smooth. The lanes are wide. By contrast, the route from a studio classroom to public-service work is a winding dirt path."

how my landscape architecture skills would be able to enrich educational programming, I further investigated the position and ultimately applied for it.

After a couple of informative telephone interviews, it became obvious to me that I had made the right decision. *Good Neighbors* is a program that aims to transform young students into designers and stewards of the built environment. Third-grade classrooms that participate in *Good Neighbors* are led through a series of carefully orchestrated hands-on activities that engage the students in a design process and teach them how and why public parkland is important to urban communities. The two park rangers within the Division of Education at Olmsted NHS, who soon became my colleagues, had been working for years to establish this program.

On the small tract of land it occupies, Frederick Law Olmsted National Historic Site is quite the sprawling complex. The site, largely restored to its 1930s condition, includes a historically furnished drafting room, a printing department, a model-building shop, and a plans vault that contains nearly one million pieces of the firm's creative work. Unifying all of this is the Olmsted-designed, lushly planted, painstakingly maintained landscape. Without overwhelming the third-graders, we do our best to introduce them, one classroom at a time, to this wealth of information before they set foot on the site.

When the students arrive, they are unfailingly surprised and intrigued by the place that Olmsted chose to move to in 1883. Surrounded by craggy rock outcrops, Olmsted's firm grew outward from a wooden farmhouse and into the property's undulating landscape. Olmsted picked a progressive suburb of Boston, his next-door neighbor being the talented, like-minded

H. H. Richardson. Many of these city-dwelling students have spent little time in even the amount of "wilderness" that a suburban landscape has to offer. One child earnestly asked if there were bears and snakes on the site, while another remarked that she had never seen so many plants.

One step of the lesson plan asks the students to observe, describe, and carefully draw one landscape plant in situ. From the very first class I worked with, it was somewhat startling just how consistently the students' field-trip jitters and anxiety evaporated as they became engaged in their work.

While exploring the grounds, the students are able to develop their ability to observe details of a landscape and to consciously, actively experience a designed environment. Another on-site activity provides the students with a unique opportunity to dabble in the design process. Each student is put into a "design team" and given a slab of cork into which topographic contours have been cut. After the students hear requests from real "clients"—prerecorded interviews with community members—the park rangers and I guide the designers through the steps of designating circulation routes, locating shelters and recreational equipment, installing site furnishings, and planting trees and shrubs.

At the end of this process, the third-graders have become park designers, and they have also become familiar with the difficult task of balancing client requests, a landscape's existing challenges, and limitations in time and materials. When finishing their designs, some students confessed that they had never before considered, when walking on a park sidewalk or sitting on a shaded bench, that some individual had planned that feature and that these things did not occur naturally. I find this realization to be especially relevant to the successful landscape architecture of the Olmsteds, as even adults often do not know that the land that is now Central Park, though green, wooded, and full of wildlife today, once held slaughterhouses, and that segments of Boston's Emerald Necklace were once nothing more than sewage-filled marshland.

Virtually all design graduates leave school with basic communication, presentation, and graphic skills that would prove valuable in just about any place of business. I expected to assist in the development of this education program by assembling visual presentations with PowerPoint, editing photos with Photoshop, and laying out information with InDesign. But, as

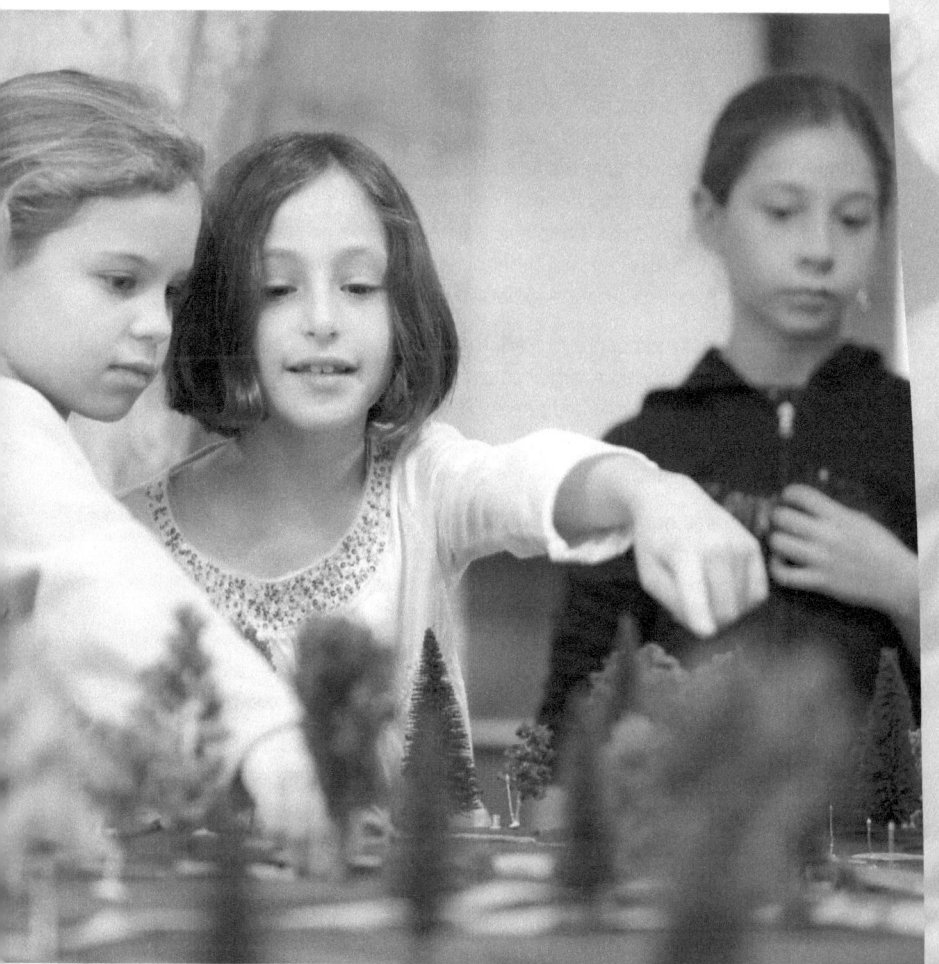

Students work collaboratively to design and construct a scale model of a city park. After the models are built these young designers are encouraged to defend their design decisions and explain how their park would address the needs of a community. (Photo: Joel Veak. Courtesy of the National Park Service, Olmsted NHS)

it turned out, several components of the *Good Neighbors* program stood to benefit from the more specific design knowledge that I had gained in school. On a somewhat regular basis, staff, adult visitors, and children called on me to identify and describe plants in the park's landscape. I applied my drafting knowledge to interpret the intentions behind century-old landscape plans and the sometimes obscure purposes of several Olmsted firm artifacts. By the end of the internship, I had even used CAD and 3D modeling programs to design precise components for the student landscape models.

It is often believed that taking a job in public service involves making a selfless sacrifice for the common good. I think that in most cases, including public school teachers, emergency personnel, public-service attorneys, and nonprofit workers, these individuals accept far lower incomes than they would have made had they gone into private-practice jobs. However, to be perfectly honest, I cannot say that my public-service experience required much of a financial sacrifice. If the compensation I received was low, it was not much below what the average entry-level designer can expect, and the experience was excellent.

In addition to my daily exposure to Park Service rangers and elementary-school teachers and students, other activities allowed me to meet and work with influential environmental designers. Through workshops, meetings, and conferences I was able to work alongside renowned modern-day landscape architects, architects, planners, and even exhibit designers.

Above all, there was one designer I encountered who made the greatest impact on me. One day, while sitting in the archives department and working to enrich a *Good Neighbors* postvisit activity, I studied the sketchy pencil lines laid down onto linen paper by Frederick Law Olmsted himself. The drawing, which I scrutinized at nose's length, was a schematic plan for one segment of the Emerald Necklace. As I peered more closely, I saw not only the bold final lines; I also could just barely discern erasures and faint gestures of marks. I felt that I was able to see his mind working as he tried to weave circulation routes through a topographically complex site. At that moment I wondered whether a more straightforward landscape architecture career path could ever have given me the opportunity to be this close to the originator of my profession.

If I had been told, even months before finishing school, that my first step after graduation would involve a two-hundred-year-old house, uniformed park rangers, and gaggles of eight- and nine-year-olds, I would likely have scoffed at the apparent irrelevance of the opportunity. I had already worked in an inspiring design office during the summer before my final year of school, and in that position I had detailed and designed landscapes that were actually being built for real clients.

"... with time, I slowly broadened the perceived boundaries of my career, and since then I have found my experience challenging, rewarding, and surprisingly relevant."

An education internship position would have seemed so far removed from my training that I probably would not have considered it.

But, with time, I slowly broadened the perceived boundaries of my career, and since then I have found my experience challenging, rewarding, and surprisingly relevant. As of this writing, I am about to start a second term of internship at Frederick Law Olmsted National Historic Site. This time, a large part of my focus will involve an in-depth study of one specific Olmsted-designed "jewel" in Boston's Emerald Necklace. I will be extracting lessons about site design, park stewardship, and community ownership from the park and its history, and I will work to teach these lessons to third-grade minds and further enrich the *Good Neighbors* program.

While I am at Olmsted NHS, delving further into the history of my profession, I will be working part-time at a nearby landscape architecture firm that truly values the important work I have been doing with the National Park Service. I am confident that I made the right choice to broaden my outlook, and I feel that my career is right on track, even if I did take a slightly scenic route to get here.

SAM VALENTINE earned his Bachelor of Landscape Architecture from the University of Georgia's College of Environmental Design in May 2009 and is a LEED Accredited Professional. He is an education intern at Frederick Law Olmsted National Historic Site, and is a design consultant for Richard Burck Associates, where he is working toward licensure.

NOTES

EDITOR'S INTRODUCTION:
GEORGIA BIZIOS & KATIE WAKEFORD

1. Internship is the period of an architect's training between receiving a professional degree and completing licensure exams. Interns work under the supervision of a licensed professional and accrue training units in sixteen design/construction categories.
2. Casius Pealer, "Nonprofit Work Experience: Beneficial for All, but Far Too Rare," *Architectural Record*, August 2007, 63–64.

CHAPTER 1: VICTORIA BEACH

1. Robert W. Gordon, "Professions and Professionalism—An Overview," in *Professionalism* (Open Society Institute Publications, forthcoming).
2. NCARB, *Intern Development Program Guidelines* (Washington, DC: NCARB, October 2010), 37.
3. Ibid., 75.
4. Ibid.
5. NCARB, "2010–2011 Rules of Conduct" (Washington, DC: NCARB, 2010).
6. The AIA's Ethical Standards are expressly unenforced and unenforceable: "The Code is arranged in three tiers of statements: Canons, Ethical Standards, and Rules of Conduct. Canons are broad principles of conduct. Ethical Standards (E.S.) are more specific goals toward which Members should aspire in professional performance and behavior. Rules of Conduct (Rule) are mandatory; violation of a Rule is grounds for disciplinary action by the Institute." AIA, "2007 Code of Ethics and Professional Conduct" (Washington, DC: AIA, 2007), 1. "E.S. 2.2 Public Interest Services: Members should render public interest professional services, including pro bono services, and encourage their employees to render such services. Pro bono services are those rendered without expecting compensation, including those rendered for indigent persons, after disasters, or in other emergencies." Ibid., 2.
7. NCARB, *Intern Development Program Guidelines*, October 2010, 33-34.
8. Ibid., 18.
9. Ibid.
10. "E.S. 5.1 Professional Environment: Members should provide their associates and employees with a suitable working environment, compensate them fairly, and facilitate their professional development. E.S. 5.2 Intern and Professional Development: Members should recognize and fulfill their obligation to nurture fellow professionals as they progress through all stages of their career, beginning with professional education in the academy, progressing through internship and continuing throughout their career." AIA, "2007 Code of Ethics and Professional Conduct," 4.

11. The Utah Architect Licensing Act Rule of 8 November 2010 indicates some governmental interest in IDP. R156-31-502 states, "'Unprofessional conduct' includes: ... (5) failing as a supervising architect to verify actual work experience when requested by a subordinate, associate or drafter of an architect who is or has been an employee," making Utah architects' registration status contingent, in part, on their responsiveness to intern requests for signatures. www.rules.utah.gov/publicat/code/r156/r156-03a.htm#T12 (accessed on 1 May 2011).

12. NCARB, *Intern Development Program Guidelines*, October 2010, 10.

13. Robert Gutman, "Professions and Their Discontents: The Psychodynamics of Architectural Practice," in *Architecture from the Outside In*, ed. Dana Cuff and John Wriedt (New York: Princeton Architectural Press, 2010), 43–60.

14. "Except as provided otherwise in this section, no person who, without compensation and as a volunteer, renders public services for a nonprofit ... or for a Commonwealth or local government agency conducting or sponsoring a public service program or project shall be liable to any person for any civil damages as a result of any acts or omissions in rendering such services." Consolidated Statutes of Pennsylvania, title 24, sec. 8332.4, available at http://www.legis.state.pa.us/WU01/LI/LI/CT/HTM/42/00.083.032.004..HTM

15. The Volunteer Protection Act of 1997, Public Law 105-19, 105th Congress (June 18, 1997), states that "no volunteer of a nonprofit organization or governmental entity shall be liable for harm caused by an act or omission of the volunteer." United States Code, Section 14503, Title 42, Chapter 139.

16. NCARB, *Intern Development Program Guidelines*, October 2010, 62.

17. Robert J. Bonner, *Lawyers and Litigants in Ancient Athens: The Genesis of the Legal Profession* (1927; repr., Chicago: University of Chicago Press, 1994), 135. Ancient Roman doctors, like Greek lawyers, were also prohibited from accepting fees. See Ralph Jackson, *Doctors and Diseases in the Roman Empire* (Norman: University of Oklahoma Press, 1988), 56–59.

18. "The true creator is necessity, who is the mother of our invention." Plato, *The Republic*, 2.396C.

19. "He's a true American original, an individualist who urged young architects to march to the beat of their own drummer. 'The way you write your signature is you,' he said, evoking that long-ago handwriting analysis that predicted his architectural ascent. 'I don't think it makes sense to be someone else.'" Blair Kamin, "Frank Gehry Holds Forth on Millennium Park, the Modern Wing and Why He's Not into Green Architecture," *Chicago Tribune*, April 7, 2010.

20. Andrea Oppenheimer Dean and Timothy Hursley, *Rural Studio: Samuel Mockbee and an Architecture of Decency* (New York: Princeton Architectural Press, 2002), 12.

CHAPTER 7: GEORGIA BIZIOS & KATIE WAKEFORD
1. Anthony Shuman, "Introduction: The Pedagogy of Engagement," in *From the Studio to the Streets: Service Learning in Planning and Architecture*, ed. Mary C. Hardin and William Zeisel (Washington, DC: American Association for Higher Education, 2005), 8.
2. Ernest L. Boyer and Lee D. Mitgang, *Building Community: A New Future for Architecture Education and Practice* (Princeton, NJ: Carnegie Foundation for the Advancement of Teaching, 1996).
3. Marvin Malecha, *The Learning Organization and the Evolution of Practice Academy Concepts* (Raleigh: North Carolina State University College of Design, 2005).
4. Boyer and Mitgang, *Building Community.*

CHAPTER 8: STEPHEN LUONI
1. Robert Gutman, "The Questions Architects Ask," in *Architecture from the Outside In: Selected Essays by Robert Gutman*, ed. Dana Cuff and John Wriedt (New York: Princeton Architectural Press, 2010), 158.
2. Paul Starr, *The Social Transformation of American Medicine* (New York: Basic Books, 1982), 180–97.
3. See *Expanding Architecture: Design as Activism*, ed. Bryan Bell and Katie Wakeford (New York: Metropolis Books, 2008) and *Good Deeds, Good Design: Community Service Through Architecture*, ed. Bryan Bell (New York: Princeton Architectural Press, 2004).
4. Michael Edwards, *Small Change: Why Business Won't Save the World* (San Francisco: Berrett-Koehler, 2008), 43.
5. Mark Brown, "Ecological Engineering: Interface Ecosystems and Adaptive Self-Organization," *Ecological Engineering: Journal of Ecosystem Restoration* 1, no. 1 (2004): 6–14.
6. Robert Gutman, "Architecture: The Entrepreneurial Profession," in *Architecture from the Outside In*, 38.
7. For an extended discussion of this point, see Beth Quinn, "Building a Profession: A Sociological Analysis of the Intern Development Program," *Journal of Architectural Education* 56, no. 4 (2003): 41–49.
8. Paolo Tombesi, "On the Separation of Design Labor," in *Building (in) the Future: Recasting Labor in Architecture*, ed. Peggy Deamer and Phillip Bernstein (New York: Princeton Architectural Press; New Haven, CT: Yale School of Architecture, 2010), 128.
9. Edwards, *Small Change*, 99.

CHAPTER 9: LEN CHARNEY & GABE BERGERON

1. David Sullivan, *DGC 2010 Architectural Study* (Woburn, MA: Dicicco, Gulman & Company, 2010).
2. AIA Young Architects Forum, "What Does It Mean to Be an Intern-Friendly or Teaching Firm?" (http://info.aia.org/nwsltr_yaf.cfm?pagename=yaf_a_061220_strategies [accessed December 3, 2009]).

CHAPTER 11: DAVID PERKES

1. Whitney Young's keynote speech to the 1968 National AIA Convention was published in the *AIA Journal*, September 1968, and reprinted in *20/20 Vision: Perspectives on Diversity and Design*, ed. Linda Kiisk AIA (Boston: Boston Society of Architects, 2003), 9–22.
2. Le Corbusier, *Towards a New Architecture* (New York: Dover Publications, 1986), 289.
3. In a recent issue of the *Chronicle of Higher Education*, Thomas Fisher, the dean of the College of Design at the University of Minnesota and the 2009–10 president of the Association of Collegiate Schools of Architecture, called for architectural education to respond to the growing need for designers to take on the challenge of working beyond the traditional paying client model. An edited and expanded version of that essay appears as chapter 2 of the current volume.
4. Theories of modernization are part of Ulrich Beck's description of "reflexive modernization" in his influential 1992 book *Risk Society: Towards a New Modernity*, and in his later writings, especially *Reflexive Modernization* (1994) and *World at Risk* (2009). Beck says, "'Reflexive modernization' means the possibility of a creative (self-)destruction for an entire epoch: that of industrial society. The 'subject' of this creative destruction is not the revolution, not the crisis, but the victory of Western modernization." See Ulrich Beck, "The Reinvention of Politics," in *Reflexive Modernization* (Stanford, CA: Stanford University Press, 1994), 2.
5. Karl Marx and Friedrich Engels, "Communist Manifesto," in *Werke* (Berlin: Volksausgabe, 1972), 5:465. Cf. also Marshal Berman, *All That Is Solid Melts into Air* (New York: Verso, 1982).
6. SEED: Social Economic Environmental Design® is the creation of an informal group of design organizations and individuals that have been working on measures for responsible design since 2005. The organization leading the effort is Design Corps. In March 2010 Design Corps launched seednetwork.org. The Web site states:

SEED is a common standard to guide, evaluate and measure the social, economic and environmental impact of design projects.

SEED maintains the belief that design can play a vital role in the most critical issues that face communities and individuals, in crisis and in every day challenges. To accomplish this, the SEED process guides professionals to work alongside locals who know their community and its needs. This practice of "trusting the local" is increasingly recognized as a highly effective way to sustain the health and longevity of a place or a community as it develops.

CHAPTER 16: BRYAN BELL
1. Credits: Design Corps Summer Studio 2008
Hosted by Neighborhood Housing Services and Tulane University
Teachers: Bryan Bell, Doug Harmon, Scott Ball
Students: Andrew Bryan, Audrey Cropp, Maggie McIntosh, Alice Phillips, Susanna Pho, Dan Stanislaw
Community Partners:
NHS: David Lessinger, Shana Sassoon, Kimberly Van Wagner, Kate Peak
Local Business Leaders: Peter Gardner, Greg Ensslen
Regional Transportation Authority: Rosalind Cook, Pat Judge
Tulane: Scott Bernhard, Emilie Taylor, Sam Richards

CHAPTER 17: HALEY LORAM
1. Darl Rastorfer, "The Community Design Collaborative: A Volunteer-Based Community Design Center Serving Greater Philadelphia," in *Expanding Architecture: Design as Activism*, ed. Bryan Bell and Katie Wakeford (New York: Metropolis Books, 2008), 104.

ABOUT THE EDITORS

GEORGIA BIZIOS, FAIA, is an ACSA Distinguished Professor in the College of Design at North Carolina State University in Raleigh. In 2004, she founded the Home Environments Design Initiative with the mission to initiate, facilitate, and coordinate scholarship, research, and outreach in quality design for home environments. In addition to teaching, Bizios has focused her practice on residential architecture and has sought to mentor and supervise architecture interns.

KATIE WAKEFORD is coeditor of *Expanding Architecture: Design as Activism* (New York: Metropolis Books, 2008), a collection of essays on design in the service of the greater public good. Wakeford is an intern architect with the NC State University School of Architecture's Home Environments Design Initiative and a LEED Accredited Professional.